Praise for *Hollywood's Blacklists*

'There has long been a need – in fact since the end of the Blacklist – ιοι a concise history of that dark period in American history, with background as to why the Blacklist happened and documentation on the personalities involved. *Hollywood's Blacklists* is precisely that work . . . highly readable, devoid of academic jargon, and scrupulously researched.'

Anthony Slide, *The Slide Area*

'I recommend *Hollywood's Blacklists* as a concise introduction to a turbulent period in American history both on and off the screen.'

Laurence Raw, *Journal of American Culture*

'Humphries's book is insightful and innovative in its approach. The author's readings of films as presented in *Hollywood's Blacklists* testify to his admirable critical acumen and encourage readers to explore further the historical period along the lines staked out in his book. Owing to the interdisciplinary charac-ter of his interpretations, Humphries's book will be useful to readers interested in contemporary film studies and to those interested in American cultural studies.'

Kate Watson, *European Journal of American Studies*

'At a time when neo-conservatives have been enjoying great success in rewrit-ing America's long history of Red Scares as crusades of freedom against tyranny Reynold Humphries's assiduously researched book is a brave and salutary corrective . . .'

Kenneth Wright, *Product* magazine

'A fascinating, well-researched and lucidly written volume that deserves wide circulation and discussion. An important contribution to the literature on the Hollywood Left, the Blacklist, and the failures of American liberalism.'

Paul Buhle, Senior Lecturer, Brown University

'*Hollywood's Blacklists* is an elegant study of the florid anti-Communist repres-sion of the American film industry as this affected the lives of the victims and the content of Hollywood films. But it is also living history, a history that comes back to haunt us in a time when the 'terrorist' is inserted into the role of Satan in the wake of communism's collapse. Because the persecutory beast was never put down then, it arises anew, and we see all the same themes replayed in different costumes and sets. Reynold Humphries has not only, then, written a fine history, but also a cautionary tale for a new epoch of reactionary repression.'

Joel Kovel, author of *Red-Hunting in the Promised Land*

In Memory of
the Abraham Lincoln Brigade
and Carey McWilliams, dissident

HOLLYWOOD'S BLACKLISTS

A Political and Cultural History

Reynold Humphries

EDINBURGH UNIVERSITY PRESS

© Reynold Humphries, 2008, 2010

First published in hardback in 2008 by
Edinburgh University Press Ltd
22 George Square, Edinburgh

This paperback edition 2010

Typeset in 11/13 pt Bembo
by Servis Filmsetting Ltd, Stockport, Cheshire, and
printed and bound in Great Britain by
CPI Antony Rowe, Chippenham, Wiltshire

A CIP record for this book is available from the British Library

ISBN 978 0 7486 2456 0 (paperback)

Contents

Acknowledgements

Many people have helped me during my research in one way or another. Thanks go first to Thom Andersen and Noël Burch who copied tapes of otherwise unavailable films for me and lent me documents. To Norma Barzman, who welcomed me into her Beverly Hills apartment in August 2002 and discussed the period and her personal memories of it. To Jean Rouverol and the late Bernard Gordon who kindly gave of their time to answer questions in writing. To Elizabeth MacRae who sent me material from the papers of her late husband, blacklisted actor/writer Nedrick Young. To Anthony Slide for his encouragement and hospitality in Los Angeles.

Thanks also to the outside readers for giving the go-ahead to this project and to Paul Buhle and Joel Kovel for their support. To Dave Wagner and Tony Williams who put at my disposal the fruits of their research and were always willing to exchange ideas. Special thanks are due to Pat McGilligan who always found the time to give help and provide invaluable information.

Much of the information used in this book was gleaned from research in various archives. Special thanks go to Ned Comstock, Doheny Memorial Library, University of Southern California, who looked out material from the Jack L. Warner Papers; and to Barbara Hall, Margaret Herrick Library, Academy of Motion Picture Arts and Sciences, who answered questions, gave advice and took invaluable initiatives in putting at my disposal material from the Special Collections. Working at the Margaret Herrick Library, in quiet and comfortable surroundings with the help of friendly staff, is one of the many pleasures of research.

I wish to thank too the staff of the American Film Institute and the Southern California Library for Social Study and Research for their hospitality during my visits. The staff of the Charles E. Young Special Collections and of the Arts Library Special Collections of the University of California at Los Angeles were most courteous and helpful. A special word in memory of the late Lisa Kernan of the Arts Library who made helpful suggestions as to what material could prove of interest. A big thank-you to Jeanette Gilkison who found me excellent accommodation in Santa Monica.

Nicola Ramsey of Edinburgh University Press has always believed in this book and I wish to thank her warmly for encouraging me to work out a coherent proposal. Thanks to all those at the Press who have seen it through to its completion. And, last but not least, thanks to my wife Martine Lannaud, called upon yet again to help out with computing matters.

The Background

On the morning of 27 October 1947 screenwriter John Howard Lawson appeared before the House Committee on Un-American Activities (HUAC) in Washington to answer questions in the context of its inquiries into Communism in the Motion Picture Industry. The Committee's Chairman was Republican Congressman J. Parnell Thomas, its Chief Investigator Robert Stripling, a southern Democrat. Lawson asked to be allowed to read a statement. Thomas examined it and refused: it was not pertinent to the Hearings. Stripling then commenced the interrogation of Lawson. After establishing his identity, he asked: 'Are you now or have you ever been a member of the Communist Party?' Lawson questioned the right of the Committee to ask that question. There then ensued a confrontation between witness and Chairman, the former trying to answer in his own way, the latter using his gavel to reduce him to silence. Finally Thomas demanded that Lawson leave the stand. Thus ended the testimony of the first of 'the Hollywood Ten'.

Things proceeded in like fashion with the other nine and resulted in the Ten being charged with and finally convicted of contempt of Congress for refusing to answer the Committee's questions. This refusal and the ensuing condemnation resulted in their employers, the various Hollywood studios, dismissing them in a statement making it clear that Hollywood would no longer wittingly hire known Communists in any capacity. Thus was created the blacklist. What began with the exclusion of ten men at the end of 1947 was to continue, after a three-year period during which the face of the world in general and of America in particular was to change dramatically, from early 1951 and to embrace the entire industry for several years. As we shall see, both the status of witnesses – already referred to at the time as 'friendly' or 'unfriendly' – and the

nature of the questioning by HUAC, illustrated these political changes and the
relations between those members of the film industry who had been briefly
united in 1947 in their opposition to the Committee.

A note of warning needs to be sounded here, given the confusion still
reigning in popular accounts of the role of the blacklist because of the Cold
War US–Soviet standoff. This confusion centres on one person, Senator
Joseph McCarthy, and the term 'McCarthyism'. Readers must therefore keep
in mind that HUAC was investigating Communism in Hollywood before the
Senator was first elected in 1946; that HUAC was a Committee of Congress
and not of the Senate; and that McCarthy did chair Senate Hearings on
Communism but that he never investigated Hollywood.[1] The Senator's
obsession with Communist subversion had been the all-consuming concern
since the early 1920s of a man who was to wield considerable power for
fifty years and whom we shall meet on more than one occasion: J. Edgar
Hoover, Director of the Federal Bureau of Investigation (FBI) from 1924 to
1972. One study asserts that by 1945 Hoover 'was fully prepared to lead the
postwar purge of American leftists that misleadingly traveled under the
banner of "McCarthyism"' (Theoharis and Cox 1993: 200). A specialist on
McCarthyism – the word was coined early in the Senator's career by a newspaper opponent of his – goes even further. Suggesting that 'Hooverism'
would best define the phenomenon of the persecution of people for their
alleged Communist attachments or sympathies, she also made the following
remark, to the implication of which we shall return constantly throughout
this study:

> Had World War II not diverted the nation's leaders from the issues of
> Communism, it is likely that some form of McCarthyism might well have
> entered American politics a full ten years before it finally did. From con-
> gressional committees to the FBI, all the machinery was in place.
> (Schrecker 1998: xxviii)

It is therefore Hoover, and not McCarthy, who will loom large in these
pages. Hoover saw any radical questioning of the status quo – such as campaigning for the rights of blacks and the struggle to organise working people
into unions – as a form of dissidence. And dissidence led inexorably to subversion, the *raison d'être* of Reds.

Writing of the ever-increasing radicalism of the working class after the Great
Crash of 1929, one writer has stated that its culture 'was marked by a sustained
sense of class consciousness, and a new rhetoric of class, by a new moral
economy, and by the emergence of a working-class ethnic Americanism'
(Denning 1998: 8). The 'Cultural Front' brought together in the 1930s
workers, artists and intellectuals committed to new forms of solidarity both

cultural and political. Foremost were anti-fascism and the fight against segregation. Theirs was a participation depending on

> reorganizing patterns of loyalty and allegiance, articulating cultural practices in a new historical bloc. Such a historical bloc attempts to forge an alliance of social groups and class fractions: by offering a new culture, a way of life, a conception of the universe, it creates the conditions for a political use or reading of cultural performances and artifacts, the conditions for symbolizing class conflict. (Denning 1998: 63)

According to circumstances, then, blacks and whites, unionists and middle-class intellectuals, musicians and writers joined forces in ways that threatened simultaneously the status quo, the supposedly classless nature of American society and the relations between groups and classes based on power structures so long in place that they were taken for granted. Those structures included, of course, the relations between the studio moguls and their employees: actors, writers, directors, set designers, manual labourers and so on. The attempts to unite employees into unions representing the various groups was, as we shall see in Chapter 1, an early source of conflict. Just how important it was for the Right to break the back of unions in general by turning worker against worker can be seen in the following incident. Commenting on the acts of violence of which Communist unionists were victims in the early 1950s at the hands of the very workers whom they represented and defended, Republican Representative Kid Clardy stated: 'This is the best kind of reaction there could have been to our hearings' (Caute 1978: 364).[2]

One of the tragedies of the post-war period – due in no small part to the behaviour and attitudes of the American Communist Party (CPUSA), as will become apparent as our own investigation proceeds – was the collapse of the alliance on the Left between liberals, radicals and Communists.[3] Liberals left the ship long before it started sinking, although the mass exodus occurred after 1947. One progressive historian has written thus of liberals:

> many of them were too eager to embrace established political and economic practices, too reluctant to reevaluate the diplomacy of the Cold War, too enamored with the role of leaders and experts, too cooperative with McCarthyism, and too obsessed with the psychological and moral agonies of the middle class – a preoccupation that led them to neglect the systemic diseases of urban decay, racism, and poverty. (Pells 1985: ix)

We return here to the question of class and race so essential to understanding the radical 1930s and the conservative reaction, both then and after the war. It became suspect to deny the existence of the 'Communist conspiracy'. Thus by 1950 the situation was parlous:

State and federal investigators grilled suspected citizens on their reading
habits, voting patterns, and church attendance. Support for racial equality became evidence of subversive leanings. Heretical literature was
banned from public and school libraries; some communities even held
book burnings. Hollywood scoured its films for the subversive taint.
Neighbors informed on neighbors, students on their teachers. Readers
of 'questionable' works hid their leftist tomes or buried them in the back
garden. Seven war-era concentration camps were dusted off, and lists prepared of the radicals to fill them. (Fariello 1995: 25)

My own first contact with Hollywood's blacklists, without realising it at
the time, was when I was about 15. I was watching a programme on BBC
television featuring, among other artists, a harmonica player. When he talked
to the live audience, I remember being surprised: I realised he was an
American but had assumed him to be British. The artist in question was Larry
Adler, an American forced to make his living in Britain after blacklisting.[4] It
was not until some years later that I discovered the blacklist: I read *Inquisition
in Eden* by Alvah Bessie, one of the Ten. Emerging dumbfounded from the
experience, I could only wonder how such things could have happened.
Hence this book: it is often necessary to step back and take a long, hard look
to convince oneself that things really did happen this way. Perhaps readers are
already wondering how it came about that men could be questioned about
their political convictions. The answers occupy Part I of this book: the
Introduction and Chapters 1, 2 and 3. Part II deals with the various Hearings
themselves and the forms witch hunting and blacklisting took. The
Bibliography includes works not actually quoted or referred to; like certain
notes it is intended to point the reader in the direction of a better understanding of the stakes on both sides of the political fence and to encourage
further reading.

NOTES

1. He did, however, interrogate certain artists who had worked occasionally in
   Hollywood, such as the composer Aaron Copland who won an Academy Award
   for *The Heiress* (William Wyler, 1949). However, this interrogation (26 May 1953)
   was made as Chairman of the Senate Permanent Subcommittee of the Committee
   of Government Investigations. Despite his explicit rejection of music being used
   politically, as in the Soviet Union, Copland was blacklisted from concert halls as a
   result of having been subpoenaed. His composition, *The Tender Land* was refused by
   the television channel which had commissioned it. He was never called upon to
   testify in public and did not compose again for Hollywood until the early 1960s
   (Minutes of the Eighty-Third Congress, vol. 2, pp. 1267–90). Michael Denning

includes Copland in a list of 'radical moderns', along with Duke Ellington, Charlie Chaplin – and John Howard Lawson of the Hollywood Ten (Denning 1998: 59).
2. David Caute places Clardy among the 'primitive bigots' of HUAC. An opponent of trade unionists since the 1930s (Donner 1961: 40), he finally joined the fascist John Birch Society.
3. At the time 'radical' and 'subversive' were other terms for Communism. I use 'radical' to designate a left-winger, particularly a Marxist, who was not a member of the CPUSA. To simplify matters, I shall henceforth use 'CP' to designate the American Communist Party.
4. He composed the music for *King and Country*, directed by fellow blacklistee Joseph Losey in 1964.

I
Drawing up the Battle Lines

Introduction

. . . we were children of the Depression, and we saw this tremen-
dous, nonsensical situation – the greatest production force in the
world was for no reason redundant, its factories were closed, the
windows were broken, there was despair and disillusion. The system
that supported it could not provide for its people. It was a faulty
system and we were radicalised.

Director Cy Endfield[1]

THE PRESIDENCY OF FRANKLIN DELANO ROOSEVELT

The Democrat Roosevelt was elected to the White House in 1932 to combat
the disastrous effects of the Depression: widespread unemployment as a result
of the Stock Exchange Crash of 1929. His electorate comprised both ordinary Americans looking desperately for someone able to return their country
to its pristine prosperity and businessmen who, fearing a socialist solution,
turned to a moderate ready to save capitalism from itself, while ushering in
an age of welfare destined to alleviate the worst suffering (Fraser and Gerstle
1989). The name given to Roosevelt's initiatives was 'the New Deal' and it
was embraced by the majority of the American electorate, including many
businessmen and the Warner Brothers. Opposition to it, however, was also
considerable and the forms this opposition took help explain the climate of
the 1930s and the post-war repercussions. Just two months after Roosevelt
took office, the ultra-conservative newspaper magnate William Randolph
Hearst stigmatised him in an editorial, denouncing 'the inequitable, tyran-
nical, Bolshevistic policy of confiscatory income taxation' (Pizzitola 2002:

282).² In 1936, with Roosevelt elected for a second term, Hearst published the following:

> The Red New Deal with a Soviet seal
> Endorsed by a Moscow hand
> The strange result of an alien cult
> In a liberty-loving land. (Vaughn 1996: 35)

This doggerel evokes the twin assumptions destined to become articles of faith for the Red-baiting Right after World War II: the equation of the New Deal with Communism; and the notion that the New Deal's radical supporters were acting at the Soviet Union's behest.³ On more than one occasion J. Parnell Thomas equated the New Deal and Communism and Hearst columnist Westbrook Pegler wrote in the *Los Angeles Examiner* on 17 November 1947, after the appearance of the Hollywood Ten before HUAC: 'Communism was the form of collectivism that most of these New Dealers had in mind.'⁴ Pegler's aim was to accuse Communists of using the New Deal for their own ends, but his remark also implies insidiously that the New Deal's economic and political options favoured such ends. It all depends on one's interpretation of 'Communism' which could mean simply 'the populist communitarianism and resistance to a corrupt society that informed the work and politics of so many in the New Deal years' (May 2000: 243). We shall see in the following chapters that, if the Warner Brothers (Jack and Harry) were the first producers to leave the fold of the Republican Party to embrace Roosevelt, they were the first to break the ranks of the opposition of the studio bosses to HUAC in 1947 and embrace a collaboration that was to prove disastrous for the Hollywood Left. The reasons for this about-turn were many and complex, like the reasons for the liberal–Communist alliances in the pre-war period.

THE 'NEGRO QUESTION'

Opposition to the prejudice and violence of which the black was a constant victim brought together Americans of very different persuasions. This in itself was sufficient after the war to create difficulties for many liberals who had joined forces with members of the CP throughout the 1930s and to throw others into the arms of Red-baiters. As this study concerns Hollywood, it should not be forgotten that Hollywood too was influenced by the racism endemic to society: it had to distribute its movies in the South to ensure a profit. What did that entail?

In 1936 Hollywood produced *The Black Legion*, a thinly disguised attack on the Ku Klux Klan (KKK). Joseph Breen – Hollywood's self-appointed censor whose brief was to defend the industry from outside criticism and therefore to forbid any mention of topics likely to cause too much controversy – originally opposed the film being produced on the grounds that race was 'inflammatory'.[5] In an article published on 21 October 1947, the conservative trade paper *The Hollywood Reporter* referred to bans in Memphis, Tennessee, on reissues of the 'Our Gang' shorts (starring children and adolescents, and made with those age groups in mind) because 'the shorts featured a negro child playing with white children'. Scriptwriter Edmund North has stated that producer Jerry Wald demanded that the black characters be eliminated from *Young Man with a Horn* (1950). Explaining that otherwise 'they couldn't show the picture in the South', North adds: 'Looking back now, it's – I don't know how we wrote anything.'[6] Producer William Fadiman recounts how he hired a black writer at MGM. Later he was summoned and told that the film had been cancelled: too expensive. Fadiman informed the writer who left the studio which promptly re-scheduled the picture for production.[7] Scriptwriter and future blacklistee Bernard Gordon – a Communist, unlike North and Fadiman – introduced the character of a black taxi-driver into a script, only to have the producer cross it out:

> it was not permitted because it would only cause trouble in the South, where theaters would refuse to play the film. There you have the smoking gun. As the House Committee on Un-American Activities had set out to prove: the Party was endeavouring to insert Red propaganda into films. (Gordon 2004: 103–4)

Should readers be bemused to learn that 'Red propaganda' meant 'defending the constitutional rights of Negroes', let us pursue this line of inquiry. One historian has written that 'the CP was for years the only primarily white organization not specifically devoted to civil rights to pay serious attention to African Americans' and that 'the CP's attempt to create a multiracial community was, at the time, exceptional' (Schrecker 1998: 32, 33). A member of the panel set up after the war to investigate the loyalty of Post Office workers (many of whom were black), remarked: '. . . the fact that a person believes in racial equality doesn't *prove* that he's a Communist, but it certainly makes you look twice, doesn't it? You can't get away from the fact that racial equality is part of the Communist line' (Schrecker 1998: 282). Frank Tavenner, counsel for HUAC, certainly agreed. He suggested to friendly witness Michael Blankfort that his defence of negro actors was due to CP influence.[8] The irony lay in the fact that Blankfort was cooperating with the Committee, yet did not offer this interpretation himself. As we shall see in Chapter 5, HUAC had to 'feed' questions to witnesses in an attempt to get the desired answer but did not always succeed.

What is crucial here is the role of the South. In an article entitled 'Who's loyal to America?', published in *Harper's Magazine* (September 1947), Henry

Steele Commager referred to Representative Williams of Mississippi who rose in the House to denounce the *Survey-Graphic* magazine which

> contained 129 pages of outrageously vile and nauseating anti-Southern, anti-Christian, un-American, and pro-Communist tripe, ostensibly directed towards the elimination of the custom of racial segregation in the South.[9]

The Congressman went on to refer to 'meddling un-American purveyors of hate and indecency'. Readers will note the use of 'custom', but of particular interest to us here is the epithet 'un-American': it was constantly used to designate opponents of racial segregation. Long before 1947 the formula already smacked of connotations of being Red. And in 1954, Red-baiter Myron Fagan called for the impeachment of Supreme Court Justice Earl Warren (a Republican nominee of President Eisenhower) for the 'crime' of desegregation, a Red plot to turn the South into 'a black Soviet Republic'.[10] This must not be construed as mere paranoid delirium: it was part of a discourse which saw racial equality as Communist and desegregation a plot to undermine a noble American institution or 'custom', which included lynching. An exhibition held in Washington's Library of Congress in the summer of 2004 to celebrate the fiftieth anniversary of that Supreme Court ruling included photographs of demonstrators in 1956 protesting against desegregation and parading with banners proclaiming 'Integration is Communism' and 'Integration is un-Christian'.

THE APOSTLES OF HATE AND THE QUESTION OF ANTI-SEMITISM

Those who continue to justify witch-hunting are embarrassed by the prevalence of anti-Semitism amongst the Red-baiters of the period. Their embarrassment is understandable, for anti-Semitism was not limited to a handful of pro-Nazi fanatics but a strong current within American society, one that had its adepts on HUAC and among those who supported it. Then as now, liberal and conservative anti-Communists denounced its most notorious practitioners for bringing anti-Communism into disrepute: the Catholic priest Father Coughlin, the evangelist Gerald L. K. Smith and HUAC member and representative from Mississippi, John Rankin. Whether calling radio commentator Walter Winchell a 'slime-mongering kike' or giving the Jewish names of Hollywood personalities on the floor of Congress, Rankin was allowed to spew forth hate because he served a purpose: he rallied the electorate of the south around him – the Democratic Party needed the southern vote to beat the Republicans – and kept alive the myth of the Judeo-Bolshevik conspiracy. This latter pathology goes back to the Red scare at the end of World War I and the fear that Jews and other aliens would take over American society, perverting its values.[11] Comparisons in 1919 between Russian Jews and 'rats infested with plague' (Bennett 1995: 189) look ahead not only to the Nazi portrayal of Jews as rats and blood-sucking spiders but significantly to Jewish mogul Jack Warner's reference to Hollywood's Communists as 'termites', indicating an unconscious fear and prejudice ready to return like the repressed among a wide variety of individuals.[12]

Henry Ford, who became a billionaire by inventing the motor car, accused the Jews of controlling Hollywood and churning out Jewish propaganda; he was awarded a medal by none other than Hitler himself. All this was perfectly conscious, as was the sympathy for Nazi ideology and anti-Semitism expressed by members of HUAC. Let us return to Rankin. Not content with opposing anti-lynch laws and ensuring, thanks to poll tax fees, that only a tiny minority of Negroes (who had a very low per-capita income) could vote, Rankin strove to defend 'white Gentiles' against the Jew and accused Hollywood of being 'in the control of aliens and alien-minded persons', in other words: Jews from Europe and Russia. In July 1942, at a time when America was at war, he denounced

> the radical, communistic elements that are trying to browbeat the Red Cross into taking the labels off the blood that is being furnished to the Army and Navy for our boys, so no one could tell whether it came from a white or colored person . . .[13]

It was official policy in the Armed Forces to segregate blood so as not to offend the sensitive, Southern mentality, a policy which continued until 1949. Rankin was therefore giving vent publicly to a prejudice that was a national disgrace, for the whole question of mingling blood raises at once the morbid fantasy of superior and inferior beings, precisely the Nazi ideology America was fighting. On another occasion, Rankin raised this issue to expose the 'schemes of these fellow travelers to try to mongrelize this nation.'[14] Rankin claimed to be fighting for Christian values, which explains why he defended Nazi military leaders after the war: they were persecuted by 'a racial minority', the Jews.[15]

Rankin was not alone. The first Chairman of HUAC to seek out Reds in Hollywood (in 1940), Texas Democrat Martin Dies, was, like Rankin, greatly admired and applauded by the Nazi Propaganda Ministry. Robert Stripling, HUAC's principal investigator, used his influence to prevent two Nazi agents from being deported. And one Edward Sullivan, nominated Chief Investigator to an earlier version of the Committee, was sentenced to fifteen years for wartime sedition.[16] A journal considered as subversive by the Justice Department and known as the 'Nazi Bible', *Scribner's Commentator*, frequently quoted J. Parnell Thomas and broadcasts from Nazi Germany.[17] Francis Walter, Chairman of

HUAC from 1955, claimed that neither the American Nazi Party nor the KKK 'constitute a threat to the liberties of Americans'. Walter was being consistent:

> Recently, Congressman Walter has been closely associated with a project which seeks to resettle American Negroes in Africa. The head of the project is New York multimillionaire Wycliffe Draper – the largest contributor to Walter's 1960 Congressional campaign. Walter served as a member of a Draper committee distributing research grants designed to prove the genetic inferiority of Negroes. (Pomerantz 1963: 74)

Also involved in this project was Richard Arens whom Walter appointed staff director of HUAC.

This racial delirium took a back seat in the strategies of J. Edgar Hoover. Close links were quickly established between the FBI and HUAC. One expert on the FBI has gone so far as to claim that the FBI really created HUAC by providing the Committee's investigators – illegally, as those summoned were not charged with any crime (Pomerantz 1963: 14) – with information from their files and responding to any request for same. As one HUAC investigator put it in 1957: 'We wouldn't be able to stay in business overnight if it weren't for the Bureau' (O'Reilly 1983: 94–7). The person quoted was an ex-FBI agent, several of whom found gainful employment working for HUAC. Indeed, one such worthy became President of the Committee between 1953 and 1955: Republican Harold Velde. His other claim to fame was in opposing the creation of a mobile library service in rural areas on the following grounds: 'The basis of Communism and socialistic influence is education of the people' (Pomerantz 1963: 57). The (Communist) plot thickens. . .

Velde's remark takes us to the heart of the matter: it betrays a contempt for, a visceral fear of, the 'little man' who might one day rise up and demand his dues. Indeed, the radical sympathies of one 'little man', Charlie Chaplin, led to his systematic persecution by Hearst, Hoover and HUAC. In 1940, when his fellow countrymen (Chaplin had retained his British nationality) were already at war but more than a year before US involvement, Chaplin wrote and directed *The Great Dictator* where he satirised Hitler and Mussolini and had a barber as his hero; in the film Hynkel/Hitler uses the Jews as scapegoats whenever he is faced with a problem. The notions of working-class solidarity between nations, closely allied to the struggle against all forms of fascism, made Chaplin a dangerous figure in the eyes of those who supported European fascism (and who cohabited happily with its American versions), all the more so as the American public, while split over the question of the US taking part in a European war, continued strongly to support social reform and to identify with Hollywood versions of the 'little man'. One historian has analysed plot samples of films of the 1930s:

As our plot samples recorded hostility to the old order and to business coupled with reformist themes, pollsters found that over 63 percent of the public expressed great fears of unemployment and wished for more security in their lives. At the same time over 65 percent felt that big businessmen and elites had too much power, and that sharp inequalities of wealth were undemocratic. They had not, however, lost faith in the possibility of progressive reform. (May 2000: 95)

Making sure that the public did lose such faith and turn to other solutions was the aim of business and social elites after the war. Thanks to the Cold War they succeeded. But I anticipate somewhat. We need to turn first to the question of fascism and anti-fascism, since it will help us understand why Communists lost support after World War II.

FASCISM, ANTI-FASCISM AND THE LIBERAL–COMMUNIST ALLIANCE

The attraction of fascism for a number of Hollywood stars and studio moguls has been well documented and shows that the latter were not averse to 'putting economics above human life' (Slide 1991: 63). Producer Walter Wanger enthused over Mussolini, claiming that he only wanted to help the Ethiopians (whose country he had illegally invaded in 1935), and the Duce's son Vittorio was invited to Hollywood by producer Hal Roach in the hope of organising a new production company. Vittorio was already a contributor to the press of pro-fascist William Randolph Hearst where his articles covered subjects ranging from how to combat the spread of Communism to advice on how to deal with gangsters in America (Pizzitola 2002: 263).[18] Hearst assured his old Republican friend, MGM boss Louis B. Mayer, that Hitler's intentions were pure, which led producer Irving Thalberg to claim, on returning from a trip to Germany in 1934, that 'Hitler and Hitlerism will pass; the Jews will still be there', while simultaneously admitting that 'a lot of Jews will lose their lives' (Gabler 1988: 338). In 1938 Leni Riefenstahl, director of the pro-Nazi *Triumph of the Will* (1935), visited the film colony and reacted thus after seeing an all-black review:

It is all breath-taking jungle ability, but no brains and no inspiration. Did a Negro ever make a great invention? . . . The Jews are backing the Negroes politically. Under their influence the Negroes will become Communists, and so the Jew and the Negro will bring bolshevism to America. (Slide 1991: 64)

John Rankin could not have put it better. Both Henry Ford and Walt Disney welcomed and entertained her. After Hitler annexed Austria in 1938, Fox, Paramount and MGM (all of whose bosses were Jewish) not only maintained their offices in that country but dismissed Jewish executives and employees in Vienna in order to appease Hitler (Slide 1991: 65, 67). Meanwhile, however, threats of boycotts and letter-writing put paid to the Roach–Mussolini idyll and the Duce's son denounced Hollywood as a 'Hebrew Communist Center' (Pizzitola 2002: 267).

One can only sympathise with readers who remain bemused and bewildered faced with this seemingly perverse blindness on the part of the Jewish moguls. In 1936 young Communist screenwriter and future blacklistee John Bright put the question to Jewish writer Samuel Ornitz (one of the Ten) who replied: 'Don't be such starry-eyed goyim about Jews. Class divisions separate us too' (Bright 2002: 48). This is an orthodox Marxist response: in the final instance class interests and economic factors will take precedence over all other considerations. I suggest we also need to evoke ideology and psychology the better to understand not only the situation described above but also the attitude of the moguls over blacklisting. Many people belonging to minorities that are constantly smeared by extremists experience the desire to belong to and thus identify with dominant positions that are objectively hostile to them. Warner's use of the word 'termites' is a classic example of this. By treating the Communists in Hollywood as pariahs to be excluded from the body politic and, so to speak, 'exterminated', he was deciding to hunt with the hounds rather than be the object of opprobrium.[19]

Just as disturbing as this ability on the part of the moguls during the 1930s to place ethics and profits in separate water-tight compartments was the open support for fascist ideology and politics given by such major stars as Gary Cooper and Victor McLaglen. Cooper promoted the 'Hollywood Hussars' (HH); McLaglen formed the 'Light Horse Cavalry':

> To be sure, there is nothing slapstick about Hollywood in dress uniforms. But when these warriors-in-make-up are financed by powerful interests, backed by civic organizations, blessed by the local ministry, and drilled by army officers, their burlesque of fascism warrants careful consideration.[20]

In the same article McWilliams cites as members of the HH a member of the Superior Court of Los Angeles – a former counsel for the Hearst *Los Angeles Examiner*, he was backed for the appointment by Hearst himself – and a certain Sheriff Eugene W. Biscailuz, later to distinguish himself in strike-breaking for Warner Brothers during the studio strikes of 1945–46 (see Chapter 3). One advertisement for the HH read: 'Now enrolling American citizens of excellent character, social and financial standing, military training'. Another specified 'American citizens only'. A booklet issued by the HH cites the Hollywood and Los Angeles Chambers of Commerce as members; it promises to provide Hollywood and Los Angeles 'with a crack military organization', one that would help in case of earthquake or 'any other emergencies menacing the property rights in our community'.[21] The formula 'property rights' highlights the questions of class and money and shows that it was the extreme Right that was ready to use violence to attain its ends and protect its wealth from the workers. This, of course, was passed off as 'Americanism', a topic which obsessed McLaglen who had recently become a US citizen: 'We consider an enemy anything opposed to the American ideal, whether it's an enemy outside or inside these boarders. If that includes the Communists in this country, why, we're organized to fight them too' (Slide 1991: 63).[22] One commentator stated that McLaglen looked 'like a combination of a Canadian Mounted Policeman, General Goering, and Mussolini'. Significantly, the actor – who was soon typecast as a drunken but good-hearted Irish soldier in John Ford Westerns – rode his troops to the building of Hearst's *Los Angeles Examiner* to express his 'good will', thus creating an ideological and political link between the Light Horse and the HH and their various sponsors and heroes.[23]

Cooper's agent had him resign rapidly from the Hussars in order to protect his client's reputation. However, Hollywood's anti-Fascists were more interested in opposing manifestations of fascism outside the community and, especially, in Europe. Nothing united personalities of widely diverging views more than the terrifying extension of fascism in Europe after the coming to power of Hitler in 1933. The plight of Jews, Mussolini's invasion of Ethiopia, the Spanish Civil War and the inexorable drive for conquest by Nazi Germany created an extreme situation that democrats everywhere – which included many conservatives – united to combat. For several years Hollywood liberals, radicals and Communists flung themselves into the battle for ideas, organising meetings and collecting funds. A leading member of the Hollywood Anti-Nazi League was actor Melvyn Douglas, an anti-Communist liberal. He

> remembered returning from Europe early in 1936 and hearing several midwestern businessmen lavishly praise Hitler and viciously attack Roosevelt. By trip's end Douglas felt 'congealed with a kind of horror' that so few seemed to be aware of the Nazi threat. (Gabler 1988: 328)

It was, however, the CP members who were the most active:

> Around here, the feeling was that you joined the CP hoping to do some good to the world, to fight fascism primarily at that point and to develop unions and so on. There was no programme of revolution, ever, that I ever heard of, except in books, theories.[24]

> I never was a Communist and disagreed with their tactics and their strategy and their policy. In fact, I was highly criticized by some of them.

Nevertheless, I have to say that during the Hitler years before we got into the war, they were the only ones that were doing any real agitation against Hitler.[25]

For the post-war witch hunters, especially those with a pro-Fascist and anti-Semitic past to hide, the touchstone for determining who was a Communist or a fellow-traveller was support for Loyalist Spain in the Civil War of 1936–39 that pitted the forces of the democratically elected, left-wing Republican government against the troops of Fascist General Franco.[26] The implications of this conflict – the victory of Franco sounded the death-knell for democracy not only in Spain but in Europe generally – were destined to return far too often and systematically from 1947 on for Spain to be seen in quite the same light as the struggle against Hitler and Mussolini. Even today apologists for post-war Red-baiting suppress the vital facts in favour of the presence of Stalin in Spain and the Spanish Republic's opposition to the Church.[27] Two things, therefore, need to be made crystal clear. Firstly, Franco rose up against the Republic to defend, not religious freedom against Communism, but the continued exploitation of the Spanish people by the ruling class, supported by the Catholic Church. Secondly, Franco was in no way neutral during World War II as his defenders claimed, but let Hitler and Mussolini use Spain as a base for their attacks on American soldiers. His being indirectly responsible for the deaths of these troops did not, however, prevent the American Legion, the self-styled guardian of 'Americanism', from pinning its Medal of Merit on Franco in 1951 (Caute 1978: 351).[28] One of the charges brought against Herbert Biberman of the Hollywood Ten was that 'he was sponsor of a benefit for Spanish Loyalist children and was contributor of an ambulance for Loyalist Spain'.[29] Americans who went to fight against Franco were part of the Abraham Lincoln Brigade, many of whose members were Communists. Among them was Alvah Bessie of the Hollywood Ten.[30]

European countries favoured non-intervention, which dealt a fatal blow to the Loyalists: Hitler and Mussolini had no hesitation in using Spain as a training ground. Remarks by another member of the Ten, Albert Maltz, put matters in perspective:

In 1935 Great Britain signed a naval treaty with Nazi Germany in violation of the Versailles Treaty to allow Germans to build submarines; Great Britain and France told Mussolini they wouldn't apply sanctions over Ethiopia . . .

A Gallup poll toward the end of the [Spanish civil] war showed 76% of Americans in favor of lifting the arms embargo, but Roosevelt needed the Catholic vote.[31]

Europe's so-called neutrality over Spain was dictated by its ongoing opposition to the Soviet Union. Ring Lardner, Jr, expressed this in another way:

> I managed to incur the wrath of Jack Warner . . . through two activities he was still fuming about a decade later when he testified before the Thomas committee. My first transgression was to organize a protest against a studio visit by Vittorio Mussolini, the Italian fascist dictator's son, who had publicly boasted about the thrill of dropping bombs on Ethiopian towns. . . . The other complaint against me involved a campaign to raise money to buy ambulances for the elected government of Spain. (Lardner 2000: 89)

Interestingly, friendly witness Richard Collins, while denouncing his own Communist past, was still unrepentantly anti-Franco, even in 1951. However, this peccadillo was not held against him.[32]

Summing up the whole sordid business of the conniving that led HUAC to count on and thus reinforce the activities of assorted fascist and anti-Semitic groups in the US, Albert Maltz said that the notion of Reds conspiring behind closed doors was 'the other side of the coin' of Hitler's thesis 'about Jews manipulating England'.[33] The embarrassing implications of such complicity did not escape even the obtuse J. Parnell Thomas. The *Los Angeles Times* of 1 December 1947 quoted Representative McDowell (Republican), chairman of a subcommittee of HUAC, to the effect 'that his group has failed to find any Fascist or Fascism in this country worth investigating'. Three days later the Los Angeles *Daily News* reported that Chairman Thomas was 'irked' at this remark, stating that HUAC would be investigating 'assertedly [sic] fascist organizations' and would later call Gerald L. K. Smith.[34] Smith was never called and never suffered the indignity of being subpoenaed for his anti-Constitutional declarations against Jews. Residents in Los Angeles mobilized in 1946 to protest the announcement that he was to make one of his speeches there. Five years later, at a time which coincided with the renewed HUAC onslaught on Hollywood, he was invited back by the California anti-Communist League to talk about HUAC; it was promised he would 'name names and cite facts'.[35] Another event of that year sums up the political climate in a way that sounds like a joke in the worst taste but which was only too tragically serious. The scene: Houston, Texas, where an immigration examiner is testifying about aliens applying for citizenship:

> Examiner: Eighteen of them formerly belonged to the Hitler Youth and similar organizations.

> Judge: Yes, but they have been thoroughly investigated. None has ever been a Communist or member of a Communist front organization, only Nazi and Fascist. (Belfrage 1989: 153)

THE END OF THE LIBERAL–COMMUNIST ALLIANCE

It was the Nazi–Soviet Pact that raised the question of allegiances and isolated Communists. In 1939 Stalin and Hitler signed an agreement not to commit aggression against each other. This was done at a time when Nazi Germany had overrun Europe, when Britain alone had declared war and where, for democrats everywhere, the very fate of civilisation was in the balance. How could such a pact come to pass and what was the effect on anti-fascists in Hollywood?

The news that Stalin had signed an agreement with Hitler to the effect that the latter would refrain from threatening the territorial sovereignty of the Soviet Union (SU), while the former would leave Hitler free to conduct his war against Britain, sowed consternation in Hollywood amongst Communists and liberals alike. The original disarray that prevailed among the Communists was soon overcome as the Party in general and its leading Hollywood members, such as director Herbert Biberman, soon found an explanation which was to dictate future conduct until Hitler invaded the SU in 1941: Britain being imperialist, this was an imperialist war and therefore Communists should have nothing to do with it. This hardly convinced liberals and the non-Communist Left: up until the Pact the CP had been the leading adversary of Nazism in Germany and its spokespersons in the US. The affair triggered off a controversy which was to be placed within parentheses for the duration of the war but which left traces that returned like the repressed once the war was over.

Many commentators have said what they thought about the Pact and the turnabout on the part of the CP: members of the Ten, Hollywood personalities who were blacklisted in the 1950s, former Communists who named names, and liberals within and outside the Hollywood community. Just as liberals saw no justification for the Pact, so Communists defended it and the two sides drifted apart. This rift proved disastrous, as the refusal of the CP to condemn the Pact made it seem that the party was playing the role of the dummy to Stalin's ventriloquist. However, it was not until 1951 that the full impact of the split was felt. The attitude of the CP betrayed a depressing inability to think. Surely it was possible to point out why Stalin had signed the Pact, while continuing to hammer home the message that Hitler remained the greatest threat?[36] At least one newspaper finally put its finger on the dilemma facing Stalin:

> On the one hand, U.S. diplomacy was stringing along with the Chamberlain policy of appeasing Hitler by negotiating trade deals with prewar Germany; on the other, it was encouraging the Russians to go all-out to stop the Nazi menace.

That this two-way operation may have had a direct bearing upon the subsequent Stalin-Hitler non-aggression pact of 1939 is at least a justifiable surmise.[37]

This cogent analysis was made at a time when the first HUAC Hearings in Hollywood had already taken place. It must not be forgotten that the West had never accepted the Bolshevik Revolution of 1917 and had frequently tried to reverse the event and to damage the Soviet economy. Western hypocrisy over Ethiopia and Spain was not lost on Stalin who understood that Europe and the US would have been delighted to see the Soviet Union and Nazi Germany at each other's throats so that the survivor could be easily dealt with. Thus the future President Truman (who came to power in 1945 on Roosevelt's death and was re-elected in 1948) said in 1941: 'If we see that Germany is winning the war, we ought to help Russia, and if Russia is winning, we ought to help Germany and in that way kill as many as possible.' And for Republican Senator Taft, speaking at the same time, '[the] victory of Communism in the world would be far more dangerous to the United States than the victory of Fascism' (Griffith and Theoharis 1974: 293n6). Former Secretary of the California CP Dorothy Healey, referring to the opening of certain British archives, evokes British negotiators being sent to the Soviet Union in 1939 'with explicit instructions that they were not to make any agreements with the Soviet Union in regard to the protective security, the protection of Czechoslovakia and Poland'.[38] Faced with this perfidy, Stalin was not being paranoid or treacherous, merely pragmatic.

Two witnesses who collaborated with HUAC, scriptwriter Isobel Lennart and director Frank Tuttle, both evoked the confusion of the time, the latter insisting on that of the CP, the former her own.[39] Blacklisted writer Bernard Gordon evokes the double standards of the West in their dealings with Fascism on the one hand and Communism on the other (Gordon 2004: 29). Blacklisted writer/director Abraham Polonsky was of the opinion that 'the American Party should have had its own independent anti-Fascist position' (Barzman 2003: 64) and blacklisted writer Walter Bernstein denounced the attitude of the CP as stupid and immoral (Bernstein 1996: 52). Blacklisted director Bernard Vorhaus put it in a nutshell:

> . . . [the Soviet Union] had tried for years to get a united front of the democratic countries against Hitler and hadn't succeeded, because they were hoping that Hitler and the Soviet Union would come to fight each other and either destroy each other or greatly weaken each other. It was only after the total inability to do this that the Soviet Union got time to build up its own defenses by signing this nonaggression pact. But I was also very much opposed to other Communist parties reducing their

anti-German activities. I must say it was a very confused period. (McGilligan and Buhle 1997: 673)

This feeling that the CP was wrong to go along unquestioningly with Stalin to the point of censoring any discussion of the Nazi–Soviet Pact was shared by other Party dignitaries. They considered that Stalin had the right to defend his homeland without this leading to so confusing and ridiculous a change of attitude by the CP (Schrecker 1998: 16). I would stress here the crucial detail referred to by Vorhaus: the Soviet Union 'got time to build up its own defenses'. Why is this so important? Hitler did finally invade the Soviet Union in 1941: the German army suffered considerable losses and many troops were immobilised, thus preventing them from fighting in Europe. Two facts are essential here. First, more than half of the losses in World War II were on the Soviet side. Secondly, their sacrifices saved many lives on the side of the Allies. One specialist has estimated 'that if Russia had been knocked out of the war, the United States would have had to cope with 150 extra German divisions and 1,000,000 soldiers' (Kovel 1997: 261n38). Soviet losses at home saved the Allies in Europe.

The behaviour and attitude of the CP after the Nazi–Soviet Pact had an ideological effect immediately and various political ones soon after. The dubious tactic of embracing what one had formerly denounced alienated non-Communists, which was to prove catastrophic after the war. Politically things were even more serious. By an overwhelming majority in 1940, Congress passed the Alien Registration Bill. Called the Smith Act after its sponsor, '[u]nder its provisions, it was no longer necessary to prove that someone was actually building bombs or collecting dynamite; simply talking about overthrowing the government by "force and violence" was enough' (Schrecker 1998: 97–8). The government in general and J. Edgar Hoover in particular had always based their anti-Communism on 'the assertion that the party and its adherents were part of an illegal conspiracy to destroy the American government by force and violence' (Schrecker 1998: 103).[40] When HUAC got into the act in earnest in 1947, the Cold War was under way, with the belief in the Soviet Union's striving for hegemony taken for granted in many quarters. As one anti-Communist liberal nicely put it:

> The failure of this terrified and growing minority to attempt any intellectual comprehension of how Communism has come to power through violent revolution in the twentieth century and therefore why that same kind of revolution cannot occur in America is a mystery to the educated anti-Communist American left. (Vaughn 1996: 31)

By 1950, however, the 'minority' was the majority: the Soviet Union had the atom bomb, China was Communist and the Korean War had started. This latter event saw the most celebrated and controversial post-war trial, that of Julius and Ethel Rosenberg, and reinforced the obsession with spies.

The Rosenbergs were accused of giving nuclear secrets to the SU and were eventually executed in 1953 in a climate of intense hatred and paranoia. Today Soviet archives have revealed that Julius was indeed a spy but that he did not hand over nuclear secrets. It is now common knowledge that members of the CP were also in the pay of the Kremlin. What does this prove? What could the American Communists do to bring capitalism crashing down about the ears of its practitioners, thus ushering in the dictatorship of the proletariat? The striving for hegemony on the part of the Soviet Union must not be confused with the very real fact of Stalin's determination to maintain law and order in his backyard, putting down brutally any questioning of his power, in the SU or the various satellites under his sway. Our assumptions about Soviet aggression have been shown by the archives to be erroneous, the result of deliberate propaganda (Kovel 1997: xi). We do know, however, that the US kept Nazis in power in post-war Germany as they were useful in the Cold War and that both US and German business had always had a soft spot for Nazism.[41] What is less well known is that leading bankers and businessmen were involved in planning a Fascist coup against Roosevelt in 1934. This act of sedition went unpunished. It is also pertinent to note that Senator James Eastland, yet another white supremacist from Mississippi, kept up the sterling work of the egregious Rankin and called on his fellow citizens not to obey the desegregation imposed by the Supreme Court in 1954.[42] This call to commit acts of sedition also went unpunished, a fact not unconnected with Eastland's membership of HUAC.

One writer has stated that the 'danger from Soviet propagandists in the United States was barely comparable to the repressive tactics of Hearst's agents, members of Congress, the FBI' (Pizzitola 2002: 418). This is perfectly true but written from a liberal standpoint today. The Hollywood Reds did represent an immense danger but not to American democracy. What they challenged was the status quo, the economic order, the power and profits of the few, worse: the ideological notion of American hegemony as going without saying. And this challenge started before the opposition to racism and fascism became the rallying cry of the forces of progress, as we shall see in Chapter 1.

NOTES

1. See Neve 2005: 117. The director was known as Cy, Cyril or C. Raker Endfield.
2. Hearst has gone down in film history as the person who inspired Orson Welles for the eponymous central figure of *Citizen Kane* (1941). As a result of Hearst's relations with J. Edgar Hoover, a file was opened on Welles who was constantly

surveyed from 1941 on. Never blacklisted, Welles found it impossible to find financial backing and left Hollywood in 1948.

3. Anti-Communists of a liberal persuasion tended to equate Communism with the Soviet Union, whereas the more reactionary anti-Communists saw liberalism, Socialism and the defence of civil rights (particularly those of blacks) as Communist. This distinction needs to be kept in mind.

4. Jack L. Warner Papers, Box 43, folder 'Red Investigation', USC. I invite readers to consult the Archival Sources (p. 164) for the abbreviations used throughout.

5. *The Black Legion*, Production Code Association (PCA) file, MHL.

6. OH, p. 55, UCLA. Interview conducted by Joel Gardner, 1986. Even more subversive in *Young Man with a Horn* (aka *Young Man of Music*) than the censored presence of blacks was the theme of jazz which harked back to the 'Cultural Front' of the 1930s when intellectuals and workers, blacks and whites, and artists from all fields were united in a collective attempt to make culture genuinely *popular* and *radical*. Welles played a key role in this period. See Denning 1998.

7. OH, pp. 46–9, UCLA. Interview conducted by Larry Ceplair, 1996.

8. *Communist Infiltration of the Hollywood Motion-Picture Industry*, HUAC Hearings, 28 January 1952, p. 2339. Hereinafter referred to as 'Hearings'.

9. Waldo Salt Papers, Box 77, folder 14, Arts Library Special Collections, UCLA.

10. William Wyler Papers, folder 694, MHL.

11. As early as 1919 Hollywood was exploiting this vein in a production which 'blended anti-Bolshevism with anti-Semitism in a story about an American girl separated from her family and raised as a Red revolutionary by Jews' (Shaw 2007: 14).

12. The anti-Communist film *The Red Menace* substituted an octopus for the spider. See Chapter 6.

13. 'Introducing Representative John Elliott Rankin'. Civil Rights' Congress Papers, Box 10, folder 17 (1947–49), SCL.

14. Anne Braden: 'HUAC. Bulwark of Segregation'. Special Collections, Young Reading Library, UCLA.

15. See below and note 41.

16. David Wesley: 'Hate Groups and HUAC'. Published by the Emergency Civil Liberties Committee in 1961. Special Collections, Young Reading Library.

17. William Wyler Papers, folder 592.

18. There is something uncanny about the juxtaposition of these topics. Gangsters already had an influence within Hollywood and Communists were systematically assimilated to gangsters in certain post-war anti-Communist films. We shall return to this subsequently.

19. We shall return to Jack Warner regularly in the following chapters where the reader will find information on his contradictory stances on the issues of the time.

20. Carey McWilliams: 'Hollywood Plays with Fascism'. *The Nation*, 29 May 1935. Carey McWilliams Papers, Box 3, 'Hollywood Hussars' folder, Special Collections, UCLA. McWilliams (1905–80) was a lawyer and chief of the Division of Immigration and Housing for the State of California from 1938 to 1942. He became editor of the progressive journal *The Nation* in 1955. One of the most

cogent and forceful opponents of the witch-hunt mentality (McWilliams 1950), he was active in the legal defence of the Hollywood Ten after their conviction, helping to draw up the *amicus curiae* brief requesting they be heard by the Supreme Court.

21. McWilliams Papers, 'Hollywood Hussars' folder.
22. Readers will notice that, for self-styled patriots, 'Americanism' goes without saying: it is what they conceive as being 'American'. This is crucial for the post-war period.
23. Slide reproduces a photo of McLaglen with his troops. Dressed in black uniforms, they resemble the Gestapo.
24. Don Gordon, OH, UCLA. Interview conducted by Larry Ceplair, 1988. Gordon is not to be confused with writer Bernard Gordon and director Michael Gordon. They had in common their membership of the CP and the fact that they were all blacklisted.
25. Vincent Sherman, OH, American Film Institute. Interview conducted by Eric Sherman, 1972. Director Sherman (1906–2006) was never blacklisted, but his career suffered during the 1950s. Returning to directing in 1957 he made several films before turning to TV. The climate created by the blacklist broke the impetus of his career.
26. By 1937 the FBI was collecting information on Hollywood personalities supporting the Loyalists against fascism in the context of its on-going surveillance of supposedly communist activity. Actor Errol Flynn is recorded as defending 'Republican Spain' and 'free men' in April 1937. In July 1937 actor James Cagney sponsored the Abraham Lincoln Brigade. Cagney had already made himself a reputation as being on the extreme Left by supporting the EPIC Campaign (see Chapter 1). See http://foia.fbi.gov/foiaindex/compic.htm and access the Cagney file.
27. Given the close collaboration between the Catholic Church and the Right in Spain in maintaining the population in poverty, this is hardly surprising.
28. We shall discuss in Chapter 5 how witnesses both friendly and unfriendly were questioned by HUAC on their support for Loyalist Spain.
29. *Variety*, 30 October 1947. Jack L. Warner Papers, Box 43, folder 'Red Investigation'.
30. Writer Ernest Hemingway also fought for the Loyalists, as did English author George Orwell whose revelations about Stalin's elimination of the non-Communist Party Left (those sympathetic to Trotsky) are still exploited by the Right against the Loyalists. The brother of Ring Lardner, Jr, of the Hollywood Ten, was killed in Spain.
31. Albert Maltz, OH, pp. 291, 432, UCLA. Interview conducted by Joel Gardner, 1976.
32. Hearings, p. 248. Collins appeared on 12 April 1951. We shall discuss his testimony in greater detail in Chapter 5.
33. OH, pp. 209–10.
34. Jack L. Warner Papers, folder 'Red Investigation'.
35. Waldo Salt Papers, Box 77, folder 14, April 1951.
36. Liberal writer Philip Dunne rightly considered that Stalin's gesture was a 'purely nationalistic one' made 'in an effort to buy time'. He estimated that the CP

'ignored the substance of history and endorsed the ephemera of propaganda' (Dunne 1992: 111).

37. *Daily News*, 14 December 1948, Civil Rights Congress Papers, Box 10, folder 13, SCL.
38. Dorothy Healey, OH, UCLA. Interview conducted by Joel Gardner, 1982.
39. Tuttle appeared before HUAC on 24 May 1951, Lennart on 20 May 1952. See Hearings, pp. 642 and 3517 respectively.
40. This is an appropriate point to remind readers that the CP was not illegal and that belonging to it did not violate any laws.
41. The publication of secret Central Intelligence Agency (CIA) documents in 2006 has lifted the corner on many dirty deeds. Of particular interest is the remark by a leading CIA official concerning who was hired by the US during the Cold War: 'It was important to use every swine, as long as he was an anti-communist.' 'Postwar German government and CIA shielded Adolf Eichmann' (www.wsws.org, 3 July 2006). It was this mentality, of course, that led former Secretary of State Henry Kissinger to use the CIA to help General Pinochet bring down yet another democratically elected government: that of Salvador Allende in Chile. An example among many others: see Kovel 1997: 245. For information on the post-war relations between the Republican Party and former Nazis, see Bellant 1991.
42. In a statement reproduced in the Library of Congress exhibition referred to above.

1

Hollywood and the Union Question

The question of unions in general and Hollywood unions in particular is a vast and complex matter which we shall find recurring throughout these pages. It was the creation of a union that sowed the seeds of the antagonisms, conflicts and trench warfare that characterised the relations not only between studios and employees in Hollywood but also between unions. These relations were to lead by a tortuous route to the Hearings and the consequent blacklist. The protracted and bitter campaigns waged to form an independent writers' union and the nature of the attempts to sabotage any such union will be the central concern of this chapter. It will be useful at this stage to document and analyse a momentous event in the politics of California which, in many ways, set the scene for what was to ensue: the EPIC (End Poverty in California) campaign of Upton Sinclair.

Sinclair was a novelist and a Socialist who stood as a Democrat for the post of Governor of California in 1934. His platform included plans to raise taxes and expand relief programmes, but also to nationalise the film industry. This last measure led Hollywood to dub him a 'Bolshevik beast' (Ceplair and Englund 1980: 91). It transpired, however, that big business and the Republicans, in whose vanguard were to be found the studio bosses, were going to need more active methods than this rhetoric to defeat Sinclair. The capitalist gambit of the 'right to work' was easy to see through as an attack on unions, at a time when there were 300,000 unemployed in Los Angeles alone and when the National Industrial Recovery Act (NIRA) had granted unions the right to organise. This had led to a wave of strikes in 1933 where wages and the recognition of unions were the key issues (Gottlieb and Wolt 1977: 204–5). Of the tactics used to discredit Sinclair, one was classic: the conservative anti-labour newspapers

misquoted Sinclair in order to give the impression of an eccentric radical with
lunatic notions on every issue. Other tactics, however, were original and
involved the studios whose bosses also indulged in economic blackmail by
letting it be known that they were thinking of leaving Southern California for
Florida. MGM and Louis B. Mayer were behind the tactic which consisted of
showing propaganda in their cinemas.

The following quote sums it up:

> Movie audiences in 1934 were enormous, and films had the power to
> reach great numbers of people. The studios, which controlled the distri-
> bution outlets, could force theater owners sympathetic to EPIC to play
> the newsreels under threat of losing the main feature.
>
> One newsreel pictured a raggedy mob scene as the announcer explained
> that crowds of unemployed were waiting at the border in the hope of
> getting into California because of the possible Sinclair victory. Though
> the EPIC newspapers pointed out that the crowd scenes were footage
> from other movies, almost all the major newspapers in the state failed to
> pick up this information. (Gottlieb and Wolt 1977: 211)

So those who claimed to believe in the 'open shop' (read: no unions) practised
cynically their own form of the 'closed shop' (read: a business monopoly). Of
considerable interest is the way the Hollywood moguls used fiction (their own
films) to put over another fiction. Fictional films became newsreels bearing the
stamp of Truth, as do documentaries.[1] There is considerable irony in this
situation when one remembers that HUAC launched its Hearings of 1947 with
the claim that there was Communist propaganda in Hollywood films. Here the
studio bosses gave the Left a lesson on how to create and exploit propaganda
for their own purposes.

Another tactic has been wryly summed up by blacklisted writer John
Wexley:

> In all the studios they had different methods of opposing EPIC, but at
> Columbia, in the central plaza, as you entered the studio, there – like a
> flagpole – was a huge thermometer thirty or forty feet high. And the
> red part, indicating the degrees of temperature, went higher as they
> got in what they called 'contributions'. It was really a tax hitting the
> employees. The studio got close to one hundred percent very quickly.
> (McGilligan and Buhle 1997: 707)

The studio workers had a choice: pay up or be fired. This had the merit of
showing where power lay, a sort of managerial closed shop where the choice
for the worker is non-existent. Wexley was under contract, so was not fired by
Columbia boss Harry Cohn until that contract ran out, whereas John Howard

Lawson could be fired at the end of the week. He was. Many were simply naive. Donald Ogden Stewart, soon to be one of the most active Hollywood Communists, has stated: 'Knowing nothing about politics, a great many of us contributed money to beat Upton Sinclair.'[2] Sinclair, although beaten, did honourably at the polls, a revealing indication of the electoral strength and ability to organise of California's progressive and radical forces.

As one historian has written, 'Upton Sinclair's campaign a year later became a flashpoint for the divisions between capital and labor, assuming symbolic proportions far greater than Sinclair's own election' (Gabler 1988: 322). A 'year later' than what? The declaration by the studios in March 1933 – the week of the inauguration of Roosevelt – that

> they weren't going to be able to meet their payrolls. Even that might not have fomented an insurrection among the stars, writers, and directors, a notoriously soft and obsequious bunch, had the studio heads not then collaborated on March 9 and decided to inflict a Draconian pay cut of 50 percent for any employee earning over fifty dollars a week – the cut to last eight weeks. (Gabler 1988: 321)[3]

Just like the 'contribution' to beat Sinclair, this pay cut was a form of imposed income-tax:

> Weary and moist-eyed, Louis Mayer collected his MGM family into the Thalberg Projection Room to lay out the grave facts about the industry's financial debility. He could barely speak. 'Don't worry, L.B. We're with you', shouted [actor] Lionel Barrymore when Mayer broke down . . . As Mayer strode back to his office, he turned to his crony Ben Thau and asked, 'How did I do?' (Gabler 1988: 321)[4]

This is an early example of downsizing: employers cut salaries and/or lay off workers to maintain profits.[5] Nobody pushed insubordination to the point of asking the studio bosses to reduce by 50 per cent the sums they gambled. They were wont to frequent a private club in Hollywood, where gambling was illegal, to assuage their lust for this particular sin (Gabler 1988: 258–61). On one occasion, in another setting, Sam Goldwyn 'bet fifty thousand on a single card' (Bright 2002: 59). One of the more tiresome and dishonest jibes made by Red-baiting journalists at the expense of Hollywood's Communists concerned the huge salaries of some of them, their swimming pools and the like. Implicit in these attacks, which smack of jealousy, is the notion that workers should not share in the vast profits made by their employers. Which brings us back to the matter of unions.[6]

Abraham Polonsky has referred to the CP's 'enormous role . . . in the organizing of unorganized labor' and Albert Maltz, one of the Ten, has stated:

'Equal pay for equal work was a CP slogan back in the 1930s, 1920s', stressing the Party's opposition to the exploitation of women by men.[7] Blacklisted actor Lionel Stander, whose virtual monologue before HUAC drove the inquisitors into the ground, attributed his radicalisation to seeing police attacking demonstrators and to reading the next day 'in the *New York Times* that this was a demonstration of the unemployed for unemployment insurance. I think it was 1931. The *Times* editorialized that the whole idea of unemployment insurance was Communistic and insane' (McGilligan and Buhle 1997: 609). When writer Michael Blankfort appeared before HUAC, he found time between attacks on his former comrades to praise the CP which 'did things like fight for unemployment insurance, for example. Unemployment insurance was a very serious thing in those days'.[8] Screen reader Don Gordon said that readers 'were the most underpaid people in the business. They [the producers] got their wages down to $25 a month.' He recounts how readers were invited to sit in on meetings held by writers trying to set up a guild and how he became chairman of a meeting to form the Screen Readers' Guild. In this capacity he went to a Screen Writers' Guild (SWG) meeting and what he said appeared the next day in the anti-labour pro-studio trade paper *The Hollywood Reporter* as 'Gordon denounces Sweatshop in Industry'. Gordon commented: 'that fixed me good'.[9] Gordon was named as a Communist by a member of the Screen Cartoonists' Guild.[10]

Writer Bernard Gordon, blacklisted in 1952, tells of an experience when President of the Guild founded by Don Gordon. Bernard Gordon led the Guild into the Conference of Studio Unions (CSU) whose militancy put it at the centre of the immediate post-war conflicts (see Chapter 3). In this capacity he participated in negotiations with the Producers' Association, in the course of which he defended the office employees who had the extra drawback of being women:

> while I was speaking my piece, I saw Charles Boren, the Paramount executive in charge of labor relations, scribble something on a piece of paper that he circulated among his buddies. Afterward I heard from one of the union people that the scrap of paper he was passing around was a crude drawing of a hammer and sickle. He was labeling me. (Gordon 1999: 6–7)[11]

Strikes also concerned the less famous and the completely anonymous, as a technicians' strike of 1933 bears witness. It also shows the corruption of the studio union at the time and sheds light on the post-war period. A sound technician had this to say of the strike:

> It started in sound, and it spread to the other IA crafts. It resulted in the complete wreckage of the IATSE, the local, not the International, as far

as the picture business was concerned. We were sold out by the heads of our locals, and a couple of them went to prison, (George) Browne and (Willie) Bioff.[12]

Stewart explained how the studios brought in people from broadcast stations because they were not organised into a union, how he was offered a contract tripling his wage if he became a strike-breaker and how those on camera continued to work, despite the strike, because they commanded higher salaries than the union scale. This question of hierarchy and how certain workers saw themselves as above the fray was a bone of contention among the writers, but it is not irrelevant in the case of actors and the creation of the Screen Actors' Guild (SAG).

Let us return to Lionel Stander, an early and active member of the SAG:

> Before the Guild got power, there were no limits on an actor's working hours. You could work till midnight or two in the morning and be called for six o'clock the next morning. And the working conditions, particularly for extras and bit players, were terrible. We'd go on location and there'd be no water, coffee, or adequate toilet facilities. (McGilligan and Buhle 1997: 611)

These views have found echoes over the years, irrespective of the political opinions of those concerned. Leon Ames stated: 'I've worked until midnight and at four in the morning been called back to makeup at seven o'clock', while Robert Montgomery remembered a film in which 'we were actually on the set and working for over thirty-five hours without a break' (Prindle 1988: 18). Both actors were conservatives: Montgomery was a key figure in strike-breaking and Red-baiting after the war, and a Republican. Nor should we assume that all actors were anxious to improve their lot. Thus Ames remembered how fellow SAG activist Ralph Morgan was denounced by another actor who was afraid of mass expulsions from the industry, whereas an early adherent to SAG, Ralph Bellamy, recalled friends saying how good MGM and Louis B. Mayer had been to them (Prindle 1988: 19). I quoted earlier the support Mayer received from Lionel Barrymore who was opposed to the creation of SAG (Prindle 1988: 21). We shall see below that certain writers shared this admiration for Mayer.

'From its founding in 1933, a struggle between progressive and conservative actors in SAG was constant but muted, with the conservatives generally dominating' (Prindle 1988: 8). The actors who joined forces as a result of the 50 per cent cut included radical Fredric March and ultra-conservative future Red-baiter Adolphe Menjou, conservative Montgomery and liberal Groucho Marx. There is no reason to assume that a conservative is going to stand idly by while

his or her standard of living is threatened. At the same time, however, conservative domination in SAG tended to give preference to those with large
salaries, rather than those who struggled to obtain a tiny role:

> Officially, at any given moment, about 85 percent of SAG members are out
> of work, and two-thirds earn less than $2,000 a year from their announced
> profession. . . . If unemployment among actual, career-oriented actors is
> only 20%, it is still horrendous from the perspective of almost any other
> profession. (Prindle 1988: 11)

In the light of the ever-increasing radicalisation of Hollywood, both Left and
Right, from the early 1930s on, what transpired within the ranks of the SAG
looked ahead to the post-war years. A radical opposition to the IATSE, the
Federation of Motion Picture Crafts (FMPC), saw the light of day in the mid-
1930s and garnered the sympathy of a number of actors, as well as the Left in
Los Angeles. The IATSE (often called IA) was the producers' union: a threat to
it was a threat to themselves. According to one historian, up until at least 1936
the SAG's board of directors denounced the IATSE's Red-baiting as 'Fascist'
and 'un-American' and sided with left-wing workers' unions. Moreover, the
SAG fought and organised without the presence of Communists: 'something
more was going on' (May 1989: 129–31). Things had changed, however, by
1938, for reasons that remain confused, although we shall propose an interpretation after discussing the SWG. A bargain was struck: the producers recognised
the SAG as sole bargaining representative, while the actors 'disavowed any
intention to join the FMPC and departed victorious' (Prindle 1988: 30). In
1938 the radical actors supported liberal Melvyn Douglas who was trounced by
the conservative candidate.[13]

Certain writers too were perfectly happy with their lot and had no desire to
be formed into a guild or a union, an unmentionable word. It is in this context
that matters become complex and the intimately linked notions of class and
hierarchy became paramount. Since we are not dealing with a classic Left–
Right opposition but with a question of the official recognition by the studios
of tasks performed (by the writers), it will be necessary to identify a number
of individuals, especially those destined to have a role to play in the post-war
showdowns, and to stress the importance of certain dates, facts and figures.

Nineteen thirty-three is the pivotal year. The Depression had been creating
misery on a massive scale since 1929. The highest wage outside Hollywood
was $33.88 a week, whereas Greta Garbo was earning $5,000 a week, and the
only unions in Hollywood were the musicians' union and the corrupt IATSE
(Schwartz 1982: 5, 8). In 1927 the producers had created the Academy of
Motion Picture Arts and Sciences, covering producers, directors, actors,
writers and technicians: 'The academy honored them with dinners and annual

affairs where it presented awards for the best films, performances, direction and scripts and hailed them all as "artists". Thalberg made it clear "artists" would never deign to organize or become members of a trade union' (Cole 1981: 119). Irving Thalberg was the brains behind Mayer at MGM and has been called 'the late, sainted union buster of history'.[14] The actors were not the only ones to react over the pay cuts. Writer John Bright has stated: 'We were making $250 a week to create millions for the company' (Bright 2002: 8). At the same time, not all writers were opposed to the producers. John Lee Mahin, young, successsful but badly paid like Bright, adopted to Mayer the same attitude as actor Lionel Barrymore: 'I think I'll go along with the studio. They'll look after me eventually' (Bright 2002: 8).[15]

Two major factors, then, separated those writers who decided to unionise and those who supported the producers. Firstly, the notion that a writer is a worker with rights and not simply an 'artist', especially as he could never be independent in Hollywood. Secondly, the reason for that lack of independence: exclusive contracts. This meant that a studio had the right to lend a writer – or an actor – to another studio without their consent and that screen credits did not necessarily go to the writer who had made a particular contribution. Moreover, the pay cuts showed that the producers would ignore the contracts if they saw fit (Schwartz 1982: 30, 11–12). Future CP member and one of the Ten, Dalton Trumbo, proposed replacing the contract system by 'a royalty system of moderate salaries and profit participation'. This suggestion 'for collectivizing movie making did not endear him to the producers' (Schwartz 1982: 7). The question of royalties meant that, say, a writer would receive financial compensation every time his or her film was projected, a notion that returns periodically today in discussions of 'pirating' films that appear on TV: unless it is specified in a contract that the actor will get a certain percentage of the profits, no monies accrue to those who helped make the film profitable in the first place.

For the purpose of discussing the betterment of conditions under which writers worked in Hollywood, motion-picture writers met on 3 February 1933. They included two members of the Ten, Lester Cole and John Howard Lawson, as well as John Bright (Cole 1981: 121–2). Bright was shortly to become one of the four founders of the Hollywood CP, along with Samuel Ornitz of the Ten (Bright 2002: xiii). The fact that none of the writers was a member of the CP at the time did not prevent the Red bogey from being yanked out of the cupboard within months. 'Pinks Plan to Stalinize Studios' was the eloquent title of an article in *Variety* in September 1933 (Ceplair and Englund 1980: 453n6). Given the reactions we have already noted to remarks made by Bernard Gordon and Don Gordon on improving working conditions, it is hardly surprising that the conservative, anti-union Republicans who ran

Hollywood saw the Trojan horse of Communism within the gates when they read the first documents produced by the writers. These included 'a statement against unfair practices of putting writers on scripts without notification of the writer already employed, and, most important, a demand writers, not producers, would control their material, as in the theater' (Cole 1981: 123).

Just how realistic was this demand, especially the reference to those writing for the stage? Many Hollywood writers came from Broadway or were novelists. Thus F. Scott Fitzgerald and Nathaniel West, Dorothy Parker and Lillian Hellman, John Dos Passos and William Faulkner all worked in Hollywood, but East Coast intellectuals such as playwrights John Howard Lawson and Donald Ogden Stewart did not have the working-class background of John Bright and Lester Cole. There is a certain incoherence in the demand, inasmuch as working in film is a collective process, whereas writing a novel or a play for Broadway is not. We are faced with a paradox, where the *collective* nature of film led the producers to behave as autocratic super-authors, which suited conservatives: they were left alone and accepted the power of the studio bosses who knew how to flatter their egos by calling them artists. Yet the writers on the Right were in a position of contradiction greater than those on the Left, for the simple reason that they repressed the fact that they were workers on a contract, at the beck and call of the moguls, whereas Cole and the others were fighting for the *artistic* status of the screenplay against the view of the moguls that this material was theirs to change if they saw fit. Thus the Right, which claimed to defend an individualistic notion of art, was in fact acting in a way detrimental to artistic endeavour, whereas the Left defended the concept of artistry in film, as in the theatre or the novel, while also insisting on the rights of workers to dispose of the products of their labour and to share in the profits.[16]

This, of course, is basically a Marxist notion, so it is intriguing to note how many writers, including impeccable conservative and Republican, Charles Brackett, rallied to the cause of the SWG.[17] One reason was the attitude of the Academy over screen credits:

> The Academy said that producers had a right to tentatively determine credits based on an assessment of substantial contributions, to be made by the producer. . . . However, even if the Academy found that the credits had been improperly allocated on the screen, the producer would not be obligated to change them. (Schwartz 1982: 49)

For a writer, a screen credit was the only form of identity he or she had: 'with the power of determining credits in the hands of the producers or the Academy, fear of obscurity was a strong enough deterrent to keep even the most outraged writer from joining with others in a unionization movement' (Schwartz 1982: 49–50).

Things came to a head in 1936 with the Academy Awards: the Academy pushed the Thalberg production *Mutiny on the Bounty*, while the SWG and the SAG lined up behind *The Informer*. The victory of the latter took everyone by surprise, as did the refusal of writer Dudley Nichols to accept the Oscar. Nichols wrote eight scripts for the film's director John Ford between 1935 and 1940 and, during the war years, wrote two major anti-Nazi films, *Man Hunt* (Fritz Lang, 1941) and *This Land is Mine* (Jean Renoir, 1943). But he also wrote scripts filmed by such right-wing directors as Howard Hawks (*Bringing up Baby*, 1938), Sam Wood (*For Whom the Bell Tolls*, 1943) and Leo McCarey (*The Bells of Saint Mary's*, 1945).[18] More importantly, he was highly respected, a staunch liberal and one of the highest paid writers in Hollywood. His letter to the Academy, turning down the award, was eloquent:

> To accept it would be to turn my back on nearly a thousand members of the Writers Guild, to desert those fellow-writers who ventured every-thing in the long-drawn-out fight for a genuine writers organization, to go back on convictions honestly arrived at, and to invalidate three years work in the Guild, which I should like to look back upon with self-respect. (Schwartz 1982: 51)[19]

The SWG executive board met in May 1936 and decided to call on its members to ratify article 12 of the Guild Code which meant refusing to sign contracts until May 1938. At the same time they would vote to amalgamate with the Authors League of America whose members in turn would then subscribe to article 12. This amounted to an embargo on the sale of all material to the studios, a collective action involving 'a nationwide confederation of authors' (Ceplair and Englund 1980: 26) which insisted on the notion of writers exer-cising control over the fruits of their labour. This would also lead to increased royalties and wages. Dark references to Communists at work abounded, although there were no Communists among the SWG members who took the decision, but the *Motion Picture Herald* wrote of a 'Writer Dictatorship' (Schwartz 1982: 58–9). However, a far more worrying event from the SWG point of view had already taken place. An opposition group to the Guild, led by James Kevin McGuinness and Howard Emmett Rogers, had been formed: the Screen Playwrights (SP). Its members took the same stance as the producers: amalga-mation with the Authors League would be to submit to Eastern domination, all the more regrettable as authors tended to despise Hollywood and everything it represented (certain writers spent part of the year in Hollywood earning big money, then returned East). The real reason was the moguls' fear of writers seeing themselves as both artists *and* workers and therefore joining forces with other unions against company unions like the IATSE. This is precisely what hap-pened, as we shall see in Chapter 3.

It was the repercussions after the war of the events of the 1930s that were significant:

> Amalgamation and Article XII together smacked of 'collectivism' to men like Rupert Hughes, Mahin, and McGuinness. In their minds the concepts of labor and union became indelibly tagged with objectionable and ideological labels. Thus the way was paved for conservatives to read 'anti-American' radicalism into tactics and strategies which were standard fare for union building. (Ceplair and Englund 1980: 37–8)[20]

Conservative elements in the SWG had in fact used a public speech by John Howard Lawson as a pretext for abandoning ship. Lawson, who could be undiplomatic and belligerent, had shown both traits by asking a most impertinent rhetorical question: 'Do you suppose it is the writers who want to put the absurdities, the repetitious paragraphs, the indecent allusions which one often finds in motion pictures? Of course not. It is the executive' (Ceplair and Englund 1980: 35). The conservatives called for the repudiation of Lawson's speech; this was refused by the SWG Board but a compromise was reached which, added to the threats from the Producers' Association, led to a mass exodus from the Guild of the more apolitical members, impressed by the departure of the well-heeled conservatives and ever mindful of that 'fear of obscurity' evoked earlier. Various writers talked of a blacklist of the more militant members of the SWG, but no proof was forthcoming: Jack Warner stated that it took place by telephone (Cole 1981: 162).[21]

Soon only the most committed writers still belonged to the SWG: seventy-five as compared to some 750 members originally! However, the SP's ideological prejudices and their inherent elitism and snobbery when it came to their socially and financially less fortunate brethren did them a disservice. For the SWG had been conceived along democratic lines of bringing all writers, famous or anonymous, under one umbrella, whereas the SP persisted in maintaining the values of its founders: let in the rich and famous and keep the riffraff out. Members had to belong to a major studio and have a certain number of screen credits; they paid high dues. As for the others, the trade paper and mouthpiece of the studios, *The Hollywood Reporter*, summed up their special status thus: 'the lesser writers will be allowed membership with nominal dues and, *while having no vote*, will nevertheless have the higher bracket scripters bonded to handle their problems with equal fervency' (Ceplair and Englund 1980: 43; emphasis added). This was a modern version of feudalism, the difference being that allegiance was now to the studios and was assured by McGuinness and Co. As a result, the SP membership never exceeded 125, leaving literally hundreds of writers out in the cold. It is a sign of the arrogance of the SP leadership and of the studio bosses that they never dreamed that anything could rock the boat. Something did.

The event that changed everything was momentous and concerned none other than the Supreme Court of the USA whose decisions are binding on all American subjects. On 12 April 1937 the Court upheld the constitutionality of the Wagner Act of 1935 which

> affirmed the right to collective bargaining but also created a National Labor Relations Board [NLRB] to mediate disputes, thus regulating the wider union formation process. Unions could indeed be formed more easily, but without the board's approval, they would have little chance of defeating a stubborn employer. (Buhle 1999: 102–3)

The SWG immediately petitioned for a hearing before the NLRB whose representatives duly came to Hollywood in late 1937 and heard witnesses from all sides for seventeen days. However, only in June 1938 did the Board issue its judgement: 'certification would be voted on in Hollywood on a studio-by-studio basis. Writers bound by a studio contract as of June 4 were eligible to cast secret ballots for the union of their choice' (Ceplair and Englund 1980: 45). The SWG won hands down, partly thanks to significant support: the newly formed Screen Directors' Guild (SDG) and the SAG whose President, Robert Montgomery, urged the hesitant to vote SWG in order to confort his Guild's past victories (Cole 1981: 162). The support of the SAG may come as a surprise to readers in the light of information earlier in this chapter. However, it is clear that this joining of ranks in order to defend a common interest – being the sole representative within a framework of collective bargaining in a context where only unionisation was feasible – can be attributed to an intelligent desire to overcome differences, without there being a genuinely radical drive behind it. Only the diehards within the writers' ranks refused to join the general movement, already engaged as they were (along with the trade papers) in Red-baiting. It is essential to remember the sentiment on the part of those who set up and ran the Screen Playwrights: they were 'artists' and not to be assimilated to manual workers such as technicians and set decorators. That the SAG was more conservative than the SWG and an ambiguous ally was to become patent during the strikes of 1945–46, but even the SWG did not vote with a single voice then (see Chapter 3). And the SDG was even more conservative, with a grand total of seven Communists. We have already seen how a right-wing figure like Hawks could support a union, not for reasons of collective solidarity, but to safeguard his enviable status within the film community.[22] It takes a genuine sense of commitment to struggle for the underdog when one is oneself among the 'happy few', socially and financially. The values that motivated the Left were to lead to their isolation and downfall.

The fact that the SWG received twice as many votes as the SP at MGM where Mayer and McGuinness ruled the roost is an indication that the anonymity of the ballot can compensate for the enforced anonymity of being a writer under contract and that democracy was being preferred to a defence of privilege. In August the NLRB ruled that the SWG was the sole bargaining representative for the industry's writers. Although management continued to haggle and to deal only with the SP, time at this particular juncture was not on the side of the studios against whom the SWG brought injunctions until the NLRB voided the studios' contracts with the SP (Ceplair and Englund 1980: 45). If some form of calm returned to the writing scene, storms were brewing on a variety of fronts, both within and outside Hollywood. It took the entry of the USA into the war in December 1941 to place them between brackets, but not to put an end to them.

NOTES

1. Hollywood resorted to this ploy in 1951 with *I Was a Communist for the FBI*. See Chapter 6 and Humphries 2006.
2. OH, UCLA. Interview conducted by Max Wilk, 1971.
3. The situation was more complex: only those earning over $100 a week were to suffer a cut of 50 per cent, whereas those earning under $50 were exempt. For those in between, the percentage rose in accordance with their weekly earnings. See Prindle 1988: 17.
4. MGM's profits in the previous quarter had been $5 million and Mayer was one of the highest-paid leaders of industry in America.
5. The moguls' threat to abandon Los Angeles for Florida was an early example of delocalisation.
6. History has an interesting tendency to repeat itself, as this anecdote concerning the IATSE (see below and note 12) indicates. After the terrorist attack on the World Trade Center in 2001, the President of the IATSE 'quickly negotiated a temporary 25 per cent pay cut for his members that was subsequently forced upon all the unions in response to the claims by the owners and producers that it was the only way to revive Broadway'. See www.wsws.org 'As Broadway stagehand talks resume, IATSE president blasts writers' strike' (19 November 2007). This is in the context of the strike of the Writers' Guild of America (WGA). I invite readers to keep this in mind when reading Chapter 3.
7. OH, p. 133, AFI. Interview conducted by Eric Sherman, 1974; Maltz, OH, p. 191.
8. Hearings, 28 January 1952, p. 467.
9. OH, pp. 7–10. Readers were hired to read scripts sent in to the studios and to choose those with potential.
10. One of the ironies of history: the Cartoonists Guild went on strike against Walt Disney in 1941 who refused to recognise it as the only legal interlocutor for collective bargaining. This fuelled his anti-Communism. See Chapter 3.

11. Bernard Gordon is interviewed in McGilligan and Buhle 1997: 260–78.
12. James G. Stewart, OH, pp. 113–14, AFI, 1971. IATSE = International Alliance of Theatrical Stage Employers. See Chapter 3.
13. Douglas, smeared later as a Jew and a fellow-traveller, was in fact always an anti-Communist liberal. His wife, Democrat Helen Gehagan Douglas, was Red-baited by Republican Richard Nixon (member of HUAC in 1947) in the climate of Cold War hysteria.
14. Leonard Spigelgass, American Film Institute Seminar, 1971, p. 9. Spigelgass was a member of the SWG from 1947 and Vice-President or Treasurer from 1949 to 1953. In October 1951 he made a speech in his capacity as a member of the Motion Picture Industry Council, set up as Hollywood's official Red-baiting organisation, in which he thanked HUAC for exposing the Communist menace in Hollywood. See MPIC Papers, 'Speeches', file 2-f.16, MHL.
15. Both then and after the war Mahin was a consistent adversary of liberals and the Left.
16. The reaction to Sinclair had already shown a feudal mentality on the part of the moguls, so 'Lawson's audacity in organizing writers . . . was viewed as akin to a rebellion of peasants with pitchforks' (Horne 2006: 99). Blacklisted writer Julian Zimet stated that studio heads 'ran their fiefs like Chinese warlords' (McGilligan and Buhle 1997: 735).
17. Brackett wrote many films in collaboration with Billy Wilder who, although no Communist, was far more radical.
18. Hawks was a conservative for reasons of elitism, both in his lifestyle and in his attitude to Hollywood. He believed in unions as long as it meant defending his independence and the large sums he was paid for his work, not out of any commitment to the collective or a belief in defending the less fortunate. But he took no part in Red-baiting. Both Wood and McCarey were virulent Red-baiters (see Chapter 4).
19. According to an article in *New Masses* (3 October 1939), Nichols and fellow Guild members Oliver Garrett and Ernest Pascal were called 'sons-of-bitches, bastards, and goddammed Reds' by the studio bosses. All were known liberals.
20. Rupert Hughes was the uncle of mogul and future Red-baiter, Howard Hughes.
21. A non-Communist progressive who knew the studios from the standpoint of the inner sanctum, producer Milton Sperling, considered that it was 'a graylist, really, a hesitation about hiring. It was emotional rather than institutional' (Schwartz 1982: 75). Blacklistee John Wexley considered Sperling one of the progressives at Warner Brothers (McGilligan and Buhle 1997: 712).
22. Similarly, the director of photography James Wong Howe, a liberal who quietly supported radical causes and the blacklistees, was dubious about unions: 'The idea of cameramen, who were artists, joining with stagehands and sound men offended his sensibility. It was a problem that would plague every talent organization in the industry' (Schwartz 1982: 13n).

2

The War Years, 1939–1945

When the US declared war on Japan on 8 December 1941 following the attack on Pearl Harbor, Nazi Germany had overrun Europe and been at war with Britain since September 1939. The controversy that raged in America between partisans and adversaries of the country's participation in the war effort was rendered more complex by the Spanish Civil War, the Nazi–Soviet Pact and attitudes within America to Nazi Germany. If Americans were united from 1941 to 1945, films made in the period 1938–40 showed that anti-Fascism brought together film-makers of very different political opinions. Before discussing certain war films, it will be useful to turn to an event that occurred in September 1941. Its repercussions were revelatory of the political climate in the US and were to return, in an inverted form, once the war was over: the Senate Sub-Committee War Films Hearings.[1]

   The Sub-Committee was created at the request of two Senators, the Democrat Burton Wheeler and the Republican Gerald Nye, to investigate what they saw as blatant propaganda films put out by Hollywood to support Roosevelt's foreign policy and create a situation where the American public would support America entering the war. The Committee was created in August 1941; the Hearings started on 9 September. Both Wheeler and Nye were isolationists: involving America in a European conflict was against American interests. They considered that war-mongering Britain had been responsible for America's participation in World War I and that the same mistake should not be made again. Isolationism tends to be assimilated to xenophobia and chauvinism, but certain progressives were also isolationists because of their opposition to the very kind of aggressive imperialism both Britain and Germany represented at the time of World War I:

In the thirties, [Hollywood actor and liberal Democrat] Will Rogers criticized the colonization of nonwhite peoples as a product of American
capitalist expansion. . . . Along the same lines Progressive historians like
Charles and Mary Beard promoted isolationism as the means to prevent
big business from advancing its class interests and power around the globe.
(May 2000: 152–3)

Nor must we confuse Wheeler with Democrats such as Rankin: he was not a
Southern racist but represented the northern state of Montana. However, a
speech by Nye brought anti-Semitism once again to the fore, along with its
bed-fellows, xenophobia and anti-Communism. What was actually said during
the War Films Hearings was uncannily prophetic of the post-war years.

The following quotation sets the scene:

From coast to coast over a nationwide radio hookup, and later in the newspapers, a speech by Senator Nye reached millions of Americans. The charge
was made that the Hollywood movies have gone into the service of war-
making, that they were part of British propaganda, and that 'international
bankers' were to blame; and Senator Nye's list of names such as Cohen,
Mayer, Goldwyn and Bernstein in his St. Louis meeting was accompanied
by howls of 'The Jews', 'The Jews' from the Nazis and Coughlinites present.

Some time ago Senator Wheeler also gave out a broadside against 'the
international bankers', listing only Jewish names.[2]

Seldes goes on to quote Nye's attack on the Hollywood moguls:

'In each of these companies there are production directors, may of whom
come from Russia, Hungary, Germany and the Balkan countries.' (This
statement was another rabble-rouser).

'The fact is that if England loses the war many of these (movie) companies will lose all their profits. . . . The question up to us is: Do we want
to send our boys to bleed and die in Europe to make the world safe for
this industry and international bankers?'

Seldes is a useful source, since his opposition to anti-Semitism was not simply
ethical but also political. Thus he points out that no mention is made by either
Senator of American banker J. P. Morgan, a Gentile, that it was he who played
a key role in getting America into World War I and that another Gentile,
Rockefeller of the Chase National Bank, controlled Twentieth Century Fox,
just as other Wall Street banks owned by non-Jews controlled various studios
such as Warner Brothers.[3] Seldes also stresses a point we have made in Chapter
1: Hollywood ached to do business with Fascist countries until the behaviour

of the dictators and the opposition within the United States put an end to such dreams of extra wealth.

The activities of newspaper magnate William Randolph Hearst are most informative. Hearst's own son claimed that his father was behind the creation of the isolationist association, 'America First'.[4] Columnist Louella Parsons raised the question of refugees employed in Hollywood, a snide and vicious way of insisting on the Jewish question and suggesting jobs should be reserved for the native-born. An out-of-work screenwriter, while professing sympathy for 'those unfortunate people' the Jews, nevertheless asked: 'Are these producers Americans or are they Jews?' After the war the question would be reformulated: 'are these Hollywood employees Americans or Communists?' Another Hearst writer linked the refugee theme with the magnate's pet crusade: 'the screen has teemed with Communist propaganda, war propaganda and alien propaganda of all kinds' (Pizzitola 2002: 385–9). Thus is formed the equation 'Jew = alien = Communist'. In HUAC parlance the last term became 'un-American'. There is a danger of over-simplification here. Thus an article in the CP paper *New Masses* (18 May 1937) entitled 'Fifth Column in America' had revealed that Nye wanted an investigation into the activities of Franco agents within the US. This suggests his isolationism was consistent and that calling him pro-Fascist misses the point. Similarly, Wheeler denounced the persecution by J. Edgar Hoover in 1940 of members of the former Abraham Lincoln Brigade who had fought Fascism in Spain. This was hardly the act of a simple isolationist and anti-Communist. He was joined in this protest by none other than Red-baiter Westbrook Pegler (O'Reilly 1983: 131). If Pegler used the War Films Hearings to denounce Stalin in the same breath as Hitler, his own opposition to Nazism and his rejection of the claims made by Wheeler and Nye are clear:

> There is no dark, mysterious reason why we have had no pro-Nazi films. The reason is that in all the record of Hitlerism there isn't enough favorable material to make a short.

> If that is the sort of entertainment that these Senators want Hollywood to produce, then it is they who are asking for false and misleading propaganda, because any such work would flout history.[5]

One commentator was critical of both Hollywood and the Committee. While deploring 'a continuous diet of drums and bugles, tanks and planes, parachutes and bombs', he warned the Committee not to see anything but a coincidence in the fact that the studio bosses were Jews, lest they 'fan the latent flames of race prejudice'.[6] Another shifted the debate onto the question of 'loyalty' and 'patriotism', asking 'Do these involve blind support for the powers-that-be in Washington?'[7] The same writer referred to Roosevelt's message to the Motion Picture Academy some months earlier 'in which he congratulated the industry and expressed his gratitude for its service to the national defense effort'. Roosevelt was walking a tightrope here: having pledged during the 1940 Presidential campaign not to involve the US in the on-going war in Europe, he nevertheless was providing Britain with invaluable support, a major bone of contention with isolationists. An influential spokesman for Hollywood, producer Darryl F. Zanuck, spelled out what Roosevelt had requested of the industry:

> We have been asked by the Government to make training pictures for the United States Army. We have made these as our patriotic duty. I am happy to say that Chief of Staff, General Marshall, has told me that these films have done an immeasurable amount of good in saving man power, material and time in organizing the Defense of America. As this committee doubtless knows, these pictures are of a strictly educational nature. I cannot believe it is an offense either for the Government to ask for this service from the industry, or for the industry to comply with such a request.[8]

This statement skilfully displaces the issue from one of movies functioning as anti-Nazi and pro-war propaganda onto the noble question of the 'Defense of America' but is disingenuous in suppressing all reference to fictional films in favour of documentaries produced to educate the armed forces. However, by also claiming that bowing to the whims of Wheeler and Nye 'would leave the American motion picture as worthless and sterile as those made in Germany and Italy', Zanuck revealed the true situation: fictional films were the Committee's real concern, although Hollywood was not indulging in propaganda like Fascist dictatorships. Zanuck was speaking the truth, but remarks by Father Coughlin showed that Hollywood's enemies were closer to another 'truth' that would become the Gospel after the war. Coughlin did not have the same axe to grind as Hearst whose anti-Communism was dictated by class and economic interests. In retrospect, Coughlin's anti-Communist remarks made when commenting on the Committee's investigations must be taken seriously, as he had put his finger on a theme that was to become the major preoccupation after the war. In his journal *Social Justice* Coughlin quoted an industry journalist as saying Hollywood was 'crawling with Communists and fellow travellers' and went on to declare that such organisations as 'The Anti-Defamation League' and 'The Anti-Nazi League' should be investigated.[9] Hollywood and the Government were to oblige by the end of the decade: both organisations were considered as Communist-controlled. Similarly, Coughlin denounced the Motion Picture Democratic Committee of Hollywood as contributing vast sums to 'Communist coffers through cocktail parties, street collection boxes and mail solicitations for the Loyalist cause in Spain' and demanded it be investigated too.[10]

Other commentators made equally prophetic remarks. Hollywood hired lawyer Wendell Willkie, a former Republican candidate against Roosevelt. Willkie demanded that he be allowed to cross-examine those witnesses who had urged the probe. *Variety* quoted Committee member Senator Clark: 'the sub-committee is not a court of law and can't be bothered about legal niceties or legal custom'.[11] Willkie challenged this assertion, but the fact remains that a Committee of Congress conducts not a *trial* but an *investigation*.[12] Also germane to our topic is Willkie's accusation that the Committee was 'badgering and threatening unprotected witnesses and refusing to allow those who are being accused from having a hearing'.[13] Two columnists spelled out eloquently the implications of the Committee's methods:

> It is going to put the entire industry before a star-chamber court in which witnesses have no benefit of counsel, for the industry's attorneys may not cross-examine witnesses.[14]

> There [*sic*] approach is not scientific, but inquisitorial. The role they have assumed is not that of judges, but of prosecutors. The defendant has been found guilty before even being brought to trial. All that is asked of him is that he confess it.[15]

This latter remark is prophetic in its use of the word 'confess', foreshadowing the tactics of HUAC from 1951 on, but journalists put their fingers on the methods that were to become the mode of functioning of HUAC in 1947: 'smearing, without chance of equal rebuttal'.[16] The formula 'witch hunt' was used both by Dorothy Thompson and *The Film Daily* of 25 September.[17] Noteworthy too was the unanimous condemnation of censorship of the movies: as unacceptable as censorship of the press itself, a theme taken up again in the wake of the 1947 Hearings (see Chapter 4). However, only one source mentioned the following fact: 'It is reported that the investigation files of the Dies' Committee have been requested by the Wheeler-Nye groups to aid in the contemplated examination.'[18] As we stated in the Introduction HUAC Chairman Martin Dies had just visited Hollywood, but it is easy to see why nobody saw a link between HUAC and the Wheeler–Nye Committee. Hollywood had already made two anti-Communist films, *Ninotchka* in 1939 and *Comrade X* in 1940, and no pro-Soviet films had seen the light of day. The feeling of outrage over the accusations launched by the isolationist Senators led to a fixation on the immediate situation which led to everything else being forgotten.

Two films in particular provoked controversy: *Blockade* (1938), written by John Howard Lawson and directed by William Dieterle; and *Confessions of a*

Nazi Spy, written by Milton Krims and future blacklistee John Wexley and directed by Anatole Litvak. Both Dieterle and Litvak were on the Left and their careers were to be seriously compromised after 1950; Dieterle stopped making anything committed, Litvak returned to Europe. Both were refugees: Dieterle (who was not a Jew) had left Germany early, Litvak, a Russian-born Jew, left Germany with the advent of the Nazis. After the war Krims wrote two anti-Communist films, *The Iron Curtain* and *One Minute to Zero* (see Chapter 6). If the hostility to *Blockade* summed up perfectly the political tensions within America, *Confessions* was a special case.

When *Blockade* went into production, Joseph Breen wrote to producer Walter Wanger on 3 February 1937, warning him that the material used was 'highly dangerous . . . from a practical standpoint, as well as distribution in Europe'.[19] The 'practical standpoint' referred to the inevitable problems that would be encountered everywhere over the evocation of the Spanish Civil War. On 22 February he wrote again, advising Wanger not to 'identify, by means of uniform or otherwise, the soldiers actively participating in the fracas' [*sic*]. On 28 February Breen wrote to Will Hays: 'The studio has taken great pains not to take sides in the matter' (which Breen significantly called the 'Spanish Revolution').[20] When the film finally premiered in 1938, the Board of Directors of the right-wing, Catholic organisation 'Knights of Columbus' sent a protest to Hays, calling the film 'historically false . . . in its complete suppression of the fact of the Communist-inspired reign of terror that preceded and precipitated armed resistance by the Spanish Nationalists'.[21] This statement is ideological not factual, but it indicates perfectly the Right's stance over the Spanish Civil War: a refusal to accept a democratic vote, a smearing as 'Communist' the Loyalists' republican values and the transformation of a fascist general into a freedom fighter.

Other reactions were diametrically opposed. Director John Ford, who had a nephew in the Abraham Lincoln Brigade but had been a member of the Knights of Columbus for years, defended the film.[22] He was followed in this by Frank S. Nugent writing in the *New York Times* (26 June 1938) and by *Box Office*, the National Film Weekly, which took issue with Hollywood's lack of courage faced with attempts to have the film withdrawn, thus preventing people from deciding for themselves. The Board of Christian Education (Presbyterian) echoed these sentiments, which led Breen to make a statement exonerating the Catholic Church and placing the blame squarely on the Knights of Columbus.[23]

If there is no ambiguity over the setting of *Blockade* – the first shot informs us we are in Spain in Spring 1936 – the result of pressure from Breen is manifest. The conflict looks like a purely internal affair, with average Spaniards on both sides, so that it is sometimes difficult to know who is fighting whom and defending what. At one point the hero, a farmer played by Henry Fonda, is decorated for bravery by the military for encouraging people to stand and fight, rather than flee. The officer in charge evokes the bombing of their cities, which for audiences at the time could only refer to the participation of Hitler and Mussolini in the conflict, but both physically and because of the uniform he wears – especially his cap – he resembles Franco! And the only political state-ment the film makes is when Fonda addresses the camera/spectators at the end to ask: 'Where's the conscience of the world?' This, however, was sufficient for the film to be welcomed or denounced as a political movie.

However, there is more to *Blockade* than a vaguely humanist message. Refusing to run away in the face of the advancing troops (since they are respon-sible for opening the hostilities, informed spectators would understand them to be Franco's), Fonda evokes the land and says to another farmer: 'this belongs to us and nobody can take it from us'. Moments later he faces the fleeing peas-ants and exhorts them to fight: 'this land belongs to us'. The script thus raises the notion of the *collective:* those who work (on the land) and produce wealth have a right to enjoy the fruits of their labours and, especially, to control its use from start to finish. Marxist in inspiration, it is one of the themes we shall see returning in the films written and directed by future blacklistees: anti-racism, sacrifice (individual or collective) for a common cause, working-class solidar-ity, trade unionism. More subtly, the script shows the confusion in which the heroine lives. Involved with the forces blockading the port and preventing food from arriving for the starving populace, she is shown at one point giving chocolate to children whose hunger she deplores, while simultaneously passing on a message aimed at preventing a relief ship from getting through the block-ade. When she sees babies dying, she is able to understand that there is a link between famine and personal gain: she opts for a socialist solution to a crisis engendered by capitalism. Lawson presumably wished her to represent a con-fused liberalism.

There is, however, a further element of the script that opens the film out and is certainly 'subversive' from the viewpoint of the Right. The heroine is accompanied by an elder man, Gabriel, who runs guns for Franco. This he does less from conviction than a desire to make money.[24] Played by the excellent character actor John Halliday, Gabriel is quite the most interesting character in this frankly leaden film: he brings to life every scene he appears in. Crucially, Lawson had put his finger on the basic ideology of capitalism: make money out of literally anything, including starving children. Gabriel is always dressed in breeches, which lends him a 'big hunter' appearance and assimilates him to Franco. This is perfectly in keeping with his role in the film: the Spaniards are so much cannon fodder, just as animals exist solely to be hunted down. It is this aspect of the film which deserves to be remembered.

Confessions of a Nazi Spy created even more controversy: the film is openly anti-Nazi, a frontal attack on the government of a country not at war with the United States. It is indicative of the divisions within American society when it came to fascism that criticism of the film came from within Hollywood in the form of a memo to Breen from one of his staff, signed 'K.L.', who considered that the script was a violation of the Hays Code as Hitler was 'unfairly represented': K.L. cited 'his unchallenged [*sic*] political and social achievements'.[25] He also asked: 'Are we ready to depart from the pleasant and *profitable* course of entertainment to engage in propaganda . . .?' (emphasis added). This was written on 22 January 1939, but on 23 November 1938 the German consul had already written to Breen after reading a clipping from *The Hollywood Reporter* stating that a Warner contract writer was to attend the German spy trial in New York to obtain first-hand information for a picture the studio was planning.[26] Luigi Laraschi of Paramount wrote to Breen on 10 December to evoke 'horrible repercussions for Jews in Germany' if the film were made. Robert Lord of Warner Brothers informed Breen (24 December) that the German–American Bund and the German consul were desperate to get their hands on the script. Breen himself contacted Jack Warner on 30 December to support the project, stating that it was honest and used material culled from the widely reported spy trial. He justified it in a letter to Will Hays the same day by comparing it to the famous newsreel documentary 'The March of Time'.[27] Such was not the opinion of one reviewer who wrote: 'Many will ask . . . how such a film could be made without the tacit consent and blessing of the U.S. Government.'[28]

If such remarks must have been sweet music to the ears of the Wheeler–Nye Committee, the *Motion Picture Daily* (29 April 1939) wrote of the film: 'only Nazi sympathizers will object'.[29] This remark is revelatory, coming as it did *before* Britain's declaration of war; it is an early indication of what was to become a majority view concerning European Fascism at the time of the Hearings. However, if the importance of the film as an anti-Nazi statement cannot be overstated, it is not the most interesting aspect of the film. I would argue that the most revealing element of the script is what certain critics consider the weakest: the use of the FBI to confound the Nazis (Buhle and Wagner 2002: 212). Prior to 1941, Hoover was more interested in unearthing Communists than Nazis. The choice of Edward G. Robinson to play the FBI agent is both perfect and grimly ironic. A very progressive Jew, he was to be hounded by the FBI and the Red-baiters after the war and brow-beaten into submission. Thus the film presents, in an unconsciously inverted form, what was to become the main concern a decade later: not the Nazi spy, but the Communist 'subversive'.

Confessions of a Nazi Spy is, in fact, a highly patriotic film. From the outset a young German woman, attending a party after a pro-Nazi speech given by the film's leading villain Dr Kassel, asks what is an innocent question for her but not for the film: 'Aren't we all supposed to be Americans?' This theme – a European who has chosen to live in the US becomes a US citizen, owes allegiance to the US and is proud to be one of its citizens – meant different things to different groups: the Left was attached to the notion, whereas the Right was either hostile or exploited it in the name of the war on 'un-Americans'. In the film, however, this seemingly progressive and humanist notion becomes something quite different and highlights all the ambiguities within Hollywood.

It is revealing that the screenwriters should have found themselves in opposite camps a decade later, for the script contains remarks that would be applied to Communists. Thus the District Attorney who prosecutes the Nazis refers to 'a world-wide spy network', destined to become HUAC's mantra of 'the world-wide Communist conspiracy'. In the film the Nazis pretend to defend the American flag, while subtly denigrating all aspects of American life. This was to become the basis of the accusation of 'un-Americanism' hurled at Communists and others once the war was over. The film's Nazis also exploit racial and religious hatred and class antagonism in order to confuse the workers and the middle class. Such tactics were later attributed to Communists in *The Red Menace* and *I Was a Communist for the FBI* (see Chapter 6). Significantly, it is not Kassel who suggests these tactics but Nazis in charge in Germany. Thus a pro-Nazi German residing in the States shows an allegiance first and foremost to Germany and Communists were constantly accused of putting the interests of the Kremlin before those of America. Most revealing, however, is a meeting where pro-Nazi Americans of German origin are challenged by their adversaries within the German-American community. One is played by Ward Bond (a leading Red-baiter after the war and already known in the 1930s for his hatred of radicals) who is a member of the American Legion! His cry 'We don't want any "isms" in this country, except "Americanism" ' is a dress rehearsal for the witch hunts.

On 19 September 1938 Harry Warner made a speech to the American Legion. Although clearly attacking Fascism and Nazism, his reference to 'organizations . . . inspired, financed, and managed by foreign interests' could just as easily apply to pro-Soviet activities in the US: 'You may have heard that Communism is rampant in Hollywood and in the motion picture industry. I tell you this industry has no sympathy with Communism, Fascism, Nazism or any "ism" other than Americanism.'[30] Such words would return to haunt the Left after 1945. On 5 June 1940 he gave a pep talk 'United We Survive. Divided We Fall' to 6,000 Warner Brothers' employees and their wives, where he hinted at 'the enemy within', and referred to 'the Fifth Column and the Trojan Horse'. Warner unmistakably had Germany in mind, but a later remark is prophetic:

> I would like a law passed that any and all members of Un-American
> Organizations, especially those sponsored and paid for by enemy foreign
> powers, would have their citizenship revoked and be deported to their
> own native lands, or the land in whose hidden employ they are.

He then evoked 'the horrors of brutal Communist, Nazi or Fascist invaders'.[31]
That Warner was defending Hollywood in general and his studio in particular
is patent, but the fact that he should have seen fit to raise the spectre of
Communism in Hollywood and lump it together with Nazism is an indication
of the ambiguities of the time and looks ahead ominously to the post-war shift
in opinion.

The confusion surrounding *Confessions* stems from the fact that interven-
tionists and isolationists alike interpreted its anti-Nazi message as a call to war.
If everyone had looked more closely, they might have reacted differently. The
final sequences of the film are devoted to the District Attorney's speech in
court denouncing the Nazi spies and to the self-congratulatory scene involving him and the FBI agent. Looking into the camera, the DA thus addresses
the film's spectators who are 'separated by vast oceans from bacteria of aggressive dictatorships and totalitarian states'.[32] More to the point in 1939, however,
is the implication of the remark: geographically we are safe, so let's keep it that
way. What is this, if not a plea for isolationism?! In the final sequence, the DA
and Robinson are having a drink when two customers start discussing the trial,
adopting, of course, an anti-Nazi attitude, much to the two men's satisfaction
(the scene is as contrived as it is revelatory). One says to the other: 'This ain't
Europe and the sooner we show 'em, the better!' This is an ambiguous remark.
It patently portrays the US as a country that can resist Nazism, but also as a
country safe from such 'bacteria'. The remark can be interpreted as both jus-
tifying intervention and making it clear that all un-American activities will be
proscribed and punished. It is hardly a simple call to arms.

Other contemporary films are less ambiguous. One is *The Man I Married*
(1940), directed by Irving Pichel. In 1932 he had co-directed *The Most
Dangerous Game*, an anti-fascist allegory whose main character, Count Zaroff,
is a cross between Mussolini and a Gestapo officer: he is dressed in black and
wears breeches. Perhaps he even inspired Victor McLaglen (see Introduction,
note 23). His mirror image in the film is a big-game hunter, Rainsford, whose
world is that of finance and whose ideology of the 'survival of the fittest',
although applied to the contest between hunter and big game, is identical to
Zaroff's who applies it to human beings: he hunts the latter only.[33] The script
of *The Man I Married* is by Oliver Garrett, a leading member of the Screen
Writers' Guild, which explains a remark surprising for the time and clearly
determined by Garrett's own liberal sympathies and the Nazi–Soviet Pact: in

the film an anti-Nazi compares Hitler to Stalin. Heroine Joan Bennett discovers gradually that the man she has married is pro-Nazi and she feels both threatened and imprisoned within her own home in Germany. A key role in the film is played by an American journalist who says at one point: 'The Nazis want to include us out of the next war', an indication that war between Germany and the US is inevitable and necessary. Moreover, he warns of the danger Nazism represents, not only to Britain and France, but also to the United States. The film is far more committed than *Confessions*. The journalist leads an ignorant society lady of a vaguely liberal disposition to discover the horrors of fascism and reject her isolationist attitude. Her disgust at the sight of German soldiers, parachutists belonging to the 'El Condor' regiment, parading on their return from Spain is more eloquent than many a speech. The film is saying that what happened in Spain is engulfing all Europe: America could be next. Breen, however, was more jittery now than over *Confessions*. In a letter to Jason S. Joy of Twentieth Century Fox (26 April 1940) he indicates anxiety that 'these avowedly anti-German pictures' harm the industry (the film was originally entitled *I Married a Nazi*)[34] and asked him to eliminate a reference to Hitler as 'the madman and his brother lunatics' as this violated the Hays Code ruling that other nations must be represented fairly.[35]

Another film directed by Pichel deserves mention here: *Colonel Effingham's Raid* (1945). Set in Georgia (the Deep South) in 1940, the script turns on the local celebration of 'Confederacy Day'. When a journalist visiting the town evokes Nazism, he is told: 'we mustn't let a war interfere with something big'. The central character is a retired soldier who describes everyone and everything in military terms: thus his black servant is his 'orderly', which symbolises black–white relations in the South. However, his devotion to the past has a positive side: he is anxious to preserve the local courthouse as being part of the town's 'common heritage'. As he speaks, a photograph of Lincoln is visible. His patriotism founders on the refusal of bankers to make a loan: it would not be in the interests of their shareholders. This attack on the profit motive shows progressive concerns alive at the end of the war.

Three other films of the period 1938–40 merit attention: *Three Comrades* (1938), *The Mortal Storm* (1940) and *Four Sons* (1940). The first two were directed by Frank Borzage, a conservative who also produced *The Mortal Storm* for that most conservative of studios, MGM. *The Mortal Storm* is even more forthright an anti-Nazi film than *The Man I Married*. The action begins in January 1933 with the celebration of the sixtieth birthday of Professor Roth who teaches biology at the university. Family, colleagues and students all join in and Roth is presented as much loved and respected. However, during the celebrations it is announced that Hitler has been nominated Chancellor and things fall apart. Roth, his wife, their daughter (Margaret Sullavan) and one of his students (James Stewart) show considerable anxiety, whereas another student (Robert Young), engaged to the daughter, and Roth's two stepsons go wild with joy. Gradually they turn against Roth, who is not only a Jew but a scientist who denounces publicly the delirium of 'racial purity'. He dies in a concentration camp. One scene shows the Nazis burning books, including those of Einstein, a most revealing choice: Einstein was simply a Jew for the Nazis, but in America he was both a Jew and a Communist in the eyes of J. Edgar Hoover of the FBI (Jerome 2003). That Roth is also a scientist is perhaps not a simple coincidence. In the course of the film Stewart helps a Jewish teacher who has been beaten up by the Nazis to escape to Austria, but Sullavan is killed when she and Stewart try to escape. The deliberately melodramatic approach that was Borzage's hallmark is far more successful in involving the audience and forcing them to take sides than the canny, pseudo-documentary approach of *Confessions* which cannot begin to match the intensity and the commitment of *The Mortal Storm*. *Variety* (10 June 1940) hailed the film as 'the most effective film exposé to date of the totalitarian idea'.[36]

Ethics and religion are as important as politics in the film. The religious element takes precedence at the end of *Three Comrades* which is set in Germany in the period 1918–20. Of the three comrades (significantly, the word has no Communist connotation in the film), Robert Taylor is an apolitical hedonist, Franchot Tone a cynic who nevertheless is committed to the notion of camaraderie, with only Robert Young showing, as soon as World War I is over, a sense of despair at the way his fellow Germans turn to hatred and violence to solve the economic problems of society. Although the film makes no overt political statement, shots of a demonstration turning violent as the marchers beat up those listening to an impassioned speech by an old man calling on Germans to hear the voice of 'reason' are clearly intended to encourage audiences to see in these violent elements the beginning of the breakdown of law and order that was both the cause and effect of Nazism. Young is shot down from behind by a thug and when Taylor's wife (Margaret Sullavan) dies from tuberculosis, Taylor and Tone leave Germany in despair for South America: the ghosts of Young and Sullavan 'accompany' them in the last shot. The presence of Sullavan in positive roles in both films, with Young portraying a progressive in one and a Nazi in the other suggests that Borzage intended the two films to be seen together as a clear warning: democracy and liberalism are destroyed by Nazism.

With *Four Sons* we return to John Howard Lawson. The film is historically interesting: it is anti-Nazi but not pro-Soviet. Lawson was Hollywood's leading Communist and the Nazi–Soviet Pact had been signed, yet there is nothing 'Stalinist' about the film. A review in *Variety* referred negatively to the Nazis and *The Hollywood Reporter* called Lawson's script 'brilliant'.[37] The family in the film is Czech and the pro-American tone is set when one of its members calls the US 'a great country': he spent ten years there. One son is a Nazi and, since the family has German origins, considers them all Germans with the Nazi occupation of the country. For another son, however, the family is and remains Czech. Here Lawson reworked the statement of the German-American woman in *Confessions* about people of that community being Americans. Yet the film was targeted as Communist by the Wheeler–Nye Hearings and provided a moment of low comedy:

> Quoting a Harrison's report on 'Four Sons', [the chairman] attempted to drag in the Communist inference by insisting the story had been changed from German to a Russian sympathy because the mother's name was 'Leontovitch'. His face flamed like a spanked baby's hams when Mr. Zanuck explained that 'Leontovitch' was not the name of the character, but that of the actress who played it.[38]

With his script for *Action in the North Atlantic* (1943) Lawson turned to the war effort of the Merchant Marine. The film is famous – infamous in right-wing circles – for a scene where a sailor, on seeing Soviet planes, shouts 'They're ours, alright!' The Left was never forgiven for extolling the Soviet war effort: when General MacArthur did so, that was patriotic, when Communists did so, that was pure propaganda. Another aspect of the film must have enraged the Right. The film is resolutely working class in its values: the sailors of the Merchant Marine belong to a Communist union. This furnished Lawson with the material for the film's big political scene where a working-class, left-wing Jew berates those who 'think America is just a place to live and sleep in', thus insisting on collective solidarity beyond the country's frontiers – the fight against fascism – and within the States: union activity to improve the workers' lot (Dick 1989: 58; Buhle and Wagner 2003b: 4). That Lawson should open the film with a quote from Roosevelt was normal in 1943, but after the war the Republican Right saw this juxtaposition as proof of the 'Communist' influences at work within the New Deal.

It was with his scripts for *Sahara* (1943) and *Counter-Attack* (1945), however, that Lawson came into his own, helped enormously by the superb direction of Hungarian Zoltan Korda. Both films reach far beyond the simple need to extol the war effort (of the British and the Americans in the former, the Soviets in the latter) and open out into complex and, in the case of *Sahara*, genuinely tragic reflections on valour, dignity and sacrifice. Based on a Soviet film called *The Thirteen*, *Sahara* recounts how Bogart manages to hold his Anglo-American team together in a seemingly doomed attempt to keep hundreds of Germans at bay until help can arrive. Although Bogart is represented as a natural leader, the script nevertheless avoids the clichés and gradually builds into a truly epic narrative of men pulling together in extreme circumstances (little food or water in the middle of the desert) to defend a common ideal. The initial tensions between the Americans and the British are overcome due to the simple fact of survival and the film even includes towards the end what was an extraordinary shot for the time and is still potent today: a British medical officer (the middle class) and a Brooklyn soldier (the proletariat) lie dead in one another's arms after their shelter has been bombed. Two aspects of the film are important. The first is the character of the African soldier who turns out to be the most resilient and courageous, Lawson taking advantage of a foreign setting to pillory the racism within American society.[39] The second is a discussion between Bogart and the British medical officer. The end for the few survivors seems imminent and the medical officer evokes the 'dignity of freedom'. Bogart does not understand and the other spells it out: the Nazi soldiers have never known it. Beyond the notion that Britain and the US refuse to regiment their troops and citizens there lies a greater truth about sacrifice and what will become of the world if Nazism wins. It is the reflection that no sacrifice is too great to save humanity from the ultimate horror. The film's Frenchman clearly represents that country's Resistance. By having an African (whom the Nazi prisoner refers to as a 'nigger') perform the film's most significant act and a Briton make its most important statement Lawson succeeded in showing the need for a genuinely cosmopolitan approach and opposition to Fascism. It is revealing that a Briton should give Bogart the American a lesson in the 'dignity of freedom'.

Counter-Attack is remarkable for Paul Muni's performance, the intensely dramatic situation and Korda's ability to exploit the setting in a cinematic way. Muni is a Soviet soldier who finds himself, along with a woman comrade, trapped underground with a small group of German soldiers: Muni and the woman are armed and they must keep awake until help arrives. The film is pro-Soviet in the sense of extolling that country's war effort and in showing Soviets as human beings. There is an exchange between one of the Nazis and Muni where the former dismisses the Soviets as weak because they are stubborn; Muni sees this as their strength. This is clearly a reference to the Soviet refusal to capitulate after the Nazi invasion, but much more: it is praise for the notion of a refusal to accept brain-washing, to submit to monstrous orders, to turn oneself into an automaton. Such arguments would soon be turned against Communists, but the political point is clear in 1945. However, the film brought complaints from religious groups because of a sarcastic reference by the Nazi to Jews walking on water. For these groups, neither Nazis nor Soviets showed any respect for religion, so it was 'dramatically unsound to have a German attempt to insult a Russian by slurs on Christianity'.[40] This protest, which is political and not religious, can be seen as part of a much wider attempt to put Nazism and Communism in the same basket.

Lester Cole, also one of the Ten, wrote two scripts dealing with war sub-jects: *Hostages* (1943) and *None Shall Escape* (1944).[41] The former's theme is similar to that of Lang's *Hangmen Also Die* (1943): the taking of Czech hostages by the Nazis in an attempt to pit the people against each other through the threat of executing said hostages.[42] The second film written by Cole recounts the struggle of the Jews and the massacre of those who were ready to stand up and fight. Both films raise the ethical and political questions posed by the remark made by the British medical officer in *Sahara* concerning the 'dignity of freedom'. In *None Shall Escape* the rabbi puts the following question to the Jews: 'Is there any greater degradation than to be tolerated?' The 'tolerance' he is berating consists of exploiting a position of power (economic and/or polit-ical) to set up a racial hierarchy which imposes inferiority on one group: they must accept it in order to be allowed to live.[43] If they refuse, they will die, which is what happens in *Hostages*: the people reply to the rabbi's call to fight and are all killed. We have here an early version of the extraordinary scene in Luis Bunuel's *The Phantom of Liberty* (1974) where one of the Spaniards defend-ing his country against the invasion by Napoleon cries 'Down with Liberty!' By doing so he rejects the 'liberty' imposed by Napoleon: capitulate and you will be free to live; resist and you will die. Death is preferable to life when the subject makes his own choice – death – instead of submitting to what the other imposes. In *Hostages* the Czech Resistance gives the order to blow up a Nazi munitions dump, knowing that this will mean the execution of the hostages. However, their sacrifice ensures the victory over Nazism and therefore a genuine freedom later.

Just as instructive as the films themselves are the ways they were received in the US. *None Shall Escape* brought a letter (17 December 1944) from a group of Marines 'somewhere in the Central Pacific'. They wrote: 'We all expected the usual flag waving, bond sellers, but to our joyous astonishment it was different. Appreciated by all. More of this sort we look forward to'. They found Marsha Hunt 'a really sensational discovery'. And the conservative trade paper *The Hollywood Reporter* praised the film to the skies for its ideals of 'truth and freedom', finding it 'fitting' that 'the simple peoples of the earth, the little fellow who has suffered most, shall be given the opportunity to voice that cry'.[44] However, Hearst's *Los Angeles Herald Express* (17 December 1943) wrote that '*Hostages* . . . is nothing less than plain Communism masquerading under the guise of Czech patriotism. The contemptible characters in the picture are the coal boss and the son of the coal boss who have the wickedness to possess money'.[45] If people of all political persuasions, united against Nazism, could respond without difficulty to *None Shall Escape*, Cole introduced into *Hostages* a class element that provoked the opposite reaction from certain quarters. The main figure is a working-class man who addresses thus the owner of a coal mine who justifies his wealth by claiming people need coal: 'you're the head of the Syndicate: you don't produce the coal. I worked in your mines for twelve years. Have you?' This recalls Fonda's remark in *Blockade* discussed earlier. And at the opening of the film those from the same monied class as the mine owner are shown fraternising with the Nazis. This accusation was too accurate historically for the Right to forgive or forget after the war.

Pride of the Marines (Delmer Daves, 1945) garnered much praise for its writer, Albert Maltz (one of the Ten). Maltz talked about how producer Jerry Wald asked him to write in a scene 'because he felt that the film needed to say things about the contemporary scene'. So Maltz added a scene concerning returning veterans' anxieties about adapting to civilian life: 'There's no question but that it was a scene with very direct political overtones.'[46] Maltz also recalls in the same interview how pleased Jack L. Warner was over a scene where a Jewish soldier was worried about what kind of job he would get after the war.[47] In another scene a returning veteran complains that a Mexican will have his job. A friend points silently to another soldier: Juan, a Mexican. In this brief encounter, Maltz managed to evoke the need for both ethnic and class solidarity.[48] The script also takes up, more explicitly, a remark made in Maltz's previous film, *Destination Tokyo* (1944). One of the veterans in *Pride of the Marines* has decided to go into politics but will refuse 'to sell oil to Japan or do business with another Hitler'. In *Destination Tokyo*, while defusing a bomb, the submarine commander (Cary Grant) notices that the fuse had 'made in USA upon it' and comments on 'the appeaser's contribution to the war effort'. Another interview with Maltz provides information on the issue at stake:

> During the late 30s leftists and pacifists vehemently protested the shipment of scrap metal to Japan. Japanese factories converted the scrap into bombs which were used against the Chinese populace. Up to late 1940 U.S. companies supplied Japan with more than 90% of its scrap iron and steel. Maltz had not forgotten: 'It is true', he says, 'that weapons that came back, and shells that came back on Pearl Harbor, came from scrap iron that we had sent; Now this was a straight political comment, but this was something that delighted Jerry Wald. Cary Grant was delighted to say it.' (Talbot and Zheutlin 1978: 15)

None of this support saved Maltz when it was discovered he was a Communist, but it does highlight the class and economic complicity between American business and fascist regimes.[49] On 3 April 1953 blacklistee Guy Endore wrote to Representative Clyde Doyle of HUAC. Evoking the demonstration in 1938 against shipments of scrap iron to Japan, he asked: 'Have you thought of blacklisting the sellers of that scrap-iron?' There was no reply.[50]

An intriguing variant on this can be found in Dalton Trumbo's script for *Tender Comrade* (1943).[51] Four married women decide to share a house rather than pay rent separately, but this does not prevent hardship. One of them gives voice to isolationist sentiments: 'We wouldn't have to ration if we'd minded our own business. Shipping food to foreigners who'll turn on us when it's over.' Thus anti-fascist solidarity (helping Britain) is decried, while making money out of fascism is looked upon as normal. Like the scripts of Cole and Maltz, Trumbo's put its finger squarely on the question of profiteering while the troops fight and die. Ginger Rogers rounds on her: 'That talk comes from Berlin. You're the sort of person Hitler counted on when he started this war.' This theme is central to *This Land is Mine*, made the same year in Hollywood by Jean Renoir from a script by Dudley Nichols. Collaborator George Sanders gets on well with the Nazi Major: both are anti-union and Sanders is opposed to 'false democratic ideas' such as strikes for a shorter working week.[52] However, the Major has nothing but contempt for the man and the town's Mayor. In a discussion with the teacher who finally stands up to be counted, the Major states that collaborators are waiting to welcome the Nazis in the US, as they are in Europe. This brings home forcefully to the audience the existence of pro-Nazi elements in the US and, in the light of the discussion between Sanders and the Major, highlights the opposition of such elements to working-class radicalism.

A number of major literary figures worked in Hollywood over the years and the most committed among them was playwright Lillian Hellman; blacklisted in the 1950s, she returned to the stage. The first of the three films that concern us here, *Watch on the Rhine* (1943) was adapted from her play by Dashiell Hammett, the celebrated creator of private eye Sam Spade (*The Maltese Falcon*).[53] *Watch on the Rhine* returns to the question of the Spanish Civil War (the Frenchman in *Sahara* fought for the Loyalists too).[54] The character played by Paul Lukas, a committed anti-Fascist who prefers to return to Nazi Germany to fight, even if it means his death, has a most revealing conversation with an Italian who expresses his delight that not all Germans and Italians are fascists. Says Lukas: 'There are many in your country and mine who fight on. I fight against fascism. *That* is my trade.' Later reference is made to Fascists who have done 'well for themselves but not by themselves. They came in on the shoulders of some of the world's most powerful men.' The script thus pillories those with a vested interest in the victory of Fascism: bankers and businessmen. The film concludes with a remark by Bette Davis, the wife of the Paul Lukas character: 'The only men worth their time on earth are those who will fight for other men.' This remark embraces the Abraham Lincoln Brigade fighting in Spain and the British officer hailing the 'dignity of freedom' in *Sahara*.

The 'world's most powerful men' are denounced again in Hellman's script for *The Searching Wind*, directed by William Dieterle in 1946. At one point a character throws a pro-Fascist out of the hotel where the action is taking place and refers to the sort of people whose money brought Mussolini to power. As it is bankers and aristocrats who are being denounced, the film makes a clear link between capitalism and Fascism, a link Cold War warriors sought to repress by hounding later those who had highlighted it. Similarly, the film ends with a character making the sort of speech certain to enrage witch hunters who had supported Fascism before the war. He denounces appeasement, pointing out that by acting thus his parents' generation condemned his to fight and die. It is interesting to note that Hollywood at the time remained true to the collective war effort: for *The Hollywood Reporter* (10 May 1946) 'no punches are pulled in indicting a section of typical American appeasers and timid politicians who might have avoided the disaster of a second World War'.[55] Even more scandalous in the Cold War climate was Hellman's other script, this time for a pro-Soviet film *The North Star* (1943).[56] Unlike *Mission to Moscow*, *The North Star* is not a paean of praise to Stalin but a hymn to the Bolshevik Revolution: not only do we hear the 'Internationale' but an old man (therefore born and brought up under the Czar) denounces those who have invaded the Soviet Union to take from them all the good they have made for themselves. Moreover, the film vaunts the merits of socialised medicine, a particular *bête noire* of the Right in the US, and finishes with a clarion call from the heroine that recalls, like the remark in *Hostages*, Fonda's remark in *Blockade*: 'The Earth belongs to us, the people, if we fight for it', she cries.

If there is much flag-waving in films made during the war, whether written by future blacklistees or not, there is also much genuine radical thought and, crucially, the belief that certain values and forms of freedom had to be defended, even if that meant fighting so that others might enjoy later what one had oneself. At the same time, however, a certain anxiety is palpable: let us make sure that all this sacrifice has not been in vain. *Pride of the Marines* adopts this line of reasoning via the theme of returning veterans, a particularly delicate question, given their number and the related problems of jobs and housing. In 1946 there appeared two films on the topic of veterans: Wyler's *The Best Years of Our Lives* and the far lesser known *Till the End of Time*. By the time of the Hearings of 1947 the very liberal Wyler was deploring the fact that it was now impossible for him to direct such a film. Nearly fifty years later the anti-Communist union leader Roy Brewer (see Chapter 3) could still denounce the film as communist propaganda because one of the characters says the US fought the wrong enemy in World War I and the film suggests that it is anti-American to criticise the Soviet Union (Fariello 1995: 118). *Till the End of Time*, directed by Edward Dmytryk of the Ten and written by anti-Communist liberal Allen Rivkin, includes a scene that leads to a bar-room brawl between returning veterans and the representatives of a veterans' association. The latter denounce 'foreign-born labor racketeers' and exclude Catholics, Jews and Negroes from their association. The Robert Mitchum character points out that a friend, Maxie Klein, was killed at Guadacanal.

This has been denounced as 'just a bit contrived' (Buhle and Wagner 2003b: 226), but hardly more so than the presence of a Mexican in *Pride of the Marines*. Both films are denouncing racism as un-American and, unwittingly, highlighting the divisive tactics soon to be used to isolate those destined to be considered 'un-American'. It is therefore interesting to note that in 1946 future professional anti-Communist Ronald Reagan was sounding warnings about precisely this kind of Fascism taking hold in the US, denouncing 'an international conspiracy' supporting it. Thus the neo-Fascist association pilloried in *Till the End of Time* bears a striking resemblance to the 'Houston-based American "Order of Patriots" which restricted membership to white Gentiles and required sidearms' (Vaughan 1994: 163).[57] However, it is even more instructive to turn to a film superficially devoid of any progressive critical intent: *The Blue Dahlia* (1945), from an original script by author Raymond Chandler. Veterans are at the centre of the film which manages to evoke the housing shortage too (a score of veterans all attempting to rent the same flat). Chandler had intended to make one of the veterans, suffering from migraines and losses of memory due to injury, the murderer of the film's *femme fatale* (the adulterous wife of the hero, played by Alan Ladd) and certain elements point to this solution until the ending. The Navy, however, was hostile to the idea and the script was duly changed. What is not clear – and this is of considerable importance – is whether the opposition to portraying a veteran as a killer (but not a cold-blooded one) stemmed from a laudable desire to present all veterans positively or from a fear that the film might arouse veterans (already under considerable pressure on their return home) to mounting a campaign, not against *The Blue Dahlia*, but the authorities who were not doing enough for them. Interestingly, the film also includes a gangster who has spent the war years making a fortune out of his night club, while ordinary men fought and died for their country. This aspect of the film was subversive of the new order overtaking the US in general and Hollywood in particular, as we shall see in the next chapter.

NOTES

1. A complete record of the Hearings, as well as coverage by the media, is available in the Academy of Motion Picture Arts and Sciences, MHL. In all quotations from this record I shall refer to 'WFH', followed by the day and the page number.
2. George Seldes, editor: *In Fact*, 25 August 1941. WFH, 'Build-up', page C. 'Coughlinites' refers to the followers of the pro-Fascist, anti-Semitic and anti-Communist priest Father Coughlin.

3. Morgan had earlier distinguished himself by participating in a plot to overthrow President Roosevelt, which would have resulted, if successful, in a Fascist America controlled by banks and big business. This had nothing to do with aliens or Jews. The plot was exposed in 1934 by a certain Major Butler, a former Army officer employed by large American firms to further their economic interests in South America and other countries in what is now known as the developing world. Unlike Seldes, Butler was no anti-capitalist.
4. It was people like WRH who succeeded in imposing definitions of what was 'American' and 'un-American'.
5. *Los Angeles Times*, 15 September 1941. WFH, Second Day, page M.
6. Arthur Robb, 13 September 1941. WFH, Fourth Day, page K.
7. Margaret Frakes: 'Why the Movie Investigation?' *The Christian Century*, 24 September 1941. WFH, Fifth Day, page G.
8. 'Darryl Zanuck Puts Out the Witch-Burners' Fire'. *The Hollywood Reporter*, 27 September 1941. WFH, Eighth Day, page B.
9. In his journal *Social Justice*. WFH, Recess after the Fourth Day, page Q.
10. In *Social Justice*. WFH, Second Recess, page X.
11. *Variety*, 10 September 1941. WFH, First Day, page A.
12. We shall return to this distinction in Chapters 4 and 5.
13. Frederick R. Barkley, *The New York Times*. WFH, Second Day, page E.
14. Dorothy Thompson, *Cleveland Plain Dealer*. WFH, Third Day, page G.
15. Barnet Nover, *The Washington Post*. WFH, Second Day, page L.
16. Arthur Robb, 13 September 1941. WFH, Fourth Day, page L.
17. WFH, Seventh Day, page E.
18. *Variety*, 'Films to Fight Nye Slurs'. WFH, 'Build-up', page C.
19. *Blockade,* PCA file, MHL.
20. Hays was responsible for the Production Code where Hollywood practised self-censorship to avoid external pressures, notable from the Catholic Legion of Decency. Breen was in charge of enforcing what was called 'the Hays Code'.
21. *Blockade,* PCA file.
22. Ford was to play an important, if ambiguous, role in the post-war period.
23. Information contained in the PCA file.
24. He is therefore a very different sort of villain from the character of Grisby in Orson Welles' *The Lady from Shanghai* (1947) who was on a pro-Franco committee, whereas the Welles character prides himself on having killed a Franco spy. In *Blockade* Fonda also kills a spy, though in self-defence and not out of conviction, given the question of censorship. This sums up the difference between the two films.
25. *Confessions*, PCA file.
26. PCA file. Interestingly, Harry Warner defended the film during the War Films Hearings by stating that it was 'a factual portrayal of a spy ring that actually operated in New York City' (Jack L. Warner Papers, USC). He thus gave the film a pseudo-documentary status, an argument that Jack Warner was to use when promoting *I Was a Communist for the FBI* (1951). See Humphries 2006.

27. PCA file. Laraschi bolstered his argument by saying Chaplin had shelved his project *The Great Dictator* for precisely this reason. Chaplin changed his mind when war broke out in 1939.

28. Clipping, PCA file: no name, date or source. Similar comments were to be made on the pro-Soviet *Mission to Moscow* (1943).

29. PCA file, MHL.

30. Jack L. Warner Papers, USC.

31. Jack L. Warner Papers.

32. In his crusade against Communism Hoover evoked 'disease' and 'contamination' as the fate awaiting Americans. I refer readers back to my discussion of Jack Warner's use of the word 'termites' in the Introduction.

33. I remind readers of my remarks on the character of Gabriel in *Blockade*. There is a fascinating visual and thematic parallel between Zaroff and Gabriel in *Blockade,* just as there is a thematic parallel between Gabriel and Rainsford.

34. A film in the 'anti-Red' cycle, *The Woman on Pier 13* (1949) was originally called *I Married a Communist*. See Chapter 6.

35. *The Man I Married*, PCA file, MHL.

36. Clipping, PCA file, MHL.

37. Clippings file, MHL. These positive reviews would seem to indicate that Lawson was not looked upon as an apologist for the Nazi–Soviet Pact. Which did not prevent Red-baiter Hedda Hopper from publishing in the conservative *Los Angeles Times* (24 November 1940) an article eloquently entitled (and harbinger of things to come) 'Cinema Fans Urged to Protest Any Signs of Un-Americanism Left in Hollywood' (Rhodes 2007: 42). Not only Communists but left-wing foreign-born actors such as Bela Lugosi were targeted (see Chapter 5).

38. WFH, Eighth Day, page A.

39. Lawson was imprisoned twice in Alabama for his anti-racist activities (Vaughan 1994: 288n32).

40. In a letter to Breen dated 1 May 1945. *Counter-Attack*, PCA file, MHL. Breen replied that the Legion of Decency had passed the film.

41. *Hostages* was directed by Frank Tuttle, one of the very few Communists in the Screen Directors' Guild. He became a friendly witness in May 1951.

42. The script of *Hangmen Also Die* was by Bertolt Brecht and John Wexley.

43. Perhaps this applies also to the way Jack Warner sided with the witch hunters in 1947.

44. *None Shall Escape*, PCA file, MHL.

45. Clippings file, MHL.

46. Albert Maltz, OH, p. 540.

47. When he testified before HUAC, Warner singled this scene out again, this time as an instance of Communist propaganda.

48. It is revealing of the mood of the time that the conservative weekly *Time*, evoking anti-Semitism, referred to the film's 'liberal polemics', without any indication of some dark Communist plot. An opinion poll of 1943 found that 62 per cent of

film commentators were in favour of 'controversial social and political issues' (Talbot and Zheutlin 1978: 21, 22).

49. And also within big business on American soil. Thus director Cy Endfield has drawn attention to private industry raising prices during the war, thus 'subverting Roosevelt's seven anti-inflationary points' (Neve 2005: 118). It was precisely this connivence between big business and fascism that provoked the rejection of *Hostages* by the Hearst press.

50. Guy Endore Papers, Box 66, folder 279, UCLA.

51. For reasons which we shall analyse in chapter 4, this film antagonised the Right as much as the pro-Soviet films of Warner Brothers and MGM.

52. As we saw in Chapter 1, the wealthy Nichols had no personal axe to grind in defending the rights of working-class people.

53. On Hammett's appearance before HUAC and the significance of the stance he adopted, see Chapter 5.

54. Hellman's play had been produced during the Nazi–Soviet Pact and denounced by the CP journal *New Masses*. After the invasion of the Soviet Union it was praised by the same journal (Wills 1976: 8).

55. *The Searching Wind*, PCA file, MHL.

56. The music was composed by Aaron Copland. See Preface, p. 4, note 1.

57. Friendly witness, actor Adolphe Menjou (see Chapter 4), stated that he would go and live in Texas (where Houston is situated) if Communists took power in the US, because Texans shot Communists on sight.

3

Hollywood Strikes, the Right Strikes Back

The title of this chapter refers to the prolonged and violent strikes that shook Warner Brothers in 1945 and 1946 and the consequent right-wing backlash within the industry (and beyond). We have seen that HUAC had investigated Communism in Hollywood as early as 1940 and the union struggles throughout the 1930s had left indelible traces within the ranks of those opposed to unionisation within the film industry. If the Motion Picture Alliance for the Preservation of American Ideals (MPA) was the explicitly right-wing manifestation of anti-Communism in Hollywood, its creation in early 1944 was not a purely local phenomenon but a sign of the times. Thus as early as January 1944 right-wing intellectuals and journalists were contending that American would be faced after the war with the expansionism of the Soviet Union, implying that World War II was a parenthesis in an on-going struggle (Lora 1974: 48). It was not until the end of the decade, however, that most liberals agreed and by the time of the HUAC Hearings of 1951 those who opposed witch hunting in the name of free speech and dissidence were few and far between.[1] The reaction of Hollywood liberals to the creation of the MPA, however, was in keeping with the anti-Fascist alliance of the war years.

The MPA advertised its birth in *The Hollywood Reporter* in February 1944. Although it denounced all forms of totalitarianism, the following remark gave the game away: 'we resent the growing impression that this industry is made up of, and dominated by, Communists, radicals and crack-pots'.[2] The MPA was the brain-child of former Screen Playwrights such as James Kevin McGuinness and many of its members worked for MGM; the old animosities of the previous decade were surfacing again.[3] So, too, were other, more sinister factors. The MPA fouled its nest in the eyes of Hollywood by contacting anti-Communist Senator Robert Rice Reynolds to denounce 'the dissemination of un-American ideas and beliefs' (Schwartz 1982: 209). Reynolds was notorious for telling the Senate: 'The dictators are doing what is best for their people. Hitler and Mussolini have a date with destiny: it's foolish to oppose them, so why not play ball with them?'[4] That Stalin was not mentioned showed that for Reynolds only fascist dictators were acceptable. The conservative Catholic journal *Tidings*, already critical of pro-Soviet movies, made the sort of remark soon to be taken up by HUAC: 'Into many motion pictures which have nothing directly to do with Soviet Russia, subtle communistic propaganda has been permitted to seep without check.'[5] As was to become the custom, no examples were given.

The reaction in Hollywood was swift and unambiguous. In June 1944 1,000 delegates representing seventeen guilds and over 20,000 workers met to denounce the MPA and vote motions. Mary McCall, President of the SWG, went back over the struggles of the 1930s and the War Films Hearings to pinpoint the reactionary nature of the Alliance, calling it 'anti-Guild, anti-Union, anti-industry', adding: '*We do not believe that union breaking is an American ideal*' (original emphasis). Oliver Garrett of the SWG pointed out the disturbing parallels between statements made by members of the Alliance and by notorious pro-Fascist and anti-Semitic figures in American politics. He then denounced the Alliance's President, director Sam Wood, for proposing an 'educational campaign' which was tantamount to dictating to the studios' story editors what should be accepted and rejected, and concluded by showing the anti-union bias of MPA member Howard Emmett Rogers.[6]

The kind of company kept by the Alliance was anathema to the guilds because of past battles and Wheeler and Nye's smears of Hollywood. Moreover, America was still at war. The Los Angeles *Citizen News* (29 June 1944) reported the Council of Guilds as calling the MPA 'a subversive and dangerous organization which comforts the enemy'. Before holding their mass meeting, the guilds had taken out an advertisement in *The Hollywood Reporter* (23 June) asking why the Alliance 'devoted so little attention to the menace of Fascism'. This point had already been made in the Los Angeles *Daily News* (6 June) by Virginia Wright who wrote that the pictures offending the MPA 'are those which support all out war against Fascism and greater understanding among the United Nations'. She also informed her readers that writer Robert Rossen had repeatedly invited McGuinness to discuss the pictures the Right found offensive but that he had declined.[7]

Present at the meeting of the Council of Guilds was Herbert K. Sorrell, President of the Conference of Studio Unions and a militant left-winger often accused of being a CP member. That this was a tactic to smear radical unionism and break up the liberal–CP alliance is a question we shall address below, but first we need to turn the clock back again to the late 1930s. The testimony of sound technician James G. Stewart (see Chapter 1) evoked the names of Bioff and Browne who controlled the IATSE and owed allegiance to the Chicago crime syndicate of Frank Nitti (Nielsen and Mailes 1995: vii). The IATSE and the studio bosses understood one another. The former was the only recognised union and therefore imposed a closed shop: one had to join the IATSE in order to work in Hollywood. The union was more interested in taking bribes from the studios in order to keep the peace – and keep wages down – than in defending the interests of its members, thus earning it the nickname of a 'sweet heart union'. This was the kind of closed shop the moguls appreciated. Jeff Kibre fought a losing battle against IA corruption, in part because of the indifference of the CP (of which he was a member): only one in six of Hollywood's Communists was a back-lot worker (Ceplair 1989: 66). Kibre was a thorn in the flesh of the IA hierarchy, prompting Browne to use the Red bogey to ward off such challenges; he claimed that 'our own native patriotism should be sufficient incentive to strive to preserve our Democracy against evil influences' (Nielsen and Mailes 1995: 66).[8]

The arrangements by which Bioff helped the producers keep profits up and wages down, with large sums going into the pocket of the Chicago crime syndicate, were finally exposed and the Producers' Association, represented by Joseph M. Schenck, President of Twentieth Century Fox, found itself in court:

> The producers claimed that they had been victims of extortion, but their payments had also been part of a deal to keep IATSE wages low and stable during the years of great gains for labor. The matter ended with Schenck, Bioff, and Browne in jail and increased executives' hatred for the radical leadership of Kibre, Lawson, and others whom they felt had been responsible for putting one of their leaders in jail, thus disgracing the entire industry. (Schwartz 1982: 132)

Soon to be in the spotlight was Herbert Sorrell who in 1938, as representative of Painters Local 644, had worked with future member of the Hollywood Ten, Herbert Biberman (representing the Screen Directors' Guild) and Dudley Nichols (SWG) when the Conference of Motion Picture Arts and Crafts called a meeting to discuss the Fair Labor Standards Act which 'established a minimum wage of 25 cents per hour and a 44-hour work week' (Nielsen and Mailes 1995: 51). By 1943 the painters were the highest paid craft-workers in the industry, thanks to Sorrell (Nielsen and Mailes 1995: 87).

The war years were a time of full employment. This soon changed:

> By the winter of 1945–46, one-quarter of all war workers had lost
> their jobs. Nearly 2 million workers found themselves unemployed by
> October 1, and real income for workers fell by an average of 15 percent
> in three months. Prospects for the future offered little hope for improve-
> ment, as 10 million servicemen and women returned to civilian life to
> join the competition for jobs. Fears of another depression, accumulated
> resentments over wartime sacrifices, and anger over postwar reverses in
> wages and working conditions ignited strikes and demonstrations from
> coast to coast. (Lipsitz 1994: 99–100)

The Hollywood strikes of 1945 and 1946 involved back-lot workers and not
actors, writers and directors, although these became involved, voluntarily or
not. The first strike began in March 1945 when the US was still at war and did
not obtain the support of the CP, in favour of a 'no-strike' attitude while the
war lasted. The strike was triggered off by a seemingly banal jurisdictional
dispute. Things, however, were anything but simple. A 'jurisdictional dispute'
occurred when one craft union, such as that representing the painters, claimed
that it alone had the right to perform a certain task, whereas another craft
union, such as that representing the set decorators, disputed this right. The
problem was compounded by rival unions – the IATSE and the CSU – being
involved. Jobs were at stake at a most difficult time and collecting dues from
members was important for a union's finances.

Sorrell was the President of the CSU, while Richard Walsh presided over
IATSE. This hardly helped matters: Walsh was a leftover from the days of gangsterism. Later he 'confessed unashamedly that he had collaborated with the
moguls to break the strike' (Horne 2001: 160), thus creating the conditions that
would lead to the break-up of the CSU by the end of 1946 and to HUAC
coming to Hollywood in 1947. However, much water – and blood – was to
flow under the bridge over the ensuing eighteen months, pitting unionist
against unionist, and unionists against strike-breakers, and leading to a radicalisation that played into the hands of the MPA and those outside Hollywood
who were increasingly determined to wage their own kind of war against the
Left. By initially standing back and refusing to bargain with the CSU because
of a counter-claim by the IATSE, the studios were in reality setting in motion
the machinery for a confrontation in the hope of eliminating the CSU and
the very idea of an independent union representing workers' interests. They
succeeded.

The first strike, involving 10,500 CSU workers, started in March and lasted
until October (Horne 2001: 160). Pickets were formed, which led to the
souring of relations between the CSU and the SAG: some actors crossed the

lines, to Sorrell's disgust, while others refused to do so. Certain actors were terrified their careers would be compromised but refused to go to work because of the violence being committed on both sides. The studios hired both 'goons' and the local police, which in turn provoked violence from the pickets. Sorrell was perfectly frank over this. Already he had resorted to violence during the period from 1937 to 1939 when faced with the presence of Nitti's gangsters from Chicago, brought in by the producers; he admitted to breaking the arms of sixteen scabs: 'One of the things that contributed to winning the strike was violence. . . . in many respects we out-thugged the thugs.'[9] According to most accounts, however, the worst and most systematic violence was committed against the pickets:

> The vicious brutality practiced against the strikers had soured a sector of public opinion which at this early date had not been sold completely on the idea that the unrest was all due to Communist machinations. The violence caused more to examine the issues of the strike, and when they discovered that the strike resulted primarily from the moguls' thwarting the will of the Local 1421 members, they were prone to sympathize with CSU. (Horne 2001: 187)

An excellent source for information on reactions to the strike and the situation created is Jack L. Warner who amassed and conserved a vast amount of material from all sides.[10] Much of it is in the form of letters sent to Warner from journalists, unionists, Warner Brothers employees and members of the general public. Letters of support for Warner Brothers tended to call the strikers 'hoodlums', whereas letters of criticism regretted the studio's retreat from fairness and liberalism and denounced violence towards the strikers as a betrayal of the progressive films of the 1930s.[11] A correspondent from Philadelphia deplored the use of 'goons and tear gas' and went so far as to refuse to attend 'any motion pictures' until the strike was ended, adding that family and friends felt the same. A collective letter from non-strikers (containing nine sheets with dozens of signatures per sheet) thanked Warner Brothers for providing them with food and beds during the strike. Another letter opened with 'The Lord Bless You', underlined several times.

Other letters were even more political in tone and content. A letter of 15 October suggested returning veterans 'be hired as they cannot be compelled to join a union', whereas an Army lieutenant wrote that he did not serve in the Army 'to fight fascism only to return to find it on the home front'.[12] IATSE President Walsh 'sought to recruit returning war veterans as strikebreakers, but the Veterans' Bureau blocked this move' (Nielsen and Mailes 1995: 113). This nicely highlights not only union rivalry but also the fact that Walsh was ready to support the kind of anti-labour measures recommended by

Warner's anti-union correspondent. The West Hollywood Democratic Club (7 October) considered the studio tactics 'Un-American and pro-Fascist' and an open letter from workers in the Columbia Unit, Screen Publicists Guild, New York City denounced the slugging of pickets by studio guards as 'un-American'. Support for the locked-out workers came from the Pacific Coast District Metal Trades Council of Seattle, with the United Federal Workers of America, Local 245, telling Warner Brothers that they should 'follow the American way . . . instead of the Nazi way'. One correspondent (8 October) wrote sarcastically: 'I am told that you and your family contributed heavily to the stinking "new deal" campaign. I am wondering how you like it now?' A hate letter in favour of the strikers refers to the Warners as 'a pack of real kikes' and 'real dirt Jews', which suggests the work of an *agent provocateur*. One letter of support called the strikes 'Un-American – it's Communism clawing itself through'.[13]

In a moving 'Open Letter to Warner Bros.', published in the Communist paper *New Masses* (6 November 1945), band-leader Artie Shaw praised the brothers for their stance against Fascism and the films they produced during the war, including those of Lawson and Maltz discussed in Chapter 2. After congratulating the Warners for helping to elect Roosevelt, he evoked their liberalism (which, unfortunately, was only skin deep), then expressed dismay over the strikes. They and the labour movement had a common enemy: Fascism.[14] Shaw was on the executive committee of the Hollywood Independent Citizens Committee of Arts, Sciences and Professions (HICCASP), along with Katharine Hepburn, Orson Welles, Frank Sinatra and Albert Einstein. Another member was Ronald Reagan with whom Shaw clashed over Reagan's incipient anti-Communism. Shaw did not survive this altercation: in 1953 he collaborated with HUAC, then withdrew from public life and music.

One letter offered Warner Brothers and the other studios a plan for 'Breaking the Stranglehold of Union Racketeers'. This was a reference, not to the gangsterism of the IATSE, but to the Communist menace. It was to be the line of attack adopted by films in the 'anti-Red cycle' (see Chapter 6). The correspondent said that it might take from two to five years for the plan to work, 'but results will begin to show within a few months' and went on to claim: 'Our efforts will be so secret and subtle the skids will be under the disturbers before they know what is going to happen.' There is no reply in the Jack L. Warner Papers, but the tone and content of the letter correspond closely to what was to happen after the collapse of the CSU at the end of 1946. Warner did, however, reply to a letter (12 October) from John Cromwell, President of the SDG. Cromwell reiterated the guild's commitment to 'the no-strike clause and our Basic Agreement' but felt that his members should not take risks by reporting for work. An irate Warner reminded Cromwell of a wire sent by him 'and 50 others' denouncing Warner Brothers for 'engaging thugs', adding that he would demand an apology in the public press. This exchange was one of the many signs of antagonism that led to Jack L. Warner collaborating with HUAC in 1947.[15]

The strike of 1945 ended in a stalemate, but everything pointed to it starting up again so that the CSU would be eliminated in favour of the IATSE: William Wilkerson, editor of *The Hollywood Reporter*, claimed the problem was not jurisdictional but Reds (Horne 2001: 184). However, if the CP had finally come to support the CSU, the relations between the Party and Sorrell were never as intimate as was claimed by those anxious to smear the CSU as Red. In a report made to the Catholic Archbishop of Los Angeles, the two priests assigned to study the strikes criticised the producers:

> Nor can we becloud the air with cries of Communism, radicalism. It is true that Communists have tried hard to infiltrate into the ranks of the CSU. But the strike is not Communist-inspired nor Communist-directed. . . . to desire the extermination of a union because of an accusation of Communism is not in keeping with the facts nor with the spirit of labor ethics. (Cogley 1956, I: 73)

This opinion was supported several years later by William F. Blowitz of the Screen Publicists' Guild who had left the CP precisely because it refused to support the CSU: 'I felt that it was a correct strike which should be won by ordinary methods of labor unions. . . . the party was opposed to Herb Sorrell all through this period' (*Variety*, 21 September 1951). This testimony was given before HUAC. *Variety* added: 'The 36-year-old publicist was then excused without further questions.' Thus a witness collaborating with HUAC gave the lie to the theory of the Communist conspiracy. What he had to say no longer interested the Committee.

Robert Kenny, former Attorney General of California and one of the Ten's lawyers, recalled that the producers and the IATSE had decided by September 1946 to crush the CSU.[16] Ben Margolis, who also represented the Ten, summed up the quandary in which unions found themselves:

> So these unions . . . were faced with the following dilemma: either they had to continue with a strike that was being lost and which threatened their very existence or they had to become strike breakers.[17]

The unions refused the latter choice; all were destroyed. Sorrell lost everything and IATSE took over. These views from the Left – Margolis was a Communist, Kenny was not – echo an article in the pro-business and anti-labour *Los Angeles Times* (16 October 1946) concerning a 'state of emergency' being declared in Local 683 by the IATSE: 2,000 members had voted to observe the CSU picket lines. President Walsh stated that 'charges of conspiracy to violate alliance orders requiring them to continue at work' would be preferred against the Local's President, Secretary-Treasurer and Business Agent, adding: 'Charges against the three are to be presented by Roy M. Brewer, international representative of the union. If sustained, the alliance then will take over the local and deal with the offenders.'

Brewer, who had joined the Motion Picture Alliance on its formation, will figure prominently in Chapter 4. Jesuit priest Father George Dunne remarked that Brewer had complained about his own union members: 'they want more money, more money, more money'. This betrays collusion between Brewer and the producers whose sole concern was to keep wages down while profits soared.[18] Dunne was explicit:

> In my judgment . . . this whole strike had been manipulated in a conspiracy between the major producers and Roy Brewer and the IATSE union . . .
>
> Brewer was guaranteeing the producers that if they forced the CSU people out on the streets, he would supply IATSE people to replace them. And he said that if the IATSE people refused to take their jobs . . . he himself would force them to do so.[19]

Dunne pointed out that he had been congratulated by Congressman Kearns, Chairman of a Sub-Committee of the Education and Labor Committee, for his 'objectivity' after Dunne had spent a day testifying. Kearns got hold of the minutes of the top secret meetings between Brewer and the producers and made public use of them, stating that 'the jurisdictional strife in September 1946 . . . is probably the result of collusion between the producers and the IATSE' (Nielsen and Mailes 1995: 160). Kearns also used the word 'conspiracy', considering that the SAG had a part to play in making the studio lockout a success. Which brings us to the actors and Ronald Reagan.

Father Dunne corroborates the views of Kearns (a Republican) by pointing out that Brewer (a Democrat) could certainly replace recalcitrant painters with eager scabs but not actors. If the latter, via their Guild, had refused to cross the picket lines, the strike would have been settled in twenty-four hours in favour of the CSU. Dunne stated this in public, which brought an immediate reaction from Reagan. Flanked by his actress wife Jane Wyman and actor George Murphy, Reagan paid a visit to Dunne and accused him of being 'a dupe for the Communists'.[20] Dunne considered Reagan 'dangerous' because he was 'obsessed' with the Communist threat.[21] Nor did Reagan go unopposed within the SAG, although the majority were more concerned with their future and their salaries than with the rights of labour, despite having fought for their own rights and their dignity a decade previously. The SAG's conservative leaders were no longer interested in the rights and dignity of other employees. Hume Cronyn criticised Reagan for being increasingly anti-CSU; John Garfield, Gene Kelly and Anne Revere were thanked by CSU for their support (Horne 2001: 212).[22] Reagan swung the SAG away from the CSU and alongside Brewer and the IATSE by pledging to keep actors working (he was elected President of the Guild soon after). His ability to speak in public was an asset. Actor Alexander Knox represented this in less positive terms: 'Reagan spoke very fast. He always did, so that he could talk out of both sides of his mouth at once' (Schwartz 1982: 249–50).[23]

One figure who disagreed with Knox was Jack Dales who retired in 1972 as the National Executive Secretary of the SAG after thirty-six years with the Union. Reagan was his hero and Dales remained convinced that Sorrell was a Communist. However, despite Reagan and Brewer being close, Dales called the latter 'a gung-ho anti-Communist' who saw 'Communists under every bush'.[24] Brewer himself confirmed this opinion of him: the Ten's lawyer Robert Kenny was secretly a Communist, as were actor John Garfield and Carey McWilliams.[25] He produced no evidence. McWilliams launched the 'Citizens' Committee' with expatriate anti-Fascist German author Thomas Mann after the strike of 1945 to support the CSU and his opinions were similar to those of Father Dunne.[26] Brewer considered that 'Sorrell was one of the greatest liars I ever saw', while admitting that conservative Robert Montgomery considered Sorrell to be honest.[27] However, Brewer damned himself for posterity as a liar with a delightful Freudian slip. Having stated that he was 'sorry for Browne' (one of the IATSE gangsters), he makes this remark: 'I had no very strong feelings against him – I mean, for him'. Which indicates that, decades after the event, Brewer could not bring himself to denounce gangsterism in the IATSE, indeed welcomed it.[28]

Brewer can be seen and heard in the documentary *Hollywood on Trial* (David Halpern, 1976), an invaluable document to which we shall return in Chapter 4. He was questioned by HUAC Chairman Thomas on the strikes and stated categorically that there would have been no strike without the Communists. Nobody else was questioned on this issue in order that Brewer's lies be accepted as fact. However, Brewer was also asked about violence on the picket lines: was it due to the presence of Communists? He hesitated before replying: 'Much of it, yes.' That hesitation betrays, not a lie, but an admission: much of the violence was also due to strike-breakers and police brought in from all over Los Angeles county by Warner Brothers.[29]

What was the role of the SWG? The Guild was not officially on strike, which meant that every member had to report to work, unless sick or having 'a contractual clause that he could work at home or out of town' (Schwartz 1982: 246). So the writers crossed the picket lines. Communist writer John

Bright expressed his amazement and disgust with this, especially as Mary McCall had proposed a motion to make a substantial contribution to the CSU strike fund (Bright 2002: 164–8). For writer/director Abraham Polonsky, the SWG and the CSU were natural allies (Ceplair and Englund 1980: 220), but he considered that Sorrell

> had allowed himself to be outmaneuvered; Sorrell unrealistically envi-
> sioned a Hollywood on the verge of industrial unionism with himself a
> sort of Harry Bridges of the studios. Instead of ducking an unwinnable
> conflict, Sorrell marched the CSU into the breach. (Buhle and Wagner
> 2001: 90)[30]

The strike and the increasingly anti-Communist mood nationwide did not help matters within the guild, where a homogeneous conservative slate challenged a liberal/radical/Communist slate led by Emmet Lavery and including Communists Lester Cole and Hugo Butler (Schwartz 1982: 248). The fact that the latter won is less important than the tensions which had become uppermost. It was but one sign among many of the times, the most significant taking place some months later, in 1947. This was the Taft–Hartley Act which forced union leaders to sign affidavits that they were not Communists. If they refused, they could no longer go before the National Labor Relations Board and ask for arbitration in the case of an intractable situation pitting employees against their employers. This fatally weakened Communist or radical unions and led to members leaving for other, ideologically safer havens. Anti-Communism thus became the dominant ideology and was soon to be made official policy.

NOTES

1. One such liberal, screenwriter Philip Dunne, has written eloquently of the cowardice of most liberals (Dunne 1992: 190–220). We shall return to Dunne in Chapter 4.
2. The complete advertisement, with the names of those holding an official position, is reproduced in Schwartz 1982: 206.
3. A famous member of the MPA was Walt Disney. See Chapter 1 note 10.
4. MPA file, MHL. This statement by Reynolds was revealed in another advertisement in *The Hollywood Reporter* (13 March 1944), this time placed by the Hollywood Writers' Mobilization which brought together liberals and Communists during the war, as well as leading industry figures like Darryl F. Zanuck. Despite the presence of the latter, the HWM was denounced as Communist during the Hearings of 1951.
5. MPA file, MHL. Following on from the strikes that are discussed in this chapter, the ultra-conservative Chicago *Herald Tribune* published, in November 1946, a series of articles denouncing the Red plot to take over Hollywood. The virulent

tone showed the shift in the post-war period. The articles can be consulted in the Jack L. Warner Papers, Box 43, folder 1.

6. Howard Estabrook Papers, MHL. Estabrook was an anti-Communist liberal and member of the SWG. See also Chapter 5.

7. MPA file, MHL.

8. Formulae such as 'native patriotism' were trotted out by assorted racists and xenophobes to justify anti-democratic measures and repression.

9. Herbert Knott Sorrell, OH, pp. 26–7, UCLA. Interview conducted in 1961.

10. Jack L. Warner Papers, Box 6, folder 10 ('Strike folder').

11. The use of the word 'hoodlums' to designate the strikers is a revealing indication of a topsy-turvy world where ideology and prejudice take precedence over reality. See Chapter 6.

12. See our discussion of veterans in Chapter 2.

13. The quotes are from a cross-section of the letters in the papers and have been chosen to give some idea of the passions aroused.

14. *New Masses* file, SCL.

15. Among those active in support of the CSU in 1945 was future member of the Hollywood Ten, Edward Dmytryk. See http://foia.fbi.gov/foiaindex/compic.htm, Part 06. Cromwell was blacklisted in 1951.

16. OH, p. 310, UCLA. Interview conducted in 1960–61.

17. OH, p. 159, UCLA. Interview conducted in 1987.

18. 'Wartime after-tax profits in the motion picture industry had increased at a far greater rate than had the wages of motion picture craft workers' (Nielsen and Mailes 1995: 139).

19. 'Christian Advocacy and Labor Strife in Hollywood', OH, p. 21, UCLA. Interview conducted in 1981. Father Dunne was the cousin of writer Philip Dunne.

20. Thirty years later the conservative Republican Murphy had not changed. He was quoted by the *Los Angeles Times* (16 July 1979) as saying 'I would be surprised if Communists weren't infiltrating [Hollywood] today.' Director William Wyler reacted thus to this claim: 'He reminds me of those Germans who still deny there was a Holocaust.' William Wyler Papers, folder 590, MHL.

21. Father Dunne, OH, pp. 23–9.

22. This support cost Garfield and Revere dearly (see Chapters 5 and 7). Kelly emerged unscathed; he was also one of the very rare liberals not to turn on the Communists after the Hearings.

23. Knox's wife, actress Doris Nolan, recounts how he poked fun of Reagan in a speech during a SAG meeting over the strikes. Brewer threatened to run Knox out of town, which he did (Slide 1999: 105–6).

24. Jack Dales, OH, pp. 20, 47, UCLA. Interview conducted in 1981. It is amusing to note how, in more liberal times, there was a tendency to turn Brewer into the villain of the piece by those closest to him. Thus producer Robert Vogel is on record as considering as 'extreme rightists' Brewer, Howard Emmet Rogers and writer Morrie Ryskind. They were all members of the Motion Picture Alliance – as was Vogel! OH, MHL. Interview conducted in 1990 by Barbara Hall.

25. Roy Brewer, OH, pp. 133–4, 168, UCLA. Interview conducted in 1981.

26. Dunne states that, in private conversations, Brewer claimed that Dunne had a homosexual relationship with Sorrell (OH, p. 19). This is not to be taken as mere gossip: homosexuality and Communism were the twin obsessions of the time. Since Brewer could hardly accuse a Jesuit of being a Red, he accused him of being gay. Moreover, Dunne's sympathies for the working class would have been seen as communist at the time.

27. Brewer, OH, pp. 117, 119. Honesty, however, was not Montgomery's strong point. Actress Marsha Hunt (blacklisted, but never a Communist) recalls how Montgomery suggested that the SAG, SDG and SWG affiliate, but 'tossed in a condition' during a meeting: Communism must be disavowed and all Communists barred from membership. This was in 1946 and therefore ushered in the Hearings of 1947 and the aftermath. (McGilligan and Buhle 1997: 313).

28. Brewer, OH, pp. 133–4, 168, 79. When Brewer appeared to testify about Communist infiltration of Hollywood before HUAC (17 and 18 May, 1952), Committee spokesman Mr Tavenner made it clear 'that the committee is not undertaking to investigate internal disputes within the labor unions' (Hearings, p. 474). Thus was avoided any discussion of the history behind the strikes and why they took place.

29. The Hearings of 1947 were held in public in Washington and filmed by newsreel cameras.

30. Harry Bridges was the president of the Longshoremen's Union and had led in 1934 a massive and successful strike concerning the entire West Coast seaboard. The Right considered him to be a Communist. See the discussion of *The Woman on Pier 13* in Chapter 6.

II
From the Hot War to the Cold War

4

The Hearings of 1947

The implications of the events which took place in Washington in October 1947 and which were to usher in a period of fear, betrayal and a concerted attack on civil liberties cannot be fully grasped without a brief discussion of the activities of HUAC during the period 1938–44 when presided over by Martin Dies, a conservative Democrat from Texas.

Dies is notorious for his denunciation of Hollywood in 1938 as a den of 'premature anti-fascists', meaning that he was not opposed to Fascist regimes until they waged war on the US. Future blacklistee, writer Paul Jarrico, was proud of the insult.[1] Research has shown that Dies maintained close relations with various Fascist and anti-Semitic organisations which supported his single-minded attacks on subversives (read: Communists). The Ku Klux Klan, the pro-Nazi American Bund, a convicted Nazi agent and William Dudley Pelley, founder of the fascist Silvershirts, all expressed their agreement with Dies' anti-Communist agenda (Pomerantz 1963: 25; O'Reilly 1983: 40–1). Two months *after* the US had entered the war, the following statement was made by the Federal Communications Commission (11 February 1942):

> Representative Dies received as many favorable references in Axis propaganda in this country as any living American public figure. His opinions were quoted by the Axis without criticism at any time. (Pomerantz 1963: 25)

On 23 May 1939 the pro-Nazi George Deatherage was called to testify before the Dies Committee in one of its rare investigations of an '-ism' other than

Communism. He refused to give any information concerning the identity of the members of his Knights of the White Camellias, including the number of members, on the grounds that to do so would be to break his oath (Pomerantz 1963: 27). This brought no reaction from HUAC, whereas appeals to the Constitution by the Hollywood Ten – a gesture more legal and serious than an oath to a secret society – brought down the full wrath of the Committee upon their heads.

Dies was a member of the white supremacist Ku Klux Klan, as was J. Parnell Thomas, HUAC Chairman in 1947. Hardly surprising, then, that Committee members John Rankin and John Wood should call the KKK '100% American' (Wesley 1961: 15). Moreover, Dies was a disciple of the first Chairman of HUAC, Hamilton Fish, an ardent pro-Nazi who considered Communists a danger because of their support for complete equality between whites and blacks, including intermarriage (Braden 1963: 17).[2] And it was Hollywood denizens close to the gangsters who invited Dies to investigate the film industry:

> it is worth nothing that it was George Brown who initially invited Dies to Hollywood and it was Herb Sorrell, a genuine hero of many rank and file workers in the studios, who fired the first volley at Dies, noting that the senator would do better to investigate Bioff than communists. (Nielsen and Mailes 1995: 65)[3]

A historian has pointed out that the presence of Dies was part of the employers' strategy to forestall radical unionism and that their union collaborators gave Dies the names of alleged Communists to be investigated (Buhle 1999: 116). Dies met with Jack L. Warner in an attempt to have an anti-Communist message slipped into *Confessions of a Nazi Spy* and writer John Wexley tells of how Warner invited him to 'work in something about the pinkos', which Wexley refused to do (McGilligan and Buhle 1997: 713).[4] On 17 February 1940 Dies published in the Hearst press an article entitled 'The Reds in Hollywood' which in turn led to an editorial 'urging the committee to look into Communism in motion pictures' (Pizzitola 2002: 367–8).[5]

If Dies finally decided that the actors he had interrogated – Humphrey Bogart, James Cagney and Fredric March – were not tainted, his investigation was only the highly visible tip of an institutional iceberg whose activities were carefully concealed: the FBI. While HUAC vociferated on stage, Hoover worked in the wings building up his files against subversives. America's leading specialist on the FBI has stated that, from the 1920s on, 'FBI investigations focused not on espionage but on Communist influence in American society' (Theoharis 2002: 139). Hoover's obsession was with cultural and ideological attacks on the social order *from within*, not with armed attacks from without. Thus in April 1941 he sent a memo to the Attorney General himself:

> These subversive groups direct their attention to the dissemination of pro-paganda and to the boring from within processes, much of which is not a violation of a Federal Statute at the time it is indulged in, but which *may become* a definite violation of law in the event of a declaration of war or *the declaration of a national emergency*. (Theoharis 2002: 140; emphasis added)

This was Hoover's mindset: a hypothetical emergency justified illegal tactics such as wiretaps and break-ins to keep tabs on people whose only crime was thinking differently. In order to cover his tracks, Hoover resorted to special procedures:

> These procedures ensured that records of illegal conduct or of the dis-semination of information were not incorporated in the FBI's Central Records System. Such records were routed to senior FBI officials and maintained in their secret office files. These dissemination activities could not have succeeded, in any event, without the witting cooperation of reporters, members of Congress, and prominent anti-Communist activists who accepted Hoover's strict condition not to disclose the FBI as their source. (Theoharis 2002: 142)

Hoover had been interested in Communism in Hollywood since the 1930s, but only the 'labour activist' variety. By 1942, however, he had come to believe that pro-Soviet and anti-Fascist films proved that the CP exerted an influence in Hollywood (Theoharis 2002: 151–3). The next step was logical: in 1943 Hoover's agents broke into the offices of the Los Angeles Communist Party and photocopied the membership files of the Hollywood section. Repeated break-ins up to 1947 enabled the FBI to verify whether Communists had con-tinued their membership and to identify new recruits:

> These lists enabled FBI agents to identify, by October 1947, 47 actors, 45 actresses, 127 writers, 8 producers, and 15 directors as former or current Communist party members. (Theoharis 2002: 155)

Readers will note the date: October 1947, the beginning of the Hearings. Hoover also received reports from the Los Angeles office of the FBI, relating how Hollywood Communists were able to 'spread propaganda', 'force the making of motion pictures which glorify the Soviet Union' and pressure pro-ducers to make 'motion pictures delineating the Negro race in most favor-able terms' (Theoharis 2002: 154). The authors of such reports were able to ignore that the Soviet Union was America's ally and to slip in their own racist prejudices hostile to the Constitution.

In October 1944 Hoover briefed the Attorney General: 'Given the ideological tenor of Hoover's report and his failure to cite any instance of illegal
conduct, an unimpressed attorney general did not even respond' (Theoharis
2002: 156). At this point in history, for the Attorney General Communist
activity was not synonymous with illegal activity.[6] That HUAC planned
to investigate Hollywood as early as 1945 suggests that the Motion Picture
Alliance, formed the previous year, had made overtures to the Committee to
return to Hollywood, but that this had fallen through because Hoover had no
intention of having the FBI linked with the investigation. He was determined
to investigate Communism in Hollywood but also to dictate his conditions.
However, Hoover's conviction of the need to expose Communism in
Hollywood led him to change his mind and to leak his information covertly –
and illegally – to HUAC Chairman J. Parnell Thomas and Robert Stripling.[7]
Both Thomas and Stripling had travelled to Los Angeles in 1945, but it was
not until 1947 that Hoover reversed his earlier decision and asked his assistant
director to extend '*every* assistance to this committee' (Hoover's emphasis).
Duly grateful, Thomas assured Hoover that no information would pass beyond
him as Chairman and 'requested leads and information of value to the
Committee' (Theoharis 2002: 157–60). The scene was set for the Hearings of
October 1947 to take place.[8]

HUAC was just one of the Committees mandated by Congress to investigate a particular topic, in this case: un-American activities, now limited to
Communist activities. A Committee was temporary and was expected to
report back to Congress and propose legislation, which Congress might act
on or not: 'Precedent, unbroken since the founding of the Republic, had
established that investigating committees are not constituted as permanent
bodies' (Donner 1961: 17). With the resignation of Dies in 1944, HUAC
risked being discontinued. This was to reckon without Representative Rankin
who, leaping onto the bandwagon of national security, managed to get
Congress to make HUAC a permanent fixture. This boost to its power
gave the members of the Committee – Southern Democrats and conservative Republicans united in their hatred of unions, civil rights and the New
Deal – the chance to devote themselves, not to partial investigation, but to
partisan exposure:

> In 1947 the Committee explained that its function was to 'expose activ-
> ities by un-American individuals and organizations which, while some-
> times being legal, are nonetheless inimical to our American concepts and
> our American future'. (Donner 1961: 56)

Legal activities were thus branded 'un-American' so that one particular vision
of American society would prevail:

It was not enough to be American in citizenship or residence – one must be American in one's thoughts. There was such a thing as Americanism. And lack of right thinking could make an American citizen un-American. (Wills 1976: 18)

There was no ambiguity concerning Chairman Thomas's vision of America – 'more business in government and less government in business' – nor was there any doubt about his (ab)use of the powers invested in him. A HUAC Chairman was potentially judge and jury: he subpoenaed citizens to appear before him and asked them questions. As this was not a court of law, witnesses did not have the right to have their lawyer cross-examine other witnesses. Moreover, what witnesses stated could not be used against them outside the room where the hearings took place, which meant that a slur on a person's character went unchallenged. We shall see this happening again and again during the 1947 Hearings:

> The committee usurped the functions of the grand jury without the protective secrecy of that body by making charges publicly in a purported effort to obtain information. The committee was able to punish people for acts or associations that would not be regarded as crimes in a court of law. The punishment was the loss of their livelihood and the annihilation of their reputations.
>
> *In this sense the committee conducted trials rather than hearings.* (Vaughn 1996: 175; emphasis added)[9]

THE HEARINGS

The Committee's brief was to investigate Communist infiltration of the motion-picture industry, but it soon transpired that the meaning of both 'Communism' and 'infiltration' was problematic. Was HUAC trying to prove members of the Hollywood community were members of the CP or that some diffuse Communist presence had led to movies being turned into propaganda? Since Jack L. Warner and Louis B. Mayer admitted that they had made pro-Soviet propaganda films during the war, other criteria had to be found. It was clear from the outset that HUAC had decided in advance who was 'friendly' (= cooperative) and who was 'hostile' (= uncooperative).[10] It was the FBI who drew up the lists of the 'friendly' and the 'hostile', which allowed HUAC, during their visit to Hollywood in May 1947, to interview those who were to appear before it in Washington in October. Many of the 'friendly' witnesses belonged to the Motion Picture Alliance, including its President, director Sam Wood, and actor Adolphe Menjou, as well as leading figures in the Screen Playwrights, such as Rupert Hughes and James Kevin McGuinness. Other key witnesses were actors Gary Cooper and Robert Taylor, writer Ayn Rand and Lela Rogers (mother of actress Ginger Rogers).[11]

Originally there had been nineteen 'unfriendly' witnesses listed, although only ten were actually called: writers Alvah Bessie, Lester Cole, Ring Lardner, Jr, John Howard Lawson, Albert Maltz, Sam Ornitz and Dalton Trumbo, directors Herbert Biberman and Edward Dmytryk, and producer Adrian Scott.[12] Those who were not called were writers Richard Collins, Gordon Kahn and Waldo Salt, director Lewis Milestone, writer-director Robert Rossen, writer-producer Howard Koch, actor-director Irving Pichel and actor Larry Parks.[13] Why these and not others, given the numbers of Communists known to the FBI (and hence to HUAC)? Several reasons have been suggested. Most of the Ten were Jews. None had a war record; after all, berating a war hero wearing his medals for the occasion would not go down well with the public. Bessie was the only member of the film community to have fought in Spain on the Loyalist side. Cole and Lawson had brought attention to themselves as militant unionists during the 1930s, Scott and Dmytryk had just made the anti-anti-Semitic *Crossfire* (1947). Trumbo was the highest-paid writer in the industry because his films were commercially successful (doubtless as propaganda too). Nor must the sheer vindictiveness of the Alliance be neglected.[14] Its members were summoned first.

Some indication of what HUAC was willing to accept as testimony and what values were being defended can be garnered from remarks made by friendly witnesses. *The Hollywood Reporter* (27 October) quoted director Sam Wood of the Alliance who named four directors who tried to 'steer us into the Red river', a supposedly witty reference to the recent Western starring Alliance member John Wayne.[15] The directors were Dmytryk of the Ten, Pichel of the Nineteen, John Cromwell and Frank Tuttle.[16] Asked whether he thought Cromwell was a Communist, actor Adolphe Menjou said he did not know, adding after prompting from Stripling: 'he acts an awful lot like one'. He then went on to refer to a discussion he had with Cromwell about the future of capitalism (Bentley 2002: 122–3). Cromwell was never given the chance to reply.[17] Menjou was both confused and confusing over the question of Communist propaganda. Firstly, he congratulated the Alliance for preventing 'an enormous amount of sly, subtle, un-American class-struggle propaganda from going into pictures', then, replying to a question about how propaganda could be portrayed, stated that it would be possible to subvert a film 'by a look, by an inflection, by a change in the voice. *I have never seen it done, but I think it could be done*' (Bentley 2002: 122; emphasis added). On the basis of a mixture of opinions, hearsay and intuition Menjou had been designated as an expert. At the outset of the proceedings, Thomas had refused Bartley Crum, one of the Ten's lawyers, the right to cross-examine, which led Crum to remark sarcastically on 'the Americanism of the procedure' (Los Angeles *Daily News*, 20 October).

Menjou indulged in some name dropping, citing actors Edward G. Robinson, Hume Cronyn, Alexander Knox and Paul Henreid as 'associates of Sorrell in the Hollywood union fight', claiming Sorrell was a Communist (Hollywood *Citizen-News*, 21 October). Thus appeared early on the dubious notion of 'guilt by association', destined to become a basic weapon with which to (brow)beat unfriendly witnesses in the future.[18] Similarly, actor Robert Taylor (who appeared the day after Menjou) talked of 'a certain group of actors and actresses whose every action would indicate to me that, if they are not Communists, they are working awfully hard to be Communists'. He then gave the names of actress Karen Morley and actor Howard Da Silva: 'He always seems to have something to say at the wrong time' (Bentley 2002: 137).[19] Taylor's testimony is revealing as an unwitting example of the complicity that existed between HUAC and the friendly witnesses. Stripling asked the actor if he had ever participated in a picture containing Communist propaganda. Taylor replied: 'I assume we are now referring to *Song of Russia*' (Bentley 2002: 137–8). 'We', not 'You'. If Taylor and Stripling had not already rehearsed the questions and answers, Taylor would not have made this revealing slip, indicating as it does an identification with Stripling's position and a common desire to incriminate the film as propaganda.[20]

Taylor was also an exponent of hearsay: 'several writers' were 'reputedly fellow travellers or possibly Communists'. However, he could give only one example: Lester Cole, 'reputedly a Communist. I would not know personally' (Bentley 2002: 139). The transcript of the Hearings fails, however, to note yet another slip of the tongue, perfectly audible in the newsreel recording of the Hearings included in the documentary *Hollywood on Trial*. Taylor does not say 'I know of several writers . . .' but: 'I know several writers – I know of several writers'. This is revealing. Taylor never accused anyone of *being* a Communist: 'of' betrays the role of hearsay which, through endless reiteration, took on the aura of truth, thus replacing an open accusation. According to *Variety* (29 October), Taylor was asked to reconcile the statement that he wouldn't work with a Communist and the fact that his last film had been written by Lester Cole. Taylor 'hemmed and hawed', then claimed his remark referred to stars only.[21] Actor Gary Cooper was also prone to discussing matters of which he had no first-hand knowledge, giving the distinct impression of being naive, even ridiculous: he was unable to remember the titles of supposedly Communist-tainted scripts he had turned down, 'because most of the scripts I read at night' (Bentley 2002: 148). Although this may seem like low but sinister farce, recent research casts new light on Cooper's testimony. Unlike other witnesses, he did not mention a single name, which infuriated Alliance President Sam Wood.

Cooper's later behaviour when making *High Noon* in 1951 – despite all forms of pressure exerted on him, he supported writer Carl Foreman, who was subpoenaed to appear before HUAC, through to the bitter end – indicated a moral sense singularly lacking at the time and a refusal to deprive people of their livelihood, despite political differences (Byman 2004: 58–60, 71–90).[22]

Lela Rogers, mother of actress Ginger, accused the film *Tender Comrade*, directed by Edward Dmytryk in 1943 from a script by Dalton Trumbo, of being Communist propaganda because of the line her daughter had to say: 'Share and share alike, that's democracy.' Mrs Rogers made this accusation on HUAC's visit to Hollywood in May 1947 and did not repeat it in October (Kahn 1948: 43–4). This is the most quoted remark of the Hearings, which is unfortunate: at *no* point in *Tender Comrade* does Ginger Rogers speak this line in this form. She suggests to three friends – each of the young married women is the 'tender comrade' of her husband, abroad fighting – that, instead of renting an apartment each, they should pool their resources and rent a house.[23] This is certainly a case of defending social housing for working people. Later Rogers makes a remark that infuriated the Right: in case of disagreement, they should take a vote.[24] These are her actual words:

> We could take a vote. We could run the joint like a democracy. If anything comes up, we'll just call a meeting . . . We could sell one car and use the other on a share-and-share-alike basis.

The notion of sharing everything, including sacrifices, in order to help the war effort is made explicit by their housekeeper, significantly a Jewish refugee from Nazi Germany. She is displeased when the butcher gives her bacon beyond the legal rations as this means depriving others, especially soldiers. So 'share and share alike' takes on an international dimension, one of solidarity. Although such elements are an obvious attack on free enterprise and profiteering, what Rogers and the housekeeper defend cannot be abstracted from the context of a World War. Trumbo was not being a Communist here but simply giving a patriotic history lesson.

That HUAC was coming to Hollywood as trouble-shooters with certain left-wingers in their sights was an open secret, and the Nineteen hired lawyers to ascertain how best to react. However, the producers too were under fire, for allegedly having allowed Communists to slip propaganda into their films. Their lawyer, Paul McNutt, requested that the Committee subpoena the films incriminated so as to prove their point concerning subversive content: 'On behalf of the producers I represent, I urge committee members not to accept second or third hand opinion on these films' (*Variety*, 21 October 1947). If I insisted on the way Mrs Rogers misquoted the remark in *Tender Comrade*, it is because such inaccuracies, however minor, when added to hearsay were to destroy careers. McNutt's request was echoed by W. R. Wilkerson, the anti-Communist editor of *The Hollywood Reporter.* With the films in their possession, the Committee had only to 'look at them and then determine the question as a result of the inspection'. Made the day before the Hearings opened, this suggestion, like the official request of McNutt, fell on deaf ears.

In this the Committee was more than helped by producer Jack L. Warner. He had already testified during the preliminary hearings held in Los Angeles in May where he gave the names of Warner Brothers writers under contract whom he suspected of attempting to '[inject] Communist propaganda' into films. By October, however, he had changed his mind on a number of cases and asked to rectify matters, but certain names remained on the list, essentially those of the Nineteen (Kahn 1948: 12–16). The Committee's main concerns were to get Warner to justify a blacklist and ask it to outlaw the CP. Representative Vail put this question to the producer: 'Would you be deeply interested in providing a livelihood for the individual who was attempting by subversive methods to destroy this form of government?' (Kahn 1948: 22). This is a convoluted way of asking 'Are you in favour of a blacklist?' Warner, however, showed no interest in the matter, so Vail's colleague Representative McDowell moved on to the matter of the CP: 'You know during Hitler's regime they passed a law in Germany outlawing Communism and the Communists went to jail. Would you advocate the same thing here?' McDowell had obviously forgotten World War II and that Warner was a Jew. Nor had he viewed *Confessions of a Nazi Spy*. To his credit, Warner riposted: 'Everyone in this room and everyone in the world knows the consequences of that type of law' (Kahn 1948: 22). However, Warner finally said he wanted the CP to be made illegal, but on the question of a blacklist he was more careful:

> I agree to it personally, Mr. Congressman, but I cannot agree so far as the [Motion Picture] Association is concerned. I can't for the life of me figure where men could get together . . . to deprive a man of his livelihood because of his political beliefs. (Kahn 1948: 26)

Outlawing the CP was HUAC's chief obsession and one of their most redoubtable adversaries was Arthur Garfield Hays, counsel for the American Civil Liberties Union (ACLU), a lawyer specialising in constitutional law and an adamant anti-Communist: he considered them 'crackbrained' (Bentley 2002: 247). He was summoned before a Subcommittee of HUAC (chaired by Richard Nixon) and allowed to make a statement which extends over five pages of Bentley's volume. Here are some of his remarks:

> The Bill of Rights guarantees the freedom to advocate changes in the American form of government, to belong to a political party for that

purpose, and to run for office. Any denial of these freedoms for Communists inevitably challenges the rights of all political minorities. (249)

We have plenty of legislation today to stop all Communist activity if we could prove that the party and the members thereof advocate force and violence. (251)

This kind of legislation [outlawing the CP] seems to me to be wholly un-American, indicates lack of faith in our institutions, would arouse fear and timidity, and invite attacks upon sincere liberal thought. (251)

The method of the Fascists, of Hitler and Mussolini, was to stir up a Red scare and then repress the liberties of the people in order to save them from the Reds. (253)

At one point he was corrected by Representative McDowell when he referred to 'the Un-American Committee'. Hays persisted: he had called it that when Dies was Chairman, accusing the latter of being 'a dangerous man' seeking to 'stir up a Red scare' (271). Thus the considerable change in the political climate over a decade had not changed the opinions of an expert on the Constitution.[25]

The Nineteen and their lawyers decided to challenge the Committee's determination to inquire into a citizen's private opinions as a violation of the First Amendment of the Constitution (1791):

Congress shall make no law respecting an establishment of religion, or prohibiting the free exercise thereof; or abridging the freedom of speech, or of the press; or the right of the people peaceably to assemble, and to petition the Government for a redress of grievances.

The lawyers had reason to believe that such a tactic had every chance of succeeding, given legal precedent. In a decision dating from 1942, Justice Hugo Black had written: 'I view the guarantees of the First Amendment as the foundation upon which our government structure rests and without which it could not continue to endure as conceived and planned' (Wagman 1991: 56). The following year Justice Robert H. Jackson had stated:

If there is any fixed star in our constitutional constellation it is that no official, high or petty, can prescribe what shall be orthodox in politics, nationalism, religion or other matters of opinion, or force citizens to confess by word or act their faith therein.[26]

Ben Margolis, one of the group's lawyers, pointed out later that taking a stand on the First was considered 'a respectable position' by 95 per cent of the population.[27] Ring Lardner, Jr has written that the unanimous decision to take the First and therefore to refuse to answer any questions was modified when another of their lawyers, Robert Kenny, suggested the following tactic: 'I want you not to refuse to answer a question but say you're trying to answer it in your own way' (Lardner 2000: 119). One reason for this argument was that a refusal to answer could lead to a citation for contempt and therefore to prison.

It is sufficient to read the transcripts of the Hearings and, especially, to view the newsreel footage to understand how things backfired for the unfriendly witnesses. It was immediately clear that the leeway granted the friendly witnesses was not to be extended to them and that they had to answer 'yes' or 'no' to the question: 'Are you now or have you ever been a member of the Communist Party?' The first to take the stand, John Howard Lawson, asked to be allowed to read a prepared statement. Thomas asked to see it, started to read it and refused, declaring it irrelevant to the Hearings.[28] When he was asked the question about membership in the CP, he started to give a speech, only to be cut off by the Chairman's gavel. The question was repeated and Lawson replied: 'I'm forming my answer in the only way any American citizen can frame', before being cut off by Thomas who said: 'Then you deny, you, you refuse to answer that question?' This is another slip of the tongue. Lawson admitted and denied nothing and his 'refusal' was relative: he refused to answer in the way imposed on him. He was told to 'stand away from the stand'.

This confrontation was repeated, with variations, when Lawson's colleagues took the stand. Lester Cole was asked if he belonged to the SWG: to have answered 'yes' would have been to concede the Committee's right to question him on his union affiliations, protected like politics and religion by the First. Cole responded thus: 'I'd be very happy to answer that question. I believe the reason the question is being asked . . .'. At this point Thomas started banging the table with his gavel and shouting 'No!' *Hollywood on Trial* shows that he wielded his gavel to the accompaniment of 'no' thirteen times. We can distinguish a slight smile (of resignation?) on Cole's face. Trumbo was luckier and succeeded in making the following remark: 'The rights of American labor to inviolably secret membership lists have been won in this country by a great cost of blood and a great cost in terms of hunger.' The mild-mannered Adrian Scott simply stated that he couldn't answer the questions put to him in the way demanded. Edward Dmytryk raised the question of the Constitution and the right to think. 'So you refuse to answer the question?', Thomas put in. 'I don't refuse, I'm answering in my own way', replied the director. Herbert Biberman engaged in what became a contest between the gavel of Thomas and the force of his own lungs.

Albert Maltz fared better, thanks to a brilliant ruse on his part. When asking to be allowed to read the statement he had prepared, he said: 'May I ask whether you asked Gerald L. K. Smith to see his statement before you allowed him to read it?' (Smith was the notorious anti-Semite and supporter of HUAC.)

Thomas read Maltz's statement, then allowed Maltz to read it. He listed the films he had written and how well they had been accepted both by the Academy of Motion Picture Arts and Sciences and the armed forces, denounced Thomas and Rankin for being opposed to anti-lynching laws and for supporting the Ku Klux Klan, stated that he would not have been hauled before the Committee if his name had been General Franco and concluded thus: 'The American people are going to have to choose between the Bill of Rights and the Thomas Committee. They cannot have both. One or the other must be abolished in the immediate future.' He was then asked the usual question about belonging to the CP, stated his belief that the question was improper and was dismissed by Thomas: 'Typical Communist line' (Kahn 1948: 87–90).

One commentator has written: 'The central rationale for guaranteeing freedom of expression is that unfettered exchanges of opinion will ultimately lead to truth' (Wagman 1991: 109). This may be idealistic but at least insists on the right to express oneself. This right was flouted by Thomas who, in his pre-liminary remarks, promised to be 'fair and impartial' but granted to the friendly witnesses rights he denied to the unfriendly ones. Present in the court were twenty-nine members of the motion-picture industry who had flown to Washington to show their hostility to the Committee's Hearings. They belonged to the Committee for the First Amendment, set up as soon as it transpired that Hollywood was under attack by HUAC. Four men were behind the CFA: directors John Huston and William Wyler, writer Philip Dunne and actor Alexander Knox.[29] Its first public petition denouncing HUAC was published in *The Hollywood Reporter* and signed by thirty-five Hollywood personalities. One week later a further petition bearing 350 signatures appeared in *Daily Variety*.[30] The most famous star present in Washington was Humphrey Bogart who made this statement (reproduced in the documentary *The Legacy of the Blacklist*, 1987):

> This is Humphrey Bogart. We sat in the Committee Room and heard it happen. We saw it. We said to ourselves: it can't happen here. We saw American citizens denied the right to speak by elected representatives of the people. We saw police take citizens from the stand like criminals after they'd been refused the right to defend themselves. We saw the gavel of the Committee Chairman cutting off the words of free Americans. The sound of that gavel, Mr. Thomas, rings across America, because every time your gavel struck it hit the First Amendment to the Constitution of the United States.[31]

The controversial nature of the Hearings and the celebrity of the accused led to much press comment. The Motion Picture Association of America made out a list of over 250 newspaper editorials 'denouncing the Thomas

Committee and/or commending the position of the motion picture industry'.[32] If these editorials make fascinating and revealing reading, certain ambiguities are already present, including the precise meaning of the formula
'commending the position of the motion picture industry'. The MPAA book
of cuttings opens with editorials from the New York *Herald Tribune* (22
October and 1 November 1947), a conservative Republican newspaper. Sober
yet sarcastic, they smote Thomas hip and thigh, referring to 'an abundance of
unsubstantiated charges' and 'some dizzying new definitions of Communism',
then pointed out:

> . . . this prying is forbidden by the Constitution . . .

> . . . Not Hollywood but Congress is being investigated here, and once
> again the testimony indicates that the system of Congressional investi-
> gating committees needs overhauling.

The editorials published in the New York *Times* (23 October and 2 November)
raised three key issues. Firstly, nobody can force a witness to declare his
affiliation to a party which is legally recognised. Secondly, even 'the most
degraded criminal' has the right to cross-examine. Thirdly, did the Committee
intend moving on to Broadway, the radio and the press, not to mention the
private convictions of 'labor unions, physicians, lawyers, scientists and country
storekeepers'?[33] This last point was also made by the Atlanta, Georgia, *Journal*
(28 October): 'the principles of free speech and free press are meaningless
unless they apply to people who disagree with the government'.

The question of the difference between a court of law and a Committee of
Congress was taken up by the Washington *Post* (5 November 1947). Stating
that 'Congress has an obligation not to encroach upon the realm of the judi-
ciary', the editorial refers to the language used by the Committee: 'One of the
committee's lawyers inadvertently told witnesses that they were 'charged' with
communism, *as if they had been before a court*' (emphasis added). The editorialist
of the Denver *Post* (22 October) was of the opinion that 'attorneys for all interested parties at all congressional hearings should be extended the privilege of
cross-examination', adding crucially: 'Some congressional committees do
allow the cross-examination of witnesses'. This particular aspect of HUAC's
behaviour and Thomas's arrogance and rudeness towards Paul McNutt and
Bartley Crum shocked many observers. One editorialist even wrote that the
'hearings more closely resemble purge trials in Russia than judicial or legisla-
tive proceedings in the United States' (Toledo, Ohio, *Blade*, 28 October).

Two striking editorials appeared in the Chicago *Sun* (23 October 1947)
and the Rutland, Vermont, *Herald* (29 October). The former was uncannily
prophetic:

When an atmosphere of suspicion and hatred is established, you get people turning on each other, questioning their friends and even themselves, wondering if their thoughts run in the accepted 'American' channel, secretly asking whether somebody's convictions are his own or those of a party line.

That is the most un-American thing of all – the silent intimidation, the unexpressed pressure to conform, the official reaching out to control thoughts. Until lately it was considered a basic element of Americanism that a man could think and speak as he pleased. Some day, when the current hysteria has passed, it may be so considered again.

The second editorial concentrated on the question of hearsay, where the person slurred could not sue for slander: the witness was protected by the status of the Committee. The editorialist went further by referring to 'prejudiced testimony', thus raising the fundamental question of the settling of scores and of antagonism based on political differences. The editorial is eloquently entitled 'The "Un-American" Committee'. The editorialist of the Marion, Ohio, *Star* (30 October) summed things up: 'Nothing the Reds can do in this country is half so fearful as the things Americans might do if they lost sight of the vital importance of their civil liberties.'

For other editorialists the problem with HUAC lay in its inability to go beyond generalities. The Philadelphia *Inquirer* (22 October 1947) took it as self-evident that Communists were influencing the content of films and accepted at face value what had been claimed by the friendly witnesses; the problem with the testimony of Menjou is that he named no films, despite the fact that 'a concerted and earnest attempt' had been made to subvert the screen. There was only one solution: 'naming names, and citing actual performances'. The Aberdeen, Washington, *World* (24 October) called for the Communists to 'be identified and their names blazoned over the country'. The Sunbury, Pennsylvania, *Item* (28 October) called on Hollywood to efface 'the red tinge' from films, while the Los Angeles *Herald and Express* (24 October) considered it the Committee's duty 'to clear the air of subversive propaganda'. The Cleveland *Plain Dealer* (29 October) accepted the Committee line that the Ten had refused to testify. Even more forthright, the New York *Daily Mirror* congratulated Thomas for uncovering the 'skulduggery' of the Communists and asked him to 'drive these *vermin* out of one of America's greatest industries' (emphasis added).

Behind many of the editorials, however, lay the implicit assumption that, should X turn out to be a Communist, then the Committee had done its job and Hollywood was within its rights to dispense with his services. Thus there crept into discourse the notions of 'guilt' and 'innocence', insidiously implying in this context that being a Communist was a sign of the former. The editorial of the Durham *Sun* (24 October 1947) was entitled 'Not Only the Guilty Who Are Made to Suffer'. Its sole concern was a fear that people 'branded as Communists' were going to see their careers suffer if they were not members of the Party, implying that it was acceptable to deprive a 'bona fide Communist' of his livelihood. Similarly, the Asheville, North Carolina, *Times* (29 October) wrote that 'such inquiries are likely to start witch-hunts, liable to work irreparable harm to individuals who are entirely innocent'. The logic is limpid: witch hunts are justifiable when they expose the 'guilty', such as Communists. The groundwork was being laid for what was to come: the abandonment by most liberals of any attempt to protect rights *as such*, only those of the 'innocent': non-Communists or ex-Communists. In his Foreword to the volume published by the American Civil Liberties Union (Miller 1952: 11), liberal playwright Robert Sherwood denounced 'the cruel and inhuman publicity to which many decent, non-Communist American artists have already been subjected'. Clearly Communist artists were not 'decent' and could be happily subjected to such 'cruel and inhuman publicity'. We shall see that this opinion, commonplace among liberals by 1950, was in the process of becoming the received wisdom once the Hearings closed.

This impression was gained from the testimony of one witness in a position to defend the Ten: Emmet Lavery, President of the SWG. He was in a unique position before HUAC: considered an unfriendly witness, while not being a member of the Nineteen. As President of the SWG he had become synonymous with Communism in the eyes of the Committee, for whom union struggles were subversive (= hostile to business); and he had been denounced as a 'Communist masquerading as a Catholic' by the vindictive writer and Alliance member, Rupert Hughes. Morrie Ryskind of the Alliance had stated before the Committee that the SWG was under Communist domination. When Lavery asked if he would have the opportunity to reply, he received from Chairman Thomas the following answer: 'Without objection, the Chair will give you permission to reply to those. That is just why you are here. Charges have been made against you and your organization' (Bentley 2002: 171). The ambiguous passive voice is as eloquent as the word 'charges': we have seen that a Committee of Congress is *not* a court of law and everyone knew who was making the charges, although Thomas could not admit it and simultaneously claim to be 'fair and impartial'.

Lavery, a lawyer by training, volunteered spontaneously that he was not a member of the CP, adding: 'I am not sure, as a student of constitutional law, whether the Committee does have the authority to demand it of me' (Bentley 2002: 172). Asked whether he was 'aware of any Communist infiltration within the Screen Writers' Guild', he replied that he was 'willing to make the assumption' that there was, adding that the SWG had members of the extreme Left and the extreme Right but that most were in the 'liberal center'. By refusing the notion of 'infiltration', Lavery was patently trying to demolish the Committee's pre-conceived notions. Similarly, when asked if 'action should be taken' to remove Communists from the Guild, he replied: 'it would be disastrous for a guild to attempt to project a standard of conduct not yet embodied in the law by the Congress of the United States' (Bentley 2002: 177). However, Lavery had already agreed with J. Edgar Hoover: outlawing the CP would drive it underground. This remark was unfortunate because it implied that for Lavery too the CP represented a threat. Likewise, when asked about the 'influence' of Lawson, Trumbo, Maltz, Bessie, Ornitz and Biberman (who had already appeared), Lavery made the mistake of replying that they did not 'control' the guild, thus placing his reply on the terrain chosen by the Committee, although he denied such control existed. Had Lavery kept to the word 'influence', he could have continued to deny the notion of 'infiltration' and thus potential control, whereas his anxiety to defend the SWG ended by giving the impression that it had indeed been infiltrated and come close to being controlled by Communists.[34]

Which brings us back to the mantra of 'Communist propaganda'. Both Jack L. Warner and Louis B. Mayer had suffered on the stand because of pro-Soviet films they had made during the war, *Mission to Moscow* by the former, *Song of Russia* by the latter. Originally, in May 1947, Warner had tried to put the blame for *Mission to Moscow* on Roosevelt and former American Ambassador to Moscow, Mr Davies. This was an excellent way of 'proving' that the New Deal was influenced by Reds and how prone to Red propaganda Hollywood was. However, by October Warner admitted that his brother Harry had contacted Ambassador Davies about turning his book *Mission to Moscow* into a film. So much was made of this because of the controversial nature of the film: not praise for the courage and sacrifice of the Soviets but a paean of praise to Stalin and a justification of his regime, including the notorious 'purge' trials where Stalin started to eliminate internal opposition to his regime.[35] Basically, however, for Warner Brothers, the film was part of the war effort, as was the MGM production *Song of Russia* which preached love and understanding (the film is a love story involving an American conductor and a Soviet peasant). What was at stake here was censorship, but in a very particular sense. During his testimony friendly witness James Kevin McGuinness stated that anti-Communist films should be made, a remark which functioned as an opening gambit. Thomas asked: 'will these public hearings aid the industry in giving it the will to make these pictures?' McGuinness concurred. The next step had also been carefully rehearsed, with the witness agreeing with the Committee that anti-Communist films might be distributed as 'a patriotic and public duty' through schools and churches, should Hollywood be approached to help such an undertaking (Suber 1966: 48–9). Thus HUAC sought to transform Hollywood and its films into a vector of propaganda, while simultaneous dictating the content of films, exactly what it was accusing the Left of doing, but without proof.

THE AFTERMATH

The Hearings over, the Committee recommended that the Ten be cited for contempt of Congress. Two major statements were made in the days that followed. One was by Emmet Lavery concerning the coming SWG election. His

> implicit message was that the Ten had knowingly harmed Guild interests by linking the writers' unions with communism in the public mind; that is, they had deliberately associated their refusal to answer the question about Guild membership with their refusal to answer the question about Communist Party membership. (Ceplair and Englund 1980: 294)

In calling for an All Guild Slate, Lavery was effectively calling for the defeat of all left-wing elements within the SWG. This was promptly denounced by four of the Nineteen – Cole, Collins, Kahn and Lardner – but supported by novelist and screenwriter James M. Cain who pointed out that the accusations of Communism were true and that the SWG had to exclude 'all politics' from its activities (Ceplair and Englund 1980: 294–5). Lavery's call was discussed in the Los Angeles *Herald Express* (7 November 1947): the Guild was 'to confine its interests in [*sic*] matters concerned with the writing profession and refrain from labor, political and other extraneous activities'. How could a Guild – or union – not be concerned with 'labor'? Elementary: by refusing to consider itself a union.[36]

The second statement was by Martin Quigley, the conservative, Catholic owner and editor of the *Motion Picture Herald* (8 November 1947).[37] Quigley raised the spectre of HUAC public hearings to come and evoked the 'disrepair' of the motion-picture industry. He considered that an investigation of 'propaganda hostile to the United States and its institutions' was proper but that HUAC appeared 'to have been supplied with a wealth of misinformation', particularly that concerning the presence of such propaganda. The pro-Soviet films of the war years now seemed 'ridiculous' but to investigate them was 'absurd'.[38] Quigley also made the telling point that distributors and public would never have accepted un-American propaganda, indicating that he rejected HUAC's claim about movies disseminating Communist propaganda. More revealing is his remark that, long before HUAC descended on Hollywood, it was known that there were Communists in Hollywood: 'The employing firms had not, of course, been hiding the accused persons and in most instances their Communistic inclinations were not only known but well-known.'

Two aspects of the Hearings had tarnished the image of the Ten: what many considered their undignified behaviour; and the 'revelation' that they were members of the CP. Actress Marsha Hunt confirmed that the members of the CFA were 'belittled and made to look foolish' by the press, that Bogart was 'angry at the way we were treated and at what we had seen', but that 'we were also sorry that a few of the Nineteen had been so shrill and defiant in their demeanor. It hadn't helped their case' (McGilligan and Buhle 1997: 317). As far as being CP members is concerned, faint-hearted liberals pretended they never knew in order to be shocked by the ghastly truth, thus presenting themselves with a sort of escape route by which they could abandon the comrades and become pure Americans again.[39] The revelation before HUAC that the Ten were card-carrying Communists, made by a former FBI agent summoned as a witness, covered up the fact that the information had been obtained *illegally* and would have caused HUAC considerable embarrassment, had the right to cross-examine been granted. But there was no way the Ten's lawyers could ascertain whether a breach of ethics was involved.[40] This was therefore a stroke of genius on the part of the FBI and HUAC. The former's records 'raise disturbing questions about how secrecy, ostensibly for counterintelligence reasons, undermined limited, constitutional government based on the rule of law and order' (Theoharis 2002: 239).

Supporters of the Ten said in private that they should have called a press conference before the Hearings and declared they were members of the CP, while insisting on their constitutional right not to answer questions on their beliefs.[41] Superficially, this would seem to be a good solution, but to have acted thus would have been to admit that there are circumstances in which one must state one's convictions in public: when under pressure to do so. It also lends credibility to unsubstantiated accusations. The suggestion also highlights the surreal situation in which members of the CP found themselves: if they admitted to belonging to the CP, they would suffer discrimination in the form of refusals of employment; at the same time their membership was an open secret for the FBI. The climate of suspicion, and worse, surrounding Communists and other 'subversives' was such that they were forever in a quandary.[42]

The citation of the Ten for contempt of Congress brought grist to the mill of the witch hunters. Hedda Hopper kept up pressure by publishing in her column extracts from letters favourable to the friendly witnesses and hostile to the CFA. Westbrook Pegler excoriated his favourite *bête noire*, actor Danny Kaye (a prominent liberal and member of the CFA), whom he accused of not 'giv[ing] exactly his all during the war' (*Los Angeles Examiner*, 7 November 1947). This is a reference to the fact the Kaye was not drafted, but Pegler carefully failed to mention two things: John Wayne did everything to avoid the draft;[43] and Hollywood was granted dispensation by the federal government, which did not call up everyone eligible for the draft so that the industry could continue to make entertaining movies as a patriotic gesture. Pegler added an anti-Semitic touch by giving Kaye's Jewish name. In the Los Angeles *Herald Express* (17 December), he referred to the Ten, stating that some of them worked under 'assumed names'. This is a reference to Lawson, whose father changed his Jewish name *before* Lawson was born. Pegler then evoked the film *Body and Soul*, stating: 'The star is known as John Garfield . . . as he calls himself.' He then gave his Jewish name, adding that his parents were 'Born in Russia'.[44] Pegler was not alone here. When she was involved in running the Hollywood Canteen – set up by stars to offer relaxation and entertainment to members of the armed forces passing through Los Angeles on their way home on leave – director John Ford's wife gave vent to anti-Semitic remarks in the context of 'leftists' trying to take over the Canteen. She too hated Garfield, referred to him by his Jewish name and called him a Communist (McBride 2003: 370).[45] Another Red-baiting Hearst columnist, George Sokolsky, had earlier deplored a court ruling to the effect that it was illegal to call someone a Communist unless 'provably true', adding: 'But judge or no judge, we shall find a way to protect Americans from treachery as well as stupidity' (*Herald Express*, 27 October). Insinuation and witch hunting had to take precedence over the rule of law.

Rankin used the same tactic as Pegler to attack the CFA in the House of Representatives: he listed several members, then gave their Jewish names. He was roundly applauded and on 24 November 1947 Congress voted over-whelmingly in favour of the citations for contempt: 346 for, 17 against. Anti-Semitism was now the sign of the true patriot. The verbal violence of the Hearings had unnerved the CFA: 'Throughout Hollywood the word went out that the era of political demonstrations was over. The studios could no longer afford, and would not longer tolerate, activism' (Ceplair and Englund 1980: 289–90). Most of the producers were Jews and politically conservative:

> though it doesn't absolve them to say so, they were also in the grip of a deep and legitimate fear: the fear that somehow the delicate rapproche-ment they had established between themselves and this country would be destroyed, and with it their lives. (Gabler 1988: 374)

This is admirably put. Nativism, xenophobia and anti-Semitism together make for a heady and explosive brew, especially at a time of mounting anti-Communist hysteria based on a security syndrome. What exactly had tran-spired to break the delicate balance among the moguls and create a blacklist?

The answer is that Eric Johnston had come to Hollywood. In 1945 Johnston, President of the American Chamber of Commerce, took over from Will Hays as President of the Motion Picture Producers and Distributors Association (MPPDA). Hostile to the very idea of trade unions, he thus arrived in Los Angeles when the massive strike broke out and came 'espousing the ideals of liberal corporate consensus' (Munby 1999: 169). Within two years his opinions were abundantly clear:

> On March 5, 1947, Johnston charged that all Communists were 'foreign agents' and asked the U.S. Congress to prevent them from holding positions of leadership in labor unions. Johnston repeated his charges before the House Committee on Un-American Activities (HUAC) on March 27, 1947. (Adler 1974: 245)

That same month Johnston declared to the industry: 'We'll have no more *Grapes of Wrath*, we'll have no more *Tobacco Roads*. We'll have no more films that show the seamy side of American life' (Munby 1999: 172). These dates are important: two months later HUAC was in Hollywood listening to testimony from friendly witnesses. In his own way Johnston was echoing the Republican equation 'the New Deal = Communism' by seeking to impose on Hollywood 'an agenda that exorcized the ghosts of New Deal political rhetoric and promoted the goals of consensus and abundance instead' (Munby 1999: 173n30). Even before Lawson inadvertently gave both the Right and the spokesman of the new 'consensus' the stick with which to beat the Left,

> Johnston had presented a memorandum of his association showing it had been proposed that the association not hire any Communists, but that legal counsel had opposed it on the grounds that such a 'blacklist' would constitute conspiracy. The association dropped the proposal, though Johnston at first had favored it.[46]

'Legal counsel' was Paul McNutt who called a press conference on the close of the second day of the Hearings and stated that a blacklist 'would be without warrant of law and was not in accord with the announced policy of Congress or the rulings of the Supreme Court, and could therefore involve the producers in serious legal difficulties' (Suber 1966: 39). The day before the Hearings opened Johnston, the producers, their lawyers and the Nineteen's lawyers met in a Washington hotel where Johnston denied any motion in favour of a blacklist: 'Tell the boys not to worry. There'll never be a blacklist. We're not going to go totalitarian to please this committee' (Schwartz 1982: 266–7).[47]

We have already seen that collusion existed between HUAC's Chief Investigator, Robert Stripling, and certain witnesses and one historian has written that his questioning of one friendly witness, writer John Charles

Moffitt, 'inadvertently revealed that he had collaborated with certain witnesses beforehand' (Suber 1966: 35). On the very day Congress handed down its citations for contempt, the producers, their lawyers and Johnston met at the Waldorf-Astoria Hotel in New York and decided on a blacklist. Not by name: no material list ever existed, since it would indeed have been proof of a conspiracy. It took them two days, however, as certain producers, Mayer and Harry Cohn, were unhappy about losing such valuable employees. However, there were threats of boycotts, both by the professional anti-Communists of the American Legion and by Latin American countries, not to mention hostility in certain towns towards such celebrated members of the CFA as Katharine Hepburn. To these considerations must be added that of the pressure exerted by the banks.

So a statement was prepared, with legal advice, whereby the Ten were to be fired by their respective employers for conduct unbecoming. The Statement declared:

> We will forthwith discharge or suspend without compensation those in our employ and we will not re-employ any of the ten until such time as he is acquitted or has purged himself of contempt and declares under oath that he is not a Communist.

The use of 'purged' showed that the United States had now incorporated a Stalinist tactic for eliminating political enemies. Moreover, it was taken for granted that Communism was illegal, thus granting the Committee a legal power which even Congress did not enjoy. The Statement went on:

> We will not knowingly employ a Communist or member of any party or group which advocates the overthrow of the government of the United States by force or by any illegal or unconstitutional methods.

That, at least, is how the Statement is reproduced in various accounts but it is not what Eric Johnston actually said when he read it out before the press. I invite readers to listen carefully to the newsreel recording of this dramatic event included in the documentary *Hollywood on Trial*. For Johnston says the exact *opposite* at one point: not 'by any illegal' but: 'by any legal – illegal'. *He thus corrects what he first said.* This is an extraordinary and revealing slip of the tongue where Johnston speaks the simple truth: the Ten had done nothing *illegal* and the CP was perfectly *legal*. A little slip whereby Johnston and the producers admitted that they were part of a conspiracy and spoke the truth while denying it. Communists were to be deprived of their rights, irrespective of legal niceties.

Pegler trumpeted triumphantly: '10 down, 100 to go' (Hollywood *Citizen-News*, 15 December 1947). The author of 'The Talk of the Town' column in

The New Yorker (6 December) adopted a different line, one which was to prove prophetic: 'If the practice of inquiring into a man's beliefs becomes general, then every writer in America knows that the words he is writing today are the words he may swing for tomorrow.'[48] The same writer quotes a delightful piece of cant on the part of Johnston, to the effect that 'creative work at its best cannot be carried on in an atmosphere of fear'. This was precisely the atmosphere the Waldorf-Astoria Statement had created. An example was provided by director-producer Otto Preminger, an adversary from the outset of the blacklist. In *Hollywood on Trial* he mentions how he had dinner with Ring Lardner, Jr, and his wife the day Lardner had been informed that he was fired. The very next day friends told Preminger that he could no longer be seen in public with Lardner.[49]

If this was the harbinger of things to come, even more revealing and sinister for the Left were two incidents involving future blacklistees, writers Ben and Norma Barzman. The first involved their neighbour Groucho Marx (a member of the CFA) who passed in front of their house while walking his baby daughter. He mentioned how hot it was, adding: 'Of course, it's doubly hot for you – with two kinds of heat. But don't ask me for anything more than ice cubes, which is as far as my sympathies go.' With hindsight, this was a clear warning: Communists were for the high jump and liberals were no longer going to support them.[50] The other incident concerned a young lady called Norma who drove up to the Barzman's residence to inform them that there was a deputy sheriff's car at the bottom of the hill. The police were stopping most cars and asking the drivers if they were going to a certain address. It turned out to be the Barzman's and the girl added: 'The sheriff's office is keeping an eye on the house. Subversive groups are meeting there.' Ben Barzman put two and two together: the CFA had called off that very morning a meeting to decide how to help the Ten (Barzman 2003: 96–9). Hollywood's Communists were being left to fend for themselves.[51]

There is evidence, however, that open opposition to Hollywood's Communists existed *before* the Hearings commenced. The organisation Americans for Democratic Action (ADA) wrote an open letter to Chairman Thomas; it was published on 25 October 1947 in *The Hollywood Reporter.* It called on HUAC not to 'help communists thru [*sic*] careless and callous investigating methods', insisting on 'fair play for all witnesses and tolerance for all viewpoints'. If not, 'you will injure both Hollywood and your committee'. The letter was signed by Hollywood's leading anti-Communist liberal, actor Melvyn Douglas and is remarkable for the way it both suspects the worst from the Committee and makes it clear that HUAC would do some good if it exposed Communists. The letter contains the following revealing observation: 'Reckless attacks on liberals committed by the House Committee on

Un-American Activities in the past have repeatedly strengthened the hand of communist agents.'[52] This desire to protect liberals alone from an irresponsible committee goes hand in hand with the kind of smear Hollywood had come to expect, not from men like Douglas, but from the Motion Picture Alliance. For the reference to 'communist agents' assumes that those who defend Communists in the belief that freedom and free speech exist for everyone are, if not actually Communists, then supporting them in some devious way. If the ADA had wanted to pre-empt the MPA, they could not have done it better – or at a worse moment for genuinely progressive ideas.

Another liberal member of the ADA was independent producer Dore Schary (see note 39), who was to distinguish himself in two very different ways in the period following the Hearings. On 24 December 1947 the Hollywood *Citizen-News* reported: 'Full support and cooperation in meeting and solving the communist menace in movie studios has been pledged a producers' committee by AFL [American Federation of Labor] studio unions.' Schary was one of the committee and Brewer a representative of the unions.[53] The tide in Hollywood had turned definitively against the Ten. In May 1948 appeared *Berlin Express*, produced by Schary. Although a curiosity belonging to pre-history by 1948, major shooting of the film had been completed by November 1947, which means that the film was in preparation and its script completed before the Hearings opened. *Berlin Express* is remarkable for its desire to promote understanding between the US and the Soviet Union and to support anti-Nazi forces in Germany. The film turns on the attempts by the American authorities to protect Dr Bernhardt, an anti-Nazi German economist, from attempts by a Nazi group to assassinate him. Thus, on the train from Paris to Berlin, an American agent pretends to be Bernhardt and the latter travels under a false identity. Also on the train are: Lindley, an American nutrition expert; Sterling, an English teacher; Perrot, a French businessman and former member of the Resistance; Maxim, a Soviet officer; and Lucienne, Bernhardt's secretary. When the false Bernhardt is killed and the real Bernhardt kidnapped, the others join forces to find him and unmask the Nazis.

If the Soviet officer is highly suspicious of everyone, the film is striking for the way it portrays people representing the Allies – including, crucially, the Soviet Union – putting differences and prejudices aside (Lindley and Sterling, but also Maxim) in a common struggle: to prevent Nazism from gaining a foothold in post-war Germany. It could be argued that the film gives the most noble role to America precisely to hide the fact that the American authorities in real life were busy using former Nazis to help them in the struggle with the new enemy, Soviet Russia. This is certainly the case, but the fact that Bernhardt is an anti-Nazi highlights rather a certain confusion in the film, one that stems from Schary's liberal views and his belief at the time in a form of entente with the Soviets. This, I would argue, is at the base of a remarkable case of ambiguity. At one point we think we are in the presence of an American soldier in a forbidden zone, a night club. However, he turns out to be a Nazi in disguise. This is clearly a warning to the spectator: the enemy is everywhere. This in turn can be interpreted as the film's anti-Communist slant: behind a reassuring, patriotic exterior hides America's worst enemy. Thus *Berlin Express* comes down unwittingly on the side of the liberal adversaries of the Ten, although the ending calls for understanding between Americans and Soviets.

Meanwhile the Ten, completely isolated and abandoned by all but the most unrepentant liberals, such as Carey McWilliams, prepared to do battle in the courts. Lester Cole filed a suit against MGM for wrongful dismissal. The trial was important for the attitude of Judge Leon Yankwich and the fact that Cole was tried by a jury which remained insensitive to anti-Communist hysteria. Thus Cole was granted the right to read the statement that HUAC had refused to hear.[54] Yankwich instructed the jury to bring in a verdict in favour of Cole because of the behaviour of none other than Eric Johnston:

> Lester Cole was made to suffer a penalty not for what his employers thought of him, but for a dogmatic attitude on the part of Johnston, who insisted his doxy was orthodoxy and everyone else's was heterodoxy. (Cole 1981: 300)

On 24 March 1948, months before the trial took place, the Los Angeles *Herald Express* reported that studio lawyers had requested the judge be disqualified from hearing Cole's suit. Eddie Mannix of MGM claimed Yankwich 'had expressed opinions favoring the 10 suspended men' during a reception at a private residence. This was denied by the hostess.[55] Nevertheless, it showed that Sokolsky was in earnest when he wrote that Red-baiters were not going to be stopped by legal niceties. In his testimony Louis B. Mayer himself defended Cole's conduct, which was decisive in the judge's instructions. The *Los Angeles Times* reported that Cole was now back on the payroll of MGM, but 'whether or not he is assigned to work on a story is beside the point'. The California *Eagle* reported that both Cole and Yankwich received threats after the verdict, the latter being told to return to Russia.[56]

The Ten were found guilty of contempt of Congress when they appeared individually before judges and were sentenced to a fine of $1,000 and a year's imprisonment, the maximum for a misdemeanour.[57] The next stage was an *amicus curiae* brief in favour of Lawson and Trumbo, an appeal to the Supreme Court, prepared by Carey McWilliams and Alexander Mieklejohn and signed not only by scores of Hollywood personalities but also writer Norman Mailer, art historian Erwin Panofsky, nuclear physicist Linus Pauling, concert pianists Arthur Rubinstein and Artur Schnabel and twenty-two law professors at Harvard Law School. Interviewed in *The Legacy of the Blacklist* Ben Margolis stated that everyone involved in their defence considered that they had a very good chance of a positive verdict being given by the Supreme Court, given the number of liberal judges sitting. However, by the time the case came up for consideration, two liberal judges had died and been replaced by more conservative ones. The Court decided not to hear the case and in 1950 the Ten started to serve their sentences.[58] When they emerged in 1951, the second round of Hearings was already under way in Hollywood. These Hearings, and the extreme changes that had taken place nationally and internationally between 1947 and 1950, are the subject of the next chapter.

NOTES

1. Jarrico, OH, p. 112, UCLA.
2. The publications of Braden and Wesley are kept in the Special Collections, Young Reading Library, UCLA.
3. Information contained in two issue of the trade journal *Variety*, January 1940.
4. On this film, see Chapter 2.
5. I refer readers to the reference to Dies in Chapter 2.
6. In 1954 the Communist Control Act made membership of the CP a violation of the law. The Act was struck down by a Supreme Court decision in 1961.
7. Stripling had worked as an investigator for Dies from 1938 and both he and Thomas were members of the committee in 1944, the date of Dies' resignation.
8. When Philip Dunne received a copy of his own file, he found an Office Memorandum addressed to Hoover, dated 13 September 1947 and 'relating to Philip Dunne which will be submitted to Congressman Thomas' (Dunne 1992: 352).
9. A similar view was expressed at the time by Alan Barth, an editorial writer for the Washington *Post*, who highlighted 'the real defect' of HUAC: 'the concept that Congress may properly punish, by publicity, activities which it cannot constitutionally declare criminal'. Quoted in Miller 1952: 134–5.
10. The trade press used the epithet 'unfriendly', which stuck.
11. Presumably Mrs Rogers was competent to judge because she was her famous daughter's mother.
12. An eleventh person was called: exiled German playwright Bertolt Brecht. As a foreigner, he could not refuse to answer questions. He denied having belonged to a Communist Party anywhere, ran rings around the Committee who thanked and excused him. He left America immediately and settled in East Germany.
13. See the chapter 5.
14. Howard Koch observed that he was not called because HUAC knew he was not a member of the CP. That fact allowed him to defend the CP, without necessarily being in agreement, which infuriated the Alliance: Koch was seen as a link between the Communist Left and the mainstream of the industry. (Howard

Koch, OH, pp. 95, 97, AFI). Moreover, on 26 November 1947, after the Hearings were over, Koch wrote a 'Letter to my fellow workers in the motion picture industry' where he stated that he reserved the right, at some future hearing of HUAC, to refuse to state that he was not a member of the CP. William Wyler Papers, folder 591.

15. Wood also claimed in his testimony that 'subversives' had made a constant effort to get control of the Guild. This elicited a telegram of protest sent to the Speaker of the House of Representatives on 22 October 1947 by the following officers of the SDG: George Stevens, John Huston, John Ford, William Wyler, Billy Wilder and George Sidney. Ford thus disavowed his fellow Alliance member Wood. Roger McDonald Papers, Box 1, HUAC folder, MHL.

16. Tuttle was named as a Communist and appeared before HUAC in May 1951 as a friendly witness, naming names. For reasons which I have been unable to discover, Pichel was neither named nor called to testify but continued making films until his death in 1954.

17. Cromwell was never named but was blacklisted in 1951. He returned to directing in 1958. See Chapter 3 for his clash with Jack Warner.

18. Cronyn took refuge on the stage for most of the 1950s. On Knox, see Chapters 3 and 7. On the others, see Chapter 7.

19. Both were named and blacklisted as a result of the Hearings of 1951–52, as was Morley's husband Lloyd Gough. His last film was *Rancho Notorious* (1952) where he played the cowboy who rapes and murders the hero's wife. Unable to eliminate Gough from the film, the producers removed his name from the credits (McGilligan and Buhle 1997: 471–2).

20. A local newspaper, the Burbank *Evening Review* (Warner Brothers Studios were located in Burbank), printed in its issue of 24 October 1947 a photo of George Murphy, Robert Montgomery and Ronald Reagan of the SAG 'conferring shortly before the hearings got under way' with Robert Stripling. They were obviously posing for photographers. Jack L. Warner Papers, Box 43, HUAC folder.

21. Jack L. Warner Papers, Box 43, HUAC folder.

22. As Byman points out, Foreman was supported by Cooper and the star's financial backer, a Republican businessman. He was abandoned by liberal producer Stanley Kramer.

23. See also Chapter 2.

24. Trumbo was a trade unionist.

25. The formula 'Un-American Committee' has been attributed to John Howard Lawson by Thom Andersen and Noël Burch. This is now confirmed by the front cover of Gerald Horne's book which shows Lawson parading with a placard bearing the inscription: 'I am a writer blacklisted by the Un-American Committee'. On the day the Hearings opened *Variety* referred to 'the Un-American Committee', calling it 'a rabble-rousing body.' Jack L. Warner Papers, Box 43, HUAC folder.

26. Alexander Knox Collection, Box 2, blacklist folder, MHL.

27. Ben Margolis, OH, p. 183, UCLA.

28. All those who took the stand made the same request. The lawyers, expecting a refusal on the part of Thomas, had seen that the statements were distributed to the press before their clients were called.

29. Dunne had the honour of being considered a Communist by the FBI for writing the script of *How Green was my Valley* (John Ford, 1941), considered pro-union.

30. Jack L. Warner Papers, Box 43, folders 8, 29.

31. The film does not say when and where Bogart made this strong statement, but it is safe to assume that it was during a radio interview or the press conference called by the members of the CFA at their hotel and which, according to actress Marsha Hunt, 'was well-attended' (McGilligan and Buhle 1997: 316).

32. The complete list, as well as copies of many of these editorials, is held in the Jack L. Warner Papers, Box 43, folders 1–3.

33. A prophetic question. This is what HUAC did from 1951 on.

34. Lavery's SWG colleague, Philip Dunne, was critical of his behaviour, then and later (Dunne 1992: 204, 213).

35. Essentially this meant Trotsky and his followers. Trotsky fled the Soviet Union for Mexico where one of Stalin's henchmen finally killed him. Trotsky's American supporters were outraged by the film, as were many liberals and conservatives.

36. We shall see in Chapter 7 how the SWG ceased even to exercise its professional commitments in its bargaining with management over such an essential point as credits.

37. Document conserved in the William Wyler Papers, folder 591.

38. In the prepared statement he read before HUAC in October Warner stated that *Mission to Moscow* 'was made for the war effort and not for posterity'. Jack L. Warner Papers, 'Red Investigation' folder.

39. Liberal independent producer Dore Schary was quoted by *The Hollywood Reporter* (30 October 1947) as being 'shocked' to discover the Ten were CP members but considered Scott and Dmytryk 'above reproach'.

40. In a court of law evidence obtained illegally would be dismissed and could lead to a mistrial.

41. Actor Gene Kelly adopted the only decent attitude concerning Lawson: 'What if he is a Communist?' (Horne 2006: xvi).

42. Hollywood in general and the studio bosses in particular knew perfectly well who the Communists were. The union activities of Lawson and the reactions to the Nazi–Soviet Pact were known to all.

43. When Wayne died in 1979, director William Wyler had a letter published in *Newsweek* (6 August) where he referred to Wayne as a 'great American hero fighting for God and country in all services in all wars. And it was all done before cameras in Hollywood and on safe location. That's damn good acting!' William Wyler Papers, folder 694.

44. After the Hearings Dalton Trumbo started to receive hate-mail addressed to 'Jew-lover Trumbo'. Incredibly, Trumbo's agent suggested to him a year later that he should meet up with Pegler in order to talk 'freely' about the motives that prompted the Ten to adopt the attitude they did before HUAC. This indicates just

how isolated the Ten were and what influence people like Pegler exerted (Trumbo 1970: 68, 114).

45. We shall see the role played by John Ford himself in Chapter 7.

46. Thomas L. Stokes, Los Angeles *Daily News*, 29 October 1947. Jack L. Warner Papers, Box 44, folder 32. Stokes deserves to be remembered as a consistent adversary of anti-Communist hysteria.

47. Friendly witness McGuinness stated in his testimony that he 'would regret that any man was deprived of his livelihood for his political opinions, no matter how abhorrent those opinions are to me' (Suber 1966: 48). The word 'regret' both avoids any accusation of conspiracy and implies that such a blacklist could come into existence.

48. William Wyler Papers, folder 591.

49. Preminger's courage can be judged from the following. Liberal writer Philip Dunne decided to resign from Fox on hearing Lardner had been fired. Lardner told him not to 'do anything foolish' and he changed his mind. Dunne was disgusted with the way his SWG colleagues attacked and abandoned the Ten and to the end of his life felt he should have resigned (Dunne 1992: 212, 220).

50. Another future blacklistee, writer Allen Boretz, confirmed this by stating that Groucho was typical of Social Democrats: people who meant well but were 'lackadaisical' (McGilligan and Buhle 1997: 118).

51. Norma was to become famous as Marilyn Monroe.

52. Document conserved in the William Wyler Papers, folder 686 ('Political').

53. Jack L. Warner Papers, Box 43, HUAC folder.

54. Civil Rights Congress Papers, Box 1, folder 31 (Lester Cole), SCL.

55. Jack L. Warner Papers, Box 43, HUAC folder.

56. Civil Rights Congress Papers, Box 1, folder 31.

57. Biberman and Dmytryk did not appear before the same judge as the others. They were fined $500 and given six months' imprisonment.

58. Trumbo has written that Supreme Court Justice Frankfurter 'went out of his way to state that refusal to hear the appeal of the Ten could not be interpreted as approval of the lower court's decision that they must go to jail' (Trumbo 1970: 366). Unfortunately, as decisions were to show for some years, not even Supreme Court Justices were exempt from the ideological prejudices of the period. Two were: Hugo Black and William Douglas. Their names deserve to be remembered.

5

None Shall Escape: The Hearings of 1951–1953

There was little cause for optimism in Hollywood in 1948, yet the events that came to pass within three years must have exceeded the worst fears. In 1949 the Soviet Union exploded its first atom bomb and the Communists seized power in China. In February 1950 Senator McCarthy claimed the State Department was harbouring 205 Communists and four months later the Korean War erupted when the Communist North invaded the pro-American South.[1] When the Rosenbergs were sentenced to death in 1951, the judge stated in court that he held them personally responsible for the American deaths in Korea.[2] He received a letter of congratulations from Hedda Hopper (Slide 2007: 211).

There is something uncanny about McCarthy's timing, as if he guessed that an international emergency was about to occur. Rather it was a case of creating in the domestic arena a state of mind so that the public would interpret the international situation in paranoid terms: the Soviets were just itching to expand their empire, even to overthrow the American government and way of life. The groundwork for this mindset had been laid in 1947 by what was called the 'Truman Doctrine'.[3] Faced with what he presented to Congress and the public as Soviet-dominated Communist insurgencies in Greece and Turkey, Truman pledged economic and military aid to the two countries in the name of democracy. This prompted certain Democrats, in both Congress and the Senate, to demand that economic aid be channelled to Greece through the United Nations and to oppose aid to Turkey. A conservative Senator opposed all aid, given the 'venal' and 'hated' monarchy in Greece and the danger that military aid to Turkey be interpreted 'as a threat to Russia from the Soviet Union's point of view, and thus as dangerous military aggression' (McAuliffe 1978: 22–5, 151n10).[4]

Certain historians have questioned both Truman's grasp of reality and his motives. The Soviet Union's horrendous losses in the war – more than half the total of all the dead, towns razed, factories and livestock destroyed, the economy in a shambles (Leffler 1991: 91) – hardly allowed her to challenge American hegemony, let alone overthrow the government. A number of liberals at the time saw the Soviet Union 'as a nation with increasingly conservative and traditional objectives' whose foreign policy could not be construed as threatening (Pells 1985: 36). Truman and his entourage tended to equate revolution with the Bolshevik Revolution and to assume that all revolutionaries were guided by the Kremlin. However, the Truman administration and its experts, unlike the Senator quoted above, never gave a thought to the Soviet viewpoint. Just as America came to cast the Kremlin in the sinister role of masterminding a 'worldwide Communist conspiracy', so Stalin would have been justified in evoking a 'worldwide imperialist conspiracy', given America's use of Nazis to make sure post-war Germany remained anti-Communist. Ultimately,

> the United States cast itself in the role of world policeman, seeking to prevent forcible social change in other countries no matter what the local conditions, and committing the nation's energies to a limitless defence of the international status quo. (Pells 1985: 66)

Of equal importance was America's economic well-being, inextricably linked to its military expansionism. Only by subsidising the economies of devastated European countries could America increase their purchasing power and, hence, US exports to them, thus ensuring high employment and a docile electorate at home: 'Corporate liberalism had one main goal: to win public approval for an interventionist foreign policy so that the U.S. economy could fulfil its overseas potential' (Jezer 1982: 80). The parallel between this observation and the philosophy expressed by Eric Johnston is striking: Hollywood's 'manifest destiny' was to be part and parcel of that 'corporate liberalism' and sell abroad not only films but the ideologies they disseminated. This meant that Hollywood films were to become an instrument of propaganda. Given the huge sums of money needed both to combat what was seen as Soviet expansionism and to give a vital boost to the economy of America's allies, however, the Truman Doctrine did not go without saying. However, its opponents held little power and were not 'plugged into . . . the world of corporate business and law'. As Truman's Secretary of State, Dean Acheson, was to admit later: 'Korea came along and saved us' (McCormick 1991: 252, 253).

Korea was the icing on the cake for Cold War warriors, yet it was simply the culminating point in their ideological war and its concomitant repression. A salvo had already been fired in 1940 with the passing of the Smith Act, which laid down the principle of 'outlawing advocating or belonging to groups advocating overthrow of the government, for all citizens, even in peacetime' (Goldstein 1978: 69).[5] Henceforth, 'it was no longer necessary to prove that someone was actually building bombs or collecting dynamite; simply talking about overthrowing the government by "force and violence" was enough' (Schrecker 1998: 98). However, in 1943 the Supreme Court ruled that 'the Justice Department had failed to show that the CP was trying to overthrow the American government'. The Justices 'raised the possibility that it might be "a tenable conclusion" ' that the CP 'desired to achieve its purpose by peaceful and democratic means' (Schrecker 1998: 103, 192). This was a setback of considerable importance. There was now jurisprudence concerning the wording of the Act and the nature of the evidence produced in court. A HUAC investigation, however, was not a court of law.

The problem was very real in 1948 when the Justice Department decided to go ahead with a new indictment of leading CP officials. At that time the FBI knew that the CP Secretary, Earl Browder, 'was aware of and encouraged Soviet efforts to recruit American Communists to steal industrial and governmental secrets'. However, Hoover had no evidence concerning other senior party members. Yet it was they, and not Browder, who were indicted and 'convicted for conspiring to overthrow the U.S. government by force or violence' (Theoharis 2002: 32). A government can hardly talk of a 'conspiracy' where one man is involved, whereas it is easier when several are indicted. The radical change in the political climate meant new jurisprudence and a stick with which to beat the CP and anyone defending it. Henceforth, it would be easier to stigmatise Communists as indulging in illegal activities orchestrated by their masters in the Kremlin, despite the total absence of any *act* that could be called 'subversive' or 'seditious'. Thus was ushered in the profoundly ideological notion of 'preventive law', whereby X is indicted for what he *might do* and not for what he has done.[6]

The Internal Security Act was voted in 1950, during the Korean War. It was sponsored by three members of HUAC: Richard Nixon, Harold Velde (a former FBI agent) and Francis Walter; Velde (a Republican) and Walter (a Democrat) were to become the Committee's Chairmen in 1953 and 1955 respectively. The Act – known as the McCarran Act as it was introduced by Senator Pat McCarran, a conservative Democrat from Nevada – was based on findings derived from testimony before HUAC, testimony accepted without any cross-examination. It became compulsory for Communist organisations or Communist-front organisations to 'provide the federal government with the names of all their members and contributors' (Schwartz 1998: 193).[7] Truman's attempt to veto the Act was rejected. Opponents of the Act considered that it violated both the First Amendment – free speech and the right to assembly – and the Fifth Amendment (against self-incrimination).[8] Supreme Court Justice Hugo Black considered that the Act implied that people were no longer 'free to talk about any kind of change in basic governmental policies they desire to talk about'. Supreme Court Justice William Douglas saw an injustice in forcing CP officials 'to violate this law before their constitutional claims can be heard and determined' (Pomerantz 1963: 103, 100).

Truman denounced the McCarran Act (which also provided for detention centres where Communists and anyone suspected of subversive ideas could be held indefinitely during a national emergency[9]), but he had already introduced a piece of legislation destined to have considerable repercussions for Hollywood: the 'loyalty oath', which came into existence *before* the Hearings of 1947:

> In March 1947, ten days after the proclamation of the Truman doctrine, the president issued an executive order authorizing the FBI to assess the loyalty of all current and prospective federal employees . . . The sources remained anonymous; the person under investigation could seldom learn the identity of those who were questioned or the substance of what they had said. Without the right to cross-examine informants, the individual found it almost impossible to rebut any damaging testimony in his dossier. . . . The FBI did not have to produce evidence of illegal or even radical acts. Membership in or 'sympathetic association' with an organization designated as subversive on the attorney general's list was enough to bar one from government service. (Pells 1985: 266–7)

The communist threat, evoked to justify what one anti-Communist liberal denounced as the equivalent of 'Nazi-Soviet jurisprudence' (Pells 1985: 267), was nothing but a pretext: 'We did not believe', former White House aide Clark Clifford recalled, 'there was a real problem. A problem was being manufactured' (Schrecker 1998: 287). A deliberate confusion was being created in the public's mind:

> . . . the allegiance of American citizens goes to the compact embodied in the Constitution and derives from the citizenship conferred by the Fourteenth Amendment. It does not imply an uncritical acceptance of the foreign policy of the government even in a critical period nor does it imply ideological conformity. We pledge allegiance to the flag, not to the profit system. (McWilliams 1950: 28)

Truman 'designated HUAC files as an official source of evidence on employees' ties' (Wills 1976: 21).

Nineteen forty-seven also saw the passing of the Taft-Hartley Act which stipulated that officers of any union desiring the services of the National Labor Relations Board to settle differences between unions and bosses had to sign an affidavit stating they did not belong to an organization advocating the overthrow of the government. In September 1947 Philip Dunne wrote for *The Screen Writer*, official organ of the SWG, an article entitled 'On "Loyalty" Affidavits' where he expressed his anxiety and indignation over the implications of the Taft-Hartley Act.[10] Stating that he had signed such an affidavit, a form of 'loyalty oath', in 1943, Dunne insisted on two facts: America was no longer at war; and the new law both specified 'one legitimate party, the Communist Party' and was 'proclaimed by its supporters to be a permanent statement of public policy'. Dunne therefore rejected the proposal of SWG President Emmet Lavery that he 'as an individual join him in signing this affidavit. As an officer of this Guild, I shall sign one only when directed by the membership'. Lavery's call to sign was based on the need to respect the law.[11] Dunne took exception to what he saw as a capitulation: 'If there is any American right which has historical, legal and moral sanction, it is the right of the individual to dissent, the right of appeal to the courts against the law itself.' Dunne considered that Lavery was hiding behind a law in order to 'clean house' and disassociate the SWG from its communist members.[12]

Dunne's stance came to naught but his remarks were prophetic. Politically and ideologically the Republican Right succeeded in sewing up America in general and Hollywood in particular between 1947 and 1950, with the help of a Democrat President and most liberals. In this context the confrontation in 1950 within the Screen Directors' Guild between arch-conservative Cecil B. De Mille and the moderate President Joseph L. Mankiewicz is eloquent (both were Republicans). The former, supported by Leo McCarey, a friendly witness in 1947, sought to impose a loyalty oath on SDG members, but by attempting to remove Mankiewicz from the presidency at the same time this move backfired, with Mankiewicz receiving overwhelming support (Ceplair and Englund 1980: 368–9).[13] Yet Mankiewicz promptly recommended to his fellow directors that they accept the loyalty oath.[14] De Mille – who was opposed ideologically to unions, while belonging to the SDG – wanted to take over the guild. The liberal and conservative members of the SWG had eliminated all left-wing members from any position of influence and the SAG was safely conservative. The SDG was not liberal; its members were simply opposed to the extreme and unacceptable methods of De Mille and his supporters. The Left was soon totally isolated in Hollywood. The Motion Picture Industry Council (to which belonged the major studies, independent producers, all the guilds and the American Federation of Labor) was cited on 29 September 1952 by HUAC Chairman Wood as supporting HUAC in its attempts 'to deal with the problem of Communist or subversive elements'.[15]

In 1951 those disinclined to answer questions about their political sympathies or affiliations faced a legal problem. The Ten had been convicted of contempt of Congress for refusing to say whether they were or had been members of the CP, so recourse to the First Amendment was impossible, unless one was willing to risk a prison sentence. The only other possibility was recourse to the Fifth Amendment, a solution rejected by the Ten. The Fifth states: 'No person . . . shall be compelled in any criminal case to be a witness against himself, nor be deprived of life, liberty, or property, without due process of law.' This guarantee against compulsory self-incrimination posed a problem exploited by Representative Moulder of HUAC who told one witness: 'your refusal to testify so consistently leaves a strong inference that you are still an ardent follower of the Communist Party and its purpose' (Vaughn 1996: 138). It was therefore HUAC which insidiously made the inference, banking on the public adopting a 'common-sense' attitude and considering the person had something to hide.

However, HUAC and its lawyers were no fools. As *The Hollywood Reporter* stated (26 April 1951): 'According to repeated committee statements, the Fifth Amendment is designed for criminal proceedings'. Since HUAC was not a court of law, there could be no question of a crime of any kind, therefore the Fifth was irrelevant:

> Should you plead the Fifth Amendment . . ., then, because you refuse to deny that you are a Communist, in the context of a HUAC hearing you are guilty by inference (it does not matter that guilt by inference has been specifically condemned by the Supreme Court – remember we are now in a HUAC hearing). Despite the fact that a plea of the Fifth is supposed to protect the *innocent* witness who fears *unfounded* prosecution, HUAC uses it to defame and disgrace the witness. (Donner 1961: 6)

Let us take the case of an individual who accepts to speak about himself and answer the question 'Are you now or have you ever been a member of the Communist Party?' But he refuses to name other party members and takes the Fifth to avoid doing so. Since he has accepted the right of HUAC to ask that question, he has waived the right to take the Fifth and can be imprisoned for contempt. The situation was as follows: the person subpoenaed by HUAC either answered all questions and named names or else took the Fifth in order to avoid both self-incrimination and incriminating others. The 'friendly witness' fell into the former category, the 'unfriendly witness' into the latter. By 1953 President Eisenhower was declaring that any federal employee resorting to the Fifth would be fired.[16] In Hollywood taking the Fifth meant automatic blacklisting.

Who named names and who took the Fifth? Certain issues must be clarified prior to any discussion of what was said by whom and why. Not all friendly witnesses fell over themselves to give HUAC what it wanted; most did, but some made unwelcome statements. Similarly, unfriendly witnesses did not limit themselves to declining to answer; they sometimes engaged in long and heated discussions with their interrogators on matters one or other of the parties considered important. Nor was refusal to collaborate with HUAC the sole reason for finding oneself without work: blacklisting also meant not receiving offers to work, irrespective of whether one had appeared before HUAC and taken the Fifth. The outspoken Philip Dunne escaped because his anti-Communism was known to all: he had publicly opposed Dalton Trumbo over the Nazi–Soviet Pact. However, fellow anti-Communist liberals who had both been President of the SWG, Sheridan Gibney and Mary McCall, found themselves on a 'graylist' and their careers petered out through lack of offers: 'the studios were periodically capable of confounding public black- and graylists with management's own private shitlists' (Ceplair and Englund 1980: 395).[17]

A case of graylisting is that of Howard Koch, who wrote *Casablanca* and the notorious *Mission to Moscow*. One of the Hollywood Nineteen, Koch was never called in 1947 and put this down to the fact that he was not a member of the CP. However, he considered that his status as a writer listened to by both liberals and Communists made him dangerous to the Right and he spent several years without work.[18] Moreover, there existed several categories of blacklistees as a result of the new Hearings. There were those who were fired upon receiving a subpoena to appear before HUAC: writers Bernard Gordon, Paul Jarrico and Michael Wilson.[19] There were those who were named by friendly witnesses but never called, simply blacklisted: writers Allen Boretz and Bess Taffel. Then there were those who, to avoid being subpoenaed, simply left the country: writer Ben Barzman and his wife Norma, directors John Berry and Jules Dassin (who all went to France), and writer Julian Zimet (who left for Mexico).[20] Director Joseph Losey was in Italy when named, and decided to settle in Britain rather than return to the US. Writer-director Abraham Polonsky, on the other hand, who was living in France in 1951, decided to return when subpoenaed and to resist HUAC. Finally, there were those who, without being subpoenaed, contacted HUAC to confess about their Communist past: writers Sylvia Richards, Bernard Schoenfeld, Budd Schulberg and Leo Townsend.

One term that occurs in the numerous discussions of the Hearings is 'ritual'. The proceedings took on a particular form determined in advance by the status of the witness: those who were known to be ready to cooperate would be both coaxed and coached and the same elements would be repeated, with variations, *ad nauseam*. Such repetition also occurred in the case of the uncooperative witness, as we shall see. An occasional witness reserved a surprise for HUAC. Actor-writer Nedrick Young did not appear until April 1953 and adopted a deliberately aggressive stance, denouncing from the outset

> any questions that are propounded to me as a result of coercion. I also will most certainly refuse to answer any questions of a committee that refuses to confront me with an accuser, the most primitive American right. Why don't you tell me what evidence you have against me?[21]

This was a trait he had in common with other unfriendly witnesses. It was the exchanges between him and Donald Jackson that set Young apart. Thus not only did he accuse Chairman Velde of lying 'in the halls of Congress', but also evoked the First Amendment (which exposed him to contempt and prison because of a Supreme Court ruling) in reply to the usual question about belonging to the Communist Party. By stating that 'to answer your question would be to concede your right to ask it, and this I do not do', Young was adopting before HUAC the stance of the Ten, one to be reiterated by the blacklistees in their later published interviews and oral histories. From 1951 on, however, the uncooperative witness was forced to evoke the Fifth, so Young was out on a limb. However, he succeeded in provoking a slip of the tongue from the irate Jackson whom he accused of 'going in the direction of Fascism'. To which the Representative replied: 'I would rather be going where I am than to be a slave and a lackey to the Communist Party.' Young taunted him over this implicit recognition of his fascist sympathies: 'your intellectual prattle is extremely revealing', indicating Young had understood the Freudian slip. Jackson tried to repair the damage by the usual equation Fascism = Communism, but the damage was done and the exchanges reveal, less the sympathies of Jackson personally than the entire mindset of HUAC and many of its supporters.[22]

Fascism brings us back to Spain, ever present on the lips of HUAC and the witnesses, friendly and unfriendly alike.[23] Agent Meta Reis Rosenberg, who testified as a friendly witness on 13 April 1951, evoked the issue spontaneously in the context of her belonging to various Communist discussion groups:

> . . . during the Spanish Civil War, I had a very strong feeling for the Loyalists, and I was interested in hearing the point of view of any organization or finding out any information that I could regarding the Loyalist fight. (Hearings: 285)

Appearing as a friendly witness on 28 January, writer Michael Blankfort stated: 'I have no hesitancy or shame or anything but a deep feeling about my views on the Spanish war. I was for the Loyalists. This is something I believe in'

(Hearings: 2348). Writer Richard Collins, a friendly witness who testified the previous day, was even more committed:

> . . . anything that had to do with loyalist Spain, I joined, *as I would join today*, because I believe in loyalist Spain. . . .

> I remember in a Gallup poll around 1938 that 74 or 75 percent of the people said they favored the Loyalists over Franco, so that to belong to an organization that was in favor of Loyalist Spain at that time was a logical position. (Hearings: 248–9; emphasis added)

A witness like Collins could allow himself the luxury of being unrepentant over Spain because he rejected every other aspect of his Communist past. The case of actor José Ferrer, who testified as a friendly witness on 21 May 1951, highlights other matters.

Questioned about the Joint Anti-Fascist Refugee Committee, Ferrer replied:

> We who called ourselves liberal Democrats considered Franco a dictator, a man who was against the democratic processes, as Hitler had been and as Stalin is today, and anytime there was an occasion to oppose him I, for one, *rather unquestioningly did so.* (Bentley 2002: 412; emphasis added)

Ferrer is clearly implying he had acted too hastily. He had already been willing to trample on his principles and those of others of like mind, referring to 'the way innocent and well-intentioned people have been deceived and lured into participation in causes which at one time seemed worthy and later on appeared unworthy' (Bentley 2002: 409). In other words: decent liberals deceived by devious Reds into supporting anti-Fascist causes. In the remark on Franco, therefore, Ferrer is trying to eat his cake and have it. This was to become explicit in Ferrer's reply to a later question, once again on Spain, concerning the American Committee for Spanish Freedom, formed after the end of the Civil War in 1939:

> I do not remember this specific organization, Mr. Tavenner. However, once more *I must plead guilty to the charge of carelessness.* If I was approached on an anti-Franco question, the chance is I would agree to sponsor it. *Without knowing, I suspect that probably the same people sponsored it*, the same set of people, as sponsored the Joint Anti-Fascist Refugee Committee, and that there was a community of activity which I accepted *without question.* (Bentley 2002: 415; emphasis added)

Here HUAC, taking advantage of having a (com)pliant witness, is determined to smear anyone who ever opposed Franco, especially in the context of an anti-Fascist organisation. Evoking 'carelessness' was Ferrer's way of insisting on how liberals like him were duped (a favourite HUAC and FBI line), going so far as to 'plead guilty' to a 'charge', as if to a crime before a court of law. 'Carelessness' had nothing to do with it but was part of the ritual referred to earlier: confess, repent and, if necessary, degrade oneself. Ferrer was the ideal witness.

This also raises the question of the 'Communist front', an organisation supposedly infiltrated by CP members in order to exploit a cause for nefarious ends.[24] Thus the above-mentioned Joint Anti-Fascist Refugee Committee and the Artists' Front to Win the War were considered by the Attorney General as subversive organisations. In reality, it was a case of smearing anti-Fascist organisations at a time when anti-Communist sympathies were demanded. This was the only 'logical' conclusion to be drawn from Dies' condemnation in 1938 of 'premature anti-Fascists'. A 'front' was simply any anti-Fascist organisation with Communists among its members.[25] Two hostile witnesses, writer-director Robert Rossen and actor J. Edward Bromberg, were asked exactly the same question:

> According to the March 29, 1938, issue of *New Masses*, the Hollywood chapter of the League of American Writers sent telegrams to President Roosevelt, Secretary of State Hull, and the French Embassy, urging them to request France to open her borders to the purchase of supplies by Loyalist Spain. (Hearings: 683, 725)[26]

The League of American Writers was a 'front', evoked here in the context of Spain. *New Masses* was a CP journal. Both witnesses denied to reply on the grounds that they might incriminate themselves. To state before HUAC that one had belonged to, given money to or helped in any way an organisation officially considered as subversive would expose one to suspicions of being a Communist and possibly entail the obligation to reply to other questions (McGilligan and Buhle 1997: 432). The only solution, as we have seen, was to take the Fifth, which Rossen and Bromberg did.[27]

Once an unfriendly witness had declined to answer questions on CP membership, support for 'subversive' organisations or having attended a meeting in the house of a known Communist or self-confessed ex-Communist, HUAC sometimes resorted to trick tactics in order to discredit him. Thus Donald Gordon was asked if he belonged to the Fascist organisation The Silver Shirts and writer Leonardo Bercovici if he was a member of the Ku Klux Klan; unthinkingly, both replied that they did not.[28] As Bercovici had just refused to answer the usual question about the CP on the grounds that it might 'incriminate' and 'degrade', he was asked why he accepted to answer the question on the KKK. The purpose is patent: present the witness to the public as devious.

There was, however, a difference between the two questions. The CP was a party on a list of subversive organisations, whereas the KKK was not a party and had never been investigated by HUAC. Bercovici was perfectly within his constitutional rights in replying to one question and refusing to reply to the other. Unfortunately for him and others, such niceties were ignored.

I referred above to HUAC's tendency to coax and coach witnesses. Coaxing was hardly necessary with friendly witnesses, but it was occasionally used in an attempt to show unfriendly witnesses the errors of their ways. One such case was that of J. Edward Bromberg who stated that HUAC deprived people of their livelihood. HUAC Counsel Frank Tavenner asked him: 'Do you know of any individual who has been deprived of his livelihood because he appeared before this committee and frankly responded to questions propounded by the committee?' (Hearings: 730). The question is loaded by the presence of 'frankly', which means different things to different people. For Tavenner it meant answering all questions, irrespective of the committee's right to answer them, a right which for him went without saying. For a witness like Bromberg, 'frankly' meant forcing a witness to grant the committee rights he did not recognise and to betray present or former comrades.[29] HUAC's coaching of witnesses, however, was limited to those known to be ready to cooperate. There were two stages in the operation: sending an investigator to talk to those about to receive a subpoena in order to test their attitude; then preparing their testimony to make sure they said what was expected of them. One unfriendly witness, writer Alfred Lewis Levitt, referred to them as the committee's 'advance men'.[30] One such was William Wheeler; he approached Donald Gordon who found him very friendly but refused to cooperate. He was served with a subpoena, was asked by HUAC to 'come clean', took the Fifth and was fired.[31] The testimony of friendly witnesses reveals a situation that would be comical if it were not so sordid.

When writer Melvyn Levy, who testified on 28 January 1952, was asked by Tavenner if he could provide the names of other members of the group who had met in the home of a known Communist, Levy replied: 'No; Bill has the names there' (Hearings: 2319). 'Bill' was none other than William Wheeler and it is logical to assume that 'there' was accompanied by Levy pointing in the direction of the person in possession of the list made out by him before giving testimony and given to Wheeler. Meta Reis Rosenberg touchingly stated how Frank Tavenner helped her explain subtle differences in CP politics depending on dates and circumstances (Hearings: 295). HUAC was adept at putting words in people's mouths to ensure the desired response. Tavenner questioned Levy on CP boss Earl Browder: 'What was the reason that Earl Browder had for taking this special interest in writers? Do you think it was to influence the course of their writings?' (Hearings: 2313). So HUAC asked a question, then gave the witness a hint, gratefully accepted, as to the necessary answer. Chairman Walter put this question to director Frank Tuttle:

> In the light of present-day world conditions, don't you feel that those well-meaning but misguided idealists who have been members of this conspiracy will find it necessary to sever their ties immediately or run the risk of being branded traitors?

To which Tuttle dutifully replied: 'I agree, sir' (Hearings: 638). HUAC fed friendly witnesses lines like fish to performing seals.

Walter's use of the word 'conspiracy' is worth considering. Prior to the above exchange, he had referred to the CP as 'a conspiracy to overthrow the democratic form of government under which you live' and suggested to Tuttle that he must have appreciated 'that they were not good Americans'. In the space of a few lines Walter brought together the mantra of the 'worldwide communist conspiracy', the belief that the CP was ready to use violence to achieve its aims and the notions of loyal Americans and un-American activities and attitudes. The last of these takes us to the heart of the matter, especially as a belief is not an act. To state that nothing will change in the US without violence is not to *commit* that act of violence. Nor does it necessarily even imply that the speaker welcomes such violence, even less that he is disloyal.

Carey McWilliams wrote:

> Loyalty is the miracle of emotion by which social unity and consent are achieved without coercion and without a blind and senseless conformity.
>
> The essence of loyalty is consent freely given. Loyalty is not subservience or slavish submissiveness or docile conformity. . . . All loyalty involves autonomous choice and, by its very nature, loyalty is protean: there are always many loyalties. (McWilliams 1950: 50–1)

Pointing out that a Communist is less of a threat to national security than someone '*who has no loyalties*' (52, original emphasis), he argued that to ask if a Communist can be a 'loyal American' meant that 'the basic principles embodied in the First Amendment have been tacitly repealed' and that there were ideas which should be suppressed as 'subversive' (52–3). Or, to put in another way, 'to what is the loyal American loyal?' (56). The first unfriendly witness to appear, actor Howard Da Silva, adopted the same standpoint:

> I will always identify myself with the interests of the American people, but I will support or oppose my Government's policies to the extent that I understand them to serve or harm the people of the country. (Hearings: 118)[32]

By equating the 'communist conspiracy' with the 'overthrow' of the government, HUAC simply equated beliefs and acts. This, of course, did not prevent HUAC from exercising rights it did not have and from attempting to violate rights enshrined in laws. Two examples must suffice. Both Melvin Levy and another friendly witness, writer Isobel Lennart, were questioned about elections to the Board of the SWG in a blatant and brazen attempt to continue to smear the Guild. Tavenner was anxious to get Levy to admit that there was a Red plot to nominate Lester Cole and Ring Lardner, Jr to the Board, whereas Levy insisted on the difference between voting to *nominate* X and voting for his *right to present his candidature*. Levy made it clear he had voted for Cole's right to express his opinion (Hearings 2324–5). Questioned by Tavenner about Albert Maltz (20 May 1952), Lennart stated that she had signed a petition calling for him to be a candidate for election and that the person who handed her the petition was not even progressive, let alone a Communist (Hearings: 3525). On 2 June 1953 Wheeler heard the testimony of actor Lee J. Cobb in executive session.[33] Wheeler asked him this question:

> Do you believe that the United States Government and Committees of Congress have the right – I am not speaking of the rights set up by the laws of the United States – but the right to investigate Communists within any environment in the United States? (Bentley 2002: 662)

Wheeler was asking a citizen to make a statement on a legal matter where he had no competence: should the CP be outlawed? This was part of HUAC's drive to obtain the implicit repeal of the First and Fifth Amendments, a drive which did not result in HUAC bringing legislation before Congress, despite such legislation being the brief of the Committee. Wheeler was asking for a blank cheque for extra-legal rights and hence the right to violate the Constitution. Cobb gave the expected positive reply.

It will be clear by now that HUAC was imposing answers that friendly witnesses were not free to give or withhold: it was part of the act, carefully staged before and during their appearance. When asked by Francis Walter if he had ever realised that communism was 'a conspiracy for world domination, controlled and dominated entirely by a foreign power', Frank Tuttle replied in the negative, which implied that this was now his opinion too. Another friendly witness, writer Bernard C. Schoenfeld, appearing on 19 August 1952, made this statement:

> And I would recommend that the Communist Party be outlawed and also that in order to keep liberals and people of good will from having my experience, a greater and greater vigilance be made in finding out what Communist-front organizations still exist and publicizing such Communist-front organizations. (Hearings: 4260)

Representative Wood congratulated the witness whose views 'coincide with the recent practices of this committee'. HUAC's real concern, however, lay elsewhere, as an exchange several months earlier between Tavenner and a friendly witness, the playwright Clifford Odets (20 May 1952) had revealed: 'this Committee has never considered [the CP] a political party. It considers that it is a conspiratorial group' (Bentley 2002: 527). HUAC therefore considered itself above the law, whereas unfriendly witnesses stood by the law of the land *against the Committee*. Questioned by Representative Doyle, Robert Lees denounced the blacklist as un-American, adding 'any infringement on perhaps [*sic*] opinions or thoughts which this committee or some other future committee might deem suddenly un-American becomes a very dangerous thing in this country' (Hearings: 214). Actress Anne Revere, appearing on 17 April 1951, made this statement:

> as the Communist Party is a political party – legal political party – in this country today, and as I consider any questioning regarding one's political views or religious views as a violation of the rights of a citizen under our Constitution, and as I would consider myself, therefore, contributing to the overthrow of our form of government as I understand it if I were to assist you in violating this privilege of mine and other citizens of this country, I respectfully decline to answer this question on the basis of the fifth amendment, possible self-incrimination, and also the first amendment. (Hearings: 319)[34]

This was water off HUAC's back. They did not hesitate to ask Ferrer if he had voted for Benjamin Davis, one of the Communists indicted in 1948 (and a Negro) and if he belonged to a church (Bentley 2002: 434). His negative reply to the latter question (he could neither lie nor refuse to answer) suggested he was an atheist (= godless Communist). However, he had already accepted HUAC's role as the priest in the confessional. HUAC also remained faithful to the tradition set up by its predecessor in 1947: the unequal treatment of witnesses.[35] When writer Paul Jarrico appeared on 13 April 1951, he was refused the right to make a preliminary statement, on the grounds that the Committee would allow him to file it after testifying (Hearings: 277), whereas Roy Huggins, appearing on 29 September 1952, was allowed to go into the greatest detail concerning his Communist past without being interrupted (Hearings: 4265–70). The Committee's golden boy, unionist Roy Brewer, appeared for two whole days (Hearings: 474–532). Like Collins before him, however, Huggins took advantage of his status as a cooperative witness and refused HUAC's rhetoric. He had chosen to become a member of the CP and was not 'induced' (Hearings: 4265). Put on the defensive, Jarrico refused to be cowed. He accused Collins, his collaborator for many years, of perjury, which was not well received. As this was not a court, Jarrico did not have the right to confront Collins nor have him cross-examined by his own attorney, yet was expected to testify according to HUAC's scheme of things. His reply is a model of dignity: 'This is not my forum, Mr. Chairman, and this is not the place for me to discuss my differences with Mr. Collins. I don't choose to do it here' (Hearings: 277).

HUAC remained faithful to another tradition handed down from 1947: allowing friendly witnesses to give opinions, without onus of proof, on any topic deemed pertinent by the Committee. As we have seen in the case of Spain, a friendly witness could reiterate a viewpoint hostile to the Right as long as he named names and confessed to past sins. Thus Clifford Odets openly rejected the central HUAC thesis that the CP was conspiring to overthrow the Government by force.[36] He even went so far as to agree with the dissenting minority among the Supreme Court judges concerning the conviction of the CP leaders under the Smith Act.[37] This show of independence and hostility to the dogmas of HUAC in no way detracted from the power of the Committee and its hold, both psychological and ideological, over witnesses and public alike. The whole point of the Hearings of 1951–53 was to create a situation where witnesses would accept the violation of their civil rights, betray their former friends and comrades in the name of the Cold War against the Soviet Union and, on occasion, congratulate the Committee for its vigilance, having already regretted their opposition to it in the weeks following on from the Hearings of 1947.[38]

The public acts of contrition, the eager replies to the leading questions, the humiliating coaching before and during the spectacle showed how far both HUAC and Hollywood had moved since late 1947. The claim that movies contained insidious Communist propaganda belonged to the past, as an astonishing exchange between Walter and Odets showed. Quoting a remark made by Odets in 1937, to the effect that it was 'difficult to do anything with social significance' in Hollywood, the Congressman continued: 'Isn't the screening so thorough that it would be an utter impossibility to slant a picture? There are so many people that examine it for that particular purpose?' To which Odets replied: 'There is nothing less possible in Hollywood' (Bentley 2002: 530). It is therefore revealing to discover that those in power in Hollywood were as loath to part with top writers as in 1947. MGM did everything to persuade Marguerite Roberts, a writer with twenty years experience, to cooperate, but had to settle her contract when she refused (McGilligan and Buhle 1997: 572). The irony of the situation is that, once back in Hollywood in the 1960s, she wrote the script for which witch hunter John Wayne won his only Oscar: *True Grit* (1969). Wayne tried to get Communist John Bright to write scripts for him, provided he named names.[39]

Twentieth Century Fox tried to keep Abraham Polonsky on but caved in under pressure from *The Hollywood Reporter.*[40] In a letter dated 2 January 1953, Frank Freeman of Paramount wrote to William Wyler to indicate his amazement that the director could associate with those named as Communists by HUAC (he mentioned writer Leonardo Bercovici and director Bernard Vorhaus).[41] He went on: 'Of course the question of guilt by association always arises and if you continue to invite identified Communists to visit you or be part of any affair that you give, then you will have charges levelled at you.'[42] In other words: the CP may not be illegal, but you do not have the right to have Communist acquaintances. Writer Howard Estabrook wrote to the California State Committee on Un-American Activities on 25 July 1952 to state how 'shocking and disgusting' it was that members of the SWG should have been secretly members of the CP 'conniving together to accomplish their own concealed purpose'. He went on to congratulate former Communists who had 'tried to make amends as far as possible by testifying before the U.S. House Committee'. On 5 November 1945, at a time when Communists were allegedly plotting to control the SWG, Estabrook had published an article on writers – prophetically entitled 'Freedom from Repression' – in *The Hollywood Reporter,* known for its hostility to progressive writers. He referred to the members of the Guild as 'serious and earnest ladies and gentlemen, who considered all matters with the utmost impartiality . . ., with no points of view expressed that have not been expressed over and over again by the majority of American citizens by their votes'.[43] In which case the Communists in the Guild must have been so well concealed that they resorted to telepathy to influence unsuspecting liberals. On 6 September 1950 'liberal' producer Walter Wanger wrote a cringing letter of thanks to John Wayne, President of the Motion Picture Alliance, congratulating him for denouncing the 'insidious conspiracy' of the Communists. He added 'that time and history have proven the correctness of the judgment of the MPA and its foresight in recognizing the Communist menace' (Bentley 2002: 293).[44] How things had changed in Hollywood since 1944! (See Chapter 2.)

Elsewhere a more extreme tone was adopted, where hatred, smear tactics and outright delirium vied with one another. In two pieces published in a popular magazine Jimmie Tarantino referred obsessively to the Abraham Lincoln Brigade, wrote enthusiastically of people being jailed or deported (the most famous example being Chaplin who never took out American citizenship), denounced a slew of Hollywood personalities and claimed mendaciously that actor Howard Duff was an unfriendly witness (he never appeared before HUAC) (Bentley 2002: 302–7).[45] Foreign-born personalities who had acquired American citizenship, such as *Dracula* star Bela Lugosi, were not free from persecution. Lugosi had participated in 1919 in the pro-Communist Bela Kun government in Hungary and maintained his radical opinions and activities in the States: he had been involved in the setting-up of an actors' trade union before coming to America and was active in the SAG (one of whose co-founders was fellow horror star Boris Karloff).[46] Lugosi obtained American citizenship in 1931, but the FBI kept a file on him from 1944 because of his left-wing statements and associates. By 1947 Immigration and Naturalization was investigating him to revoke his citizenship (and hence deport him). Although this was dropped in 1948, in April 1955 'immigration agents arrived at the County Hospital [where Lugosi was being treated for drug addiction] to interview Lugosi about his possible Communist affiliation' (Rhodes 2007: 33–52, 194).

On 9 September 1952 that unrepentant liberal Dudley Nichols wrote to Carey McWilliams:

> The super loyalists, the bigoted and ignorant, the scared reactionaries, the corrupt and militant totalitarians, the men using patriotism as an ugly club to cow or kill whoever doesn't knuckle under to them – these people are bent on blacklisting every decent free-minded man who works in the Hollywood field.[47]

If this remarkable statement shows that, for Nichols, refusing to answer questions was a matter of principle, it also implies that taking the Fifth was also a way of protecting friends and colleagues, irrespective of whether they or the person under interrogation were or had been Communists. Thus screenwriter and novelist Dashiell Hammett (*The Maltese Falcon*) refused to answer certain questions about the Civil Rights Congress, considered a communist 'front', notably concerning the Spanish Loyalists.[48] In reality, Hammett did not have the information requested but refused to answer and make this clear, since doing so 'meant conceding that the state had a right to ask such questions in the first place' (Pells 1985: 322).[49] Hammett went to jail.

That same year the State Department banned from its overseas libraries all materials, including paintings, by 'any controversial person, Communist, fellow-travellers, et cetera' (Schwartz 1997: 45). There was no definition of 'controversial' and 'et cetera' indicates that the list of the proscribed could be extended indefinitely. Certain points will help to clarify the situation. Firstly, a non-Communist who was named might choose not to defend herself out of a feeling of solidarity with those already blacklisted and a deep-seated repugnance over the undemocratic methods of HUAC. Referring to how the Actors' Lab was targeted by the California Un-American Activities Committee,[50] Rose Hobart explained that she and four colleagues 'were finally tapped' in February 1948, which shows that the local witch hunters were active as soon as the Ten were cited for contempt. Asked why she refused to answer 'the question', she replied:

> Because there were several members of the Actors' Lab who were
> Communist members. We didn't want them to get harmed, so we
> decided that we would all have to do the same thing. We refused as a
> group. (Slide 1999: 44)

One Communist member was J. Edward Bromberg. Actor Phil Brown was also
a member of the Lab. Although he did not appear before the Committee, 'he
was labeled a liberal and, therefore, a possible Communist, primarily because
of his involvement with the Actors' Lab' (Slide 1999: 14). Brown was one of
those who steadfastly refused, even in interviews decades later, to name friends
who had been Communists (Slide 1999: 29). Paul Jarrico adopted the same
stance. Stating how his applications after Pearl Harbour as a combat correspondent were turned down because he was a known Party member, he also
declared: '. . . I'm still not prepared to talk about other people and whether
they were Communists or not' (McGilligan and Buhle 1997: 338–9, 333).
Both Albert Maltz and Abraham Polonsky, who worked anonymously while
blacklisted, refused to give the titles of certain films and TV series so as not to
compromise their collaborators (Talbot and Zheutlin 1978: 48, 92).

   A special case was that of writer Guy Endore. A leading Marxist theoreti-
cian in the Hollywood of the 1930s, he turned away from anything to do with
the CP, mainly for religious reasons.[51] Endore was nominated for an Oscar in
1946 for the highly regarded war film *Story of G.I. Joe* (1945).[52] He was named
in September 1951 by writer Martin Berkeley who had the dubious distinction of naming more colleagues than any other person: some 160. Endore
knew he was blacklisted when a project he was to work on was cancelled. His
agent suggested he get in touch with attorney Martin Gang who 'represented
more informers than any other lawyer in Los Angeles' (Navasky 1980: 98):

> My reply was that inasmuch as I was opposed to any kind of political
> screening in order to secure work, and inasmuch as such screening was
> forbidden by law, I did not want to engage in any kind of subterfuge
> which would only result in one individual escaping the blacklist while the
> blacklist itself and the principle involved would not be touched.[53]

When his agent insisted, Endore complied, only to find that, for Gang, there
was no such thing as the blacklist, only studios scared stiff by threats from
organisations such as the American Legion to picket films featuring those
named. This was bad for business and the banks would not lend money to make
such films. Endore's reply was forthright:

> It seemed to me, I told Mr. Gang, that those who accused me of subver-
> sive activities ought to avail themselves of the law of the land and bring
> me to court charged with specific wrong-doing and bring forward their
> evidence.[54]

Gang took the view that ex-Communists and non-Communists could not plead the Fifth. For Gang, if a person 'had been a member of the Communist Party and had gotten out, he had no right to plead the Fifth Amendment because he was not guilty of any crime' (Navasky 1980: 104). This attitude explicitly concedes that being a Communist was a crime and that those who were still Communists were 'guilty' of that fact, a novel interpretation of the Constitution, but one that fitted in nicely with HUAC's. It also forgets the simple but essential ethical dimension of the dilemma: pleading the Fifth was also the choice of those who refused to name names, *irrespective of whether they themselves and the people concerned were Communists or not.* Ironically for Endore, he was not in favour of the Fifth. On 1 May 1958 he wrote to William Wheeler, HUAC's investigator:

> I have always felt that the implication of taking the 5th Amendment was that one had something to conceal which was of a criminal nature. I may indeed have in my past many things that I am not too proud of, but I know of nothing criminal in my past, and therefore would have no valid reason to seek the protection of the 5th Amendment.[55]

The difference between Endore and Gang concerned the question of membership in the CP. Endore went so far as to sign an affidavit in 1958 to the effect that membership of the CP was 'now happily long past'.[56] Yet he refused to name names and preferred to stay on the blacklist rather than abandon friends 'when the charge of treason was laid upon the Party'.[57]

An unusual case was that of actor Sterling Hayden. After appearing as a friendly witness in 1951, he regretted his action and paraded before the building where the Hearings were being held, bearing a placard asking people not to name names. Although this did not affect his career, he decided to leave Hollywood in 1958 and returned to films only in 1963, playing the paranoid anti-Communist General Jack D. Ripper in *Dr. Strangelove*. Other special cases, their significance and their impact will concern us in the next chapter.

NOTES

1. Three days after the invasion Westbrook Pegler was demanding in his syndicated column that Communists and fellow-travellers be executed. Leo Gallagher Papers, Box 2, folder 32, SCL.
2. The Rosenbergs were convicted of communicating nuclear secrets during a war but to an *ally*: the Soviet Union. They were executed during a war where nuclear power was not at stake and in which the Soviet Union was not directly implicated. It is doubtful they would have been executed if tried before the Korean War.
3. Truman became President following the death of FDR in April 1945. Against all odds, he was re-elected in 1948.

4. The insurgency in Greece failed, for the simple reason that Stalin kept his promise to Churchill and refused to help the Greek Communists who had distinguished themselves in the resistance to the Nazis during the war (Kovel 1997: 245n2). Talk of 'Soviet subversion' in the West was therefore a lie: a pro-West undemocratic monarchy had to be returned to power.

5. This was during the Nazi–Soviet Pact, a time when President Roosevelt had no reason to feel sympathetic towards the CP.

6. I remind readers of Hoover's 1941 memo to the Attorney General quoted in Chapter 4.

7. The full significance of the formula 'Communist front' will emerge later.

8. This is crucial for understanding the behaviour of certain witnesses called before HUAC in 1951 and is discussed below.

9. Peter Watkins' *Punishment Park* took as its starting point the fact that the McCarran Act was still in force in 1971.

10. This essential document is preserved in the Michael Wilson Papers, Box 45, folder 11, Arts Library Special Collections, UCLA.

11. See the Emmet Lavery Papers, Box 84, folder 14, Arts Library Special Collections, UCLA.

12. It is one of the paradoxes of the period that Senator Robert Taft, co-author of the Act, would probably have agreed with Dunne, despite being a conservative and a Republican. A staunch anti-Communist, he was less anti-labour than opposed to any form of government intervention. Yet he was in favour of public housing: only decent living conditions would enable America to be the land of economic freedom. His hostility to excessive power being given to the President and his opposition to sabre rattling to impose American hegemony meant that, on certain issues, he had more in common with people like Carey McWilliams than with Cold War liberals and conservatives. See Paterson 1971: 167–204.

13. Mankiewicz owed his survival to the support of John Ford. For a detailed analysis of Ford's behaviour and statements during this period – his ambiguities, contradictions and opportunism – see McBride 2003: 261–87.

14. They all did, except John Huston and Billy Wilder. There is evidence, however, that Mankiewicz was not happy with what happened. In his film *People Will Talk* (1952) Cary Grant plays an academic whose career is threatened by unpleasant rumours. His adversary is a venomous philistine (very much like De Mille), played by pro-CSU actor Hume Cronyn (see Chapter 3).

15. Hearings, pp. 4262–3. The MPIC had made similar statements on 21 March 1951 (when the Hearings opened) and 17 September 1951.

16. As HUAC member Donald Jackson put it: 'If we didn't have the Fifth Amendment, we would find out' who the subversive elements were in the country. (*Variety*, 24 September 1951, Jack L. Warner Papers, Box 44, folder 152). For Supreme Court Justice William Douglas, the Fifth was 'our way to escape from the use of torture' (Pomerantz 1963: 49).

17. Gibney was President of the SWG when the Guild initiated legal action against the blacklist.

18. Howard Koch, OH.
19. Gordon explains that he 'was scheduled to appear in public as a 'Fifth Amendment Witness', which meant that he was expected to be 'unfriendly'. It transpired that those called before Gordon fought with the Committee who 'ran out of time and never called some of the last Hollywood people, like myself, who remained to be nailed' (Gordon 1999: 53).
20. As did Albert Maltz and Dalton Trumbo, as well as later blacklistees: writers Gordon Kahn and Hugo Butler (who worked twice there with director Luis Bunuel).
21. *Film Culture*, special issue on blacklisting, p. 2.
22. But not all: anti-Communist liberals had no truck with fascism but simply believed the country was under siege, from within and without.
23. By 1950 even those who had never been involved politically were worrying about the consequences of having given money to Spanish Civil War veterans in the 1940s, when Fascism was the enemy (Anhalt 2001: 18).
24. If, as Richard Collins claimed, most Americans were anti-Franco, then are we to assume they were all victims of a 'front' and, if so, should they all have been requested to recant?
25. Questioned by Representative Doyle about one supposed front, the Hollywood Democratic Committee, Paul Jarrico pointed out that it had campaigned for Doyle's re-election and written speeches for him. 'I don't think I had any knowledge of it', replied the Congressman (Hearings: 282).
26. Rossen and Bromberg testified on 25 June and 26 June 1951 respectively.
27. We shall return to Rossen and Bromberg in Chapter 7.
28. Gordon, OH, p. 26; Bercovici, Hearings: 450.
29. Certain witnesses, such as Bercovici, were ready to state that they were not members of the CP but refused to talk about either past membership or activities. The result was the same: blacklisting.
30. OH, p. 231, UCLA.
31. OH, pp. 21–2, 26–7.
32. The choice of Da Silva as the first witness was not fortuitous. In 1947 friendly witness Robert Taylor singled him out as a trouble-maker in the SAG. See Chapter 4.
33. This meant that nobody else was present but that HUAC reserved the right to make the testimony known, which it did.
34. Revere had appeared in the film that convinced HUAC that there was a Communist conspiracy because of the radicals and Communists who worked on it: *Body and Soul* (1947). Director Robert Rossen, writer Abraham Polonsky and actors Lloyd Gough and Canada Lee were all blacklisted. On its star, John Garfield, see Chapter 7.
35. The Chairman in the period 1949–52 was Southern Democrat John Wood, from February 1953 Republican Harold Velde, an ex-FBI agent. The Chairman of a Committee of Congress always belonged to the party controlling Congress.
36. How is it possible to overthrow a government by force when one has no troops?

37. Those dissenting included Justices Black and Douglas. The latter was quoted in the St Louis *Post-Dispatch* on 20 June 1951 where he pointed out that the CP leaders were not charged with an attempt to overthrow the Government but with conspiring to use speech and publications 'to teach and advocate the forcible overthrow of the Government'. Black considered the First Amendment forbade such an indictment and that the Smith Act was unconstitutional. Documents conserved in the Ring Lardner, Jr Papers, Box 15, folder 229, MHL.

38. The various reasons for these betrayals have been listed and exhaustively analysed by Victor Navasky.

39. Bright, OH, p. 26.

40. Polonsky, OH, p. 176. Doubtless the trade paper saw in Polonsky 'a very dangerous citizen', as he was called by HUAC member Harold Velde. See Buhle and Wagner 2001.

41. Bercovici worked uncredited as a writer after being blacklisted, whereas Vorhaus settled in Britain but never made films again. See the interviews with them in McGilligan and Buhle 1997.

42. William Wyler Papers, folder 688.

43. Howard Estabrook Papers, MHL. He also wrote these fine words, destined to be repressed by him and others: 'Public prints may smear the screen writer without pretense of proof, and may then enjoy Freedom of Repression by failing to print any whisper of authentic refutation on the other side.'

44. As I write these lines, a remarkable German film entitled *Das Leben der Anderen* has won an Oscar. It tells of the activities of the East German secret police, the Stasi. The parallels between what the film shows and the Hearings of 1951 give an uncanny feeling of *déjà vu*. In the film betraying friends and naming names is the highest act of patriotism; those who talk are congratulated, those looked upon as subversive are deprived of the right to work. For the Stasi, those denounced are the 'enemies of socialism', for HUAC members of the 'communist conspiracy'.

45. Duff had signed the *amicus curiae* brief asking the Supreme Court to consider the cases of Lawson and Trumbo (and therefore the conviction of the Ten). Chaplin had also signed.

46. Paul Buhle has called Karloff a 'doughty anti-fascist' (Buhle 1995: 107), but the actor clearly slipped through the witch hunters' net.

47. Carey McWilliams Papers, Box 13. Nichols also remarked that, once blacklisting started, there was no stopping it, an opinion shared by Emmet Lavery (OH, UCLA). An early FBI report referred to Nichols as being 'long a fellow traveller'. See http://foia.fbi.gov/foiaindex/compic.htm Part 1b.

48. See the discussion of Lillian Hellman's anti-Fascist scripts in Chapter 2.

49. Hammett was co-founder of the Motion Picture Artists Committee formed to support Loyalist Spain. Other members included actress Gale Sondergaard (wife of Herbert Biberman of the Hollywood Ten) and writer Donald Ogden Stewart. Both were blacklisted.

50. Chaired by Jack Tenney, a former liberal Democrat who swung to the right, joined the Republican Party and, in 1952, joined the presidential ticket of fascist anti-Semite Gerald Smith.
51. Guy Endore Papers, Box 66, Ray Stark folder, UCLA.
52. Endore's co-writers were Leopold Atlas, who named names, and Philip Stevenson, who was blacklisted. Endore also contributed to several major horror films in the mid-1930s, such as *Mark of the Vampire* and *The Devil-Doll*, a fact which he failed to mention in his Oral History.
53. Written statement given to the SWG by Endore on 8 February 1952. Guy Endore Papers.
54. Writer Robert Lees made a similar point (Hearings: 213).
55. Guy Endore Papers, Box 66, folder 279.
56. Guy Endore Papers, Box 66, folder 279. Endore signed the affidavit for one reason only: he needed a passport in order to visit Europe to do research for a novel and could not obtain one otherwise (Endore, OH).
57. Guy Endore Papers, Box 66, Ray Stark folder.

6

The Anti-Communist Crusade on the Screen

Of all the friendly witnesses, two in particular have taken on a special symbolic status because of the circumstances and the repercussions of their testimonies: director Edward Dmytryk of the Ten and writer-director Elia Kazan. Kazan's case is of interest because of the film he made two years after his testimony, *On the Waterfront* (1954), and his 'Life Achievement' Academy Award in 1999. This latter event encountered an opposition in the form of public demonstrations on the part of former blacklistees who were not ready to forget the implications of Kazan's testimony.[1] As blacklisted writer Walter Bernstein put it, 'it was as a director that he testified, hurting other directors, writers, and everyone who was blacklisted' (McGilligan and Buhle 1997: 54). The symbolic importance of Dmytryk lies elsewhere.

Dmytryk's testimony, in April 1951, worked over the cliché of outlawing the CP (Bentley 2002: 399). However, the director was to return constantly to his act in an attempt to justify himself. Thus in the documentary *Hollywood on Trial* (1976), he states: 'I didn't want to be a martyr for a cause I didn't believe in.' This remark exposes Dmytryk to criticism. Firstly, he displaces the question from one of keeping faith with those who were blacklisted – irrespective of whether they were members of the CP or not, as we saw in the last chapter – onto one of no longer believing in the CP. Let us remember Guy Endore, who kept faith with the victims of blacklisting long after leaving the CP. Thus Dmytryk used his disillusionment with the CP and the Soviet Union to justify condemning many people to the blacklist, whereas he named them in order to be able to work again. Secondly, he disavowed his own testimony during the Hearings of 1947 where he attempted to answer the notorious question by a reference to the Constitution. 'So you refuse to answer the question?' his interrogator stated, to which Dmytryk replied: 'I don't refuse, I'm answering it in my own way.' If Dmytryk was saying that defending the Constitution was being a 'martyr' to the CP, then he had sunk low in his own esteem and had an original view of the Constitution.

Another aspect of Dmytryk's testimony is revelatory of the problem of the reliability of a witness. More than twenty years after his testimony, Dmytryk claimed he had named no person who had not already been named, a common ploy used to justify betrayal and to pass off naming names as a banal act devoid of consequence (Navasky 1980: 283). It transpired that he was the first to name directors Michael Gordon and Bernard Vorhaus.[2] Both denounced Dmytryk as a liar; he had stated when and where he had seen them at a Party meeting, whereas both were elsewhere.[3] Neither ever denied belonging to the CP. A third blacklistee, writer Sidney Buchman, took the First and not the Fifth – thus risking imprisonment – so as to refute Dmytryk's naming writer George Corey. Buchman, who explained that Corey often dined at his house, chose this tactic to save Corey (who was not an American) and his wife from being deported. Dmytryk had said: 'the man's name, I believe, is George Corey, a writer' (Bentley 2002: 390).

We can only speculate as to what Dmytryk meant by 'I believe'. It is logical to suppose that he was unsure of the exact name, whereas he was sure Corey was present in Buchman's house. Was Dmytryk lying or was his memory defective? There is no easy answer to this. Abraham Polonsky was surprised to learn that few people had named him, whereas he believed thirty or forty had (Navasky 1980: 284). Memory is a treacherous thing. At the risk of upsetting the victims of people like Dmytryk, who was a self-serving opportunist, I would suggest both friendly witnesses and blacklistees were, in certain cases, *victims of memory*. Let us take the example of writer Budd Schulberg. Questioned in the 1970s about his testimony, he claimed: 'These people, if they had had it in them, could have written books and plays. There was not a blacklist in publishing' (Navasky 1980: 243). And yet Angus Cameron of the publishing house Little, Brown and Co. was blacklisted.[4] Schulberg was not so much lying as trying to justify his act by claiming that any blacklisted writer could find an outlet elsewhere. Remarks made by Cameron in an interview show that the situation was less simple. He wrote for help to various leading publishers: none replied (Fariello 1995: 355). It is doubtful that they would have accepted manuscripts by the proscribed, lest they suffer the same fate as Cameron. Schulberg's argument is a piece of casuistry, like Dmytryk's claim that he never named anybody not already named. Both were denying responsibility for the suffering of others. Both had created a 'screen memory' to lend a noble veneer to an act of betrayal.

As already stated, Dmytryk recanted in order to be able to work again. In 1952 he was hired by producer Stanley Kramer, the liberal who had abandoned

Carl Foreman at the time of *High Noon*. The film he directed was *The Sniper* and starred Adolphe Menjou, whom we have already met. Ironically, the film was liberal in tone. Dmytryk's turnabout was soon complete, however. On 28 September 1954 he wrote in the following terms to columnist Hedda Hopper (who counted Hoover, McCarthy and Nixon among her friends): 'Please accept this as a rather belated "thank you very much".'[5] In an interview decades later Dmytryk executes another turnabout, or perhaps had simply forgotten this letter of thanks. He blamed all the blacklisting problems on the Motion Picture Alliance and refers to Sam Wood, John Wayne – and Hedda Hopper! (Fariello 1995: 297).

Abraham Polonsky always insisted on the pragmatic side of naming names: it enabled you to continue working. For every friendly witness who claimed that acting, writing or directing was the only thing they knew how to do, however, there were many who refused to play the game:

> . . . while Martin Berkeley wrote a succession of mediocre screenplays for Universal and United Artists, Sidney Buchman ran a car park; while Roy Huggins and Meta Reis Rosenberg went on to fine producing careers, Robert Lees, Fred Rinaldo, Alfred Levitt, and Edward Huebsch struggled to make themselves over into maître d's, newsprint salesmen, photographers, and TV repairmen. (Ceplair and Englund 1980: 378)[6]

One person named by Kazan made a sarcastic reference to the lucrative film contract he was able to sign as a result of deciding to name names.[7] Kazan would not have obtained that contract otherwise. At the same time, Lillian Hellman – who both worked in Hollywood and wrote for Broadway – chose the Fifth and put an end to her lucrative career in films. Kazan, who, like Hellman, had gained his laurels in the theatre, could have done likewise but chose not to. Instead, 'he named eight members of his Group Theatre unit and some Party functionaries' (Navasky 1980: 202). Therefore he chose to destroy those who had helped him achieve fame and fortune. Kazan also chose to remain silent in the following years, but *On the Waterfront,* written by Schulberg, speaks out eloquently in favour of testifying. However, it has a sting in the tail for both men, one they had certainly not entertained.

The film turns on the dilemma faced by Terry Malloy when he decides to take on union boss Johnny Friendly who runs the union like a gangster: how to square his belief in the need to defend the interests of himself and his fellow workers with the sentiment that 'ratting' to the Crime Commission will make him a 'stoolie'. The film takes up the cudgels in defence of the Constitution and of informing. When served with a subpoena, Terry is told: 'You can bring a lawyer, if you wish. And you're privileged under the Constitution to protect yourself against questions which could implicate you in crimes.' This is a legal argument in favour of the Fifth. However, Terry is a friendly, not an unfriendly, witness and the irony of the statement lies in the fact that what happens to Terry – blacklisted by his union – is precisely what befell those named by Kazan and dozens of others before HUAC. Terry talks and is blacklisted. Kazan talked and got others blacklisted. It is also revealing that Terry is thanked by the investigator of the Crime Commission in terms similar to those used by HUAC.

Terry symbolises those who, like Kazan and Schulberg, talked and named names. The corrupt unionists clearly symbolise the CP, both within Hollywood and without. Leading CP members regularly went by aliases in a futile attempt to keep their identities a secret and Kazan gave HUAC the name of the person who recruited him into the Party, adding his alias for good measure. 'Friendly' is also an alias. At one point in the film Terry's elder brother, a union official, makes the remark that 'stooling is ratting on your friends'. This is precisely what Kazan did by giving the names of his comrades in the New York theatre of the 1930s who were also members of the same CP cell as himself. By putting these words into the mouth of a corrupt official, Kazan and Schulberg try to justify naming names when done for reasons that are honest and noble in their eyes. By a similar reversal the film hides the fact that the corrupt union in Hollywood in the 1930s was the gangster-controlled IATSE. That Terry giving evidence against his own union parallels Kazan giving evidence against the CP can only mean in the public mind that Communist-dominated unions are corrupt and that corrupt unions are Communist. This was not the case, in Hollywood or nationally.

Another key character in the film is Father Barry, based on a real-life priest who waged his own war against left-wing union officials on the waterfront in an attempt to lead the workers away from un-Americanism; he is a clerical Roy Brewer. It is interesting to speculate on why Hollywood preferred priests to Protestants. The Catholic Church has always favoured confession as a private moment, whereas Calvinism insisted on the role of public confession. Thus the inquisition in the post-war period in general and Hollywood in particular condensed the two religions in a holy war against the Red infidel: first the *private* confession orchestrated by men like HUAC investigator Wheeler, then the *public* confession before the cameras, the press and HUAC. Father Barry refers to each murder ordered by Friendly as a 'crucifixion', whereas in reality HUAC and its friendly witnesses 'crucified' the unrepentant 'sinners'. Clearly, however, Barry's main role is to lead Terry to recognise the error of his ways. Significantly, Kazan films the body of Terry's brother – executed on Friendly's orders for failing to bring Terry back onto the straight and narrow – by having him hung up on a hook in a clear reference to a crucifixion.

The film has always been denounced by the Left for the way it pillories unions at a time when any remotely radical union fighting for workers' rights was systematically demolished from within and without by anti-Communist unionists. This is the most damning indictment of the film. However, it is precisely here that *On the Waterfront* becomes ambiguous, indeed subverts its own right-thinking ideological thrust. At one point it becomes clear that Friendly is working for outside forces, represented explicitly in the film, not as Reds, but as corporate business: one of his henchmen refers to a phone call from 'Mr. Upstairs'. Doubtless the film is anxious to show Friendly as following the Party line, but in fact he is serving business interests as corrupt as himself. The film presents us, perhaps unwittingly, with the real capitalist exploiters of labour. It is also possible to read the workers' enforced return to work at the end as the victory of the IATSE over the CSU. Thus the final shot is of the doors of the warehouse closing ominously behind them and shutting them in, very much like the doors of a studio lot, a studio collaborating with gangsters against the interests of the workers.

It is through the name of the corrupt union boss that Kazan and Schulberg give themselves away, albeit unconsciously. Friendly is played by Lee J. Cobb who, after a period of resistance to HUAC resulting in financial hardship and family problems, capitulated and named names. I suggest we have an instance of Freud's return of the repressed, but in an inverted form. Friendly is a repellent character (and Cobb excelled in such characters).[8] In this he corresponds to how blacklistees saw the friendly witnesses. The parallel between 'Friendly' and 'friendly' may not be conscious, but we are surely entitled not to interpret it as a mere coincidence. Thus Friendly comes to represent the unconscious guilt Kazan and Schulberg really felt, not about having been Communists, but about having betrayed their former comrades and collaborators. And as 'Friendly' is an alias, this suggests that it was the friendly witnesses, and not the Communists, who really wore the mask of Janus.

Let us return now to the religious dimension of the film, crucial for the HUAC rigmarole and for a number of films in the anti-Communist cycle. When Larry Parks, a hesitant friendly witness, finally caved in under pressure and named names, he earned the following tribute: 'We appreciate your cooperation. You are excused.' Clearly 'excused' meant 'you may leave the witness stand', but it can also signify 'you are *forgiven*'. In his Oral History, Catholic Emmet Lavery sarcastically refers to ex-Communists as wearing 'sack cloth and ashes' and, through naming names, being 'purged, tempered, and purified'. At one point in *The Iron Curtain* (1948) – set in Canada and based on the real-life defection to the West of a Soviet official and his wife – the couple is visiting the town when the wife becomes impressed by the sound of hymns emanating from a church. In *The Red Menace* (1949) it is a priest who succeeds in bringing CP member Molly back into the arms of mother Church; we see her entering a church where, miraculously, she finds her mother kneeling in prayer for her. Such were the ruses of screen writing. A priest also figures prominently in *I Was a Communist for the FBI* (1951). The Communist in *My Son John* (1952) swears to his mother on the Bible that he's not a Red, but of course that does not count: he is an atheist! However, it is in its portrayal of corrupt union officials as gangsters that *On the Waterfront* carries on the tradition of the explicitly anti-Communist films.

Two such films place at the centre of the action Communist trade unionists and their adversaries (a 'moderate' unionist in one case, an undercover FBI man in the other): *The Woman on Pier 13* (1949) and *I Was a Communist for the FBI* (1951).[9] In both cases real-life unionists are smeared: Harry Bridges of the Longshoremen's union and leading Communist official, Steve Nelson. The union leader is portrayed as cynical and unscrupulous in *I Was a Communist* and is beaten up by the FBI agent at the end of the film (the act has no real justification, except as an encouragement to use violence against Communists: this is how heroes must behave). However, he pales in comparison to Vanning, the CP thug in the former who has those who disobey him bound hand and foot and thrown into the harbour, the film's equivalent of the 'concrete overcoat' beloved of real-life gangsters. *Woman on Pier 13* also exploits *film noir* codes where a sexually experienced Party member – or *femme fatale* – entices and seduces a naive and honest young worker in the hope of getting him to stir up trouble in the mistaken belief that he is defending workers' rights.[10] This tactic had already been used in *The Iron Curtain* where a secretary in the Canadian CP succeeds in persuading the defector to visit her apartment where she turns on the charm. In this film the CP boss waits for his comrades in a big car, as we would expect a gang boss to do. A similar situation occurs in *Big Jim McLain* (1952) where the CP boss in Hawaii has a chauffeur-driven car (a scene accompanied by suitably sinister music).[11] In *Woman on Pier 13* Reds who come looking for the hero look and behave like hoodlums: we are treated to a car, dark streets, plus a drive by night and a secret assignation. And in *Walk a Crooked Mile* (1948), Reds resort to beatings in the best gangster tradition.

When Reds are not taking over unions to incite peaceful workers to go on strike, they adopt the same tactics with blacks.[12] Here Hollywood adopted the favourite argument of John Rankin, for whom civil rights activists were in the South to stir up trouble: everyone knew the blacks were happy with their lot. *The Red Menace* (1949) resorts to low cunning: it is a black man who warns how Reds exploit the race issue. As he is addressing his son, this endows him with the voice of Truth, a sort of black John Wayne.[13] And lest such cynicism on the part of Reds were insufficient, two films make them racists too: *Big Jim McLain* and *I Was a Communist*. The former has a working-class Communist who states that working in cotton fields is for 'white trash and niggers', an attempt to show the contempt of Communists from the north for those in the

Deep South. The latter has the Steve Nelson character refer to 'niggers', which provokes the undercover agent to reply: 'Don't you mean "Negroes"?' This inversion of a real-life situation, where Communists were the first to take risks in standing up for the rights of blacks, is the politics of the gutter.[14]

Trial (1955) is more sophisticated but no less dishonest. A lawyer, whom we later learn to be a Communist, defends a young Mexican accused of murder. He puts him on the stand, knowing that this will compromise his case and lead to the boy's being found guilty and sentenced to death, thus becoming a good martyr for the Communist cause. The All Peoples' Party Club – a carefully chosen name for a Communist 'front' – organises a great charity rally which brings in a huge sum of money, little of which is used to defend the boy.[15] This has nothing to do with race and justice on the film's part but is an attack on well-heeled Reds living it up in Hollywood and contributing to Party funds. That *Trial* is really putting the Ten on trial again can be gauged from a ludicrous scene where the communist lawyer denounces the black judge as biased. By having the lawyer evoke 'constitutional rights' the film shows its hand: he is clearly a stand-in for John Howard Lawson attacking J. Parnell Thomas. However, as we saw in Chapter 4, HUAC was not a court of law, whereas the scene takes place in court. No lawyer would be so moronic as to run the risk of being disbarred by smearing a judge, and in court of all places! The film reeks of contrivance. The fact that the charity rally is presented as a Hollywood spectacle, complete with dancing girls and a black preacher nobody listens to, exposes the film for the cynical charade it is.

Lying and smearing was part of Hollywood's overall strategy of presenting Communists as eager to exploit grievances. In *I Was a Communist* they try to blame violence on the Jews so as to set Jews and Catholics at each other's throats. This would be hilarious if it weren't so obscene, but it does shed light on the notion of what 'Americanism' had become. The hero of *I Was a Communist* is lent extra credibility for the audience in a scene where he gives a boy advice on how to play baseball. He is clearly a true American (Ronald Reagan had in important role in the film tribute to the sport of football, the significantly titled *Knute Rockne – All American*, and Wayne was a former football player).[16] *The Red Menace* – which has a voice-over commentary to lend it credibility, as in a documentary, and to encourage spectators to react in the appropriate fashion at key moments – is the most elaborate example of how Communists supposedly exploited grievances. The CP defends war veterans being fleeced by estate agents and the film has characters expressing understandable bitterness over having to face a housing problem after risking their lives for years for their country. Although such a problem was real for veterans, as we saw in Chapter 2, the film quickly forgets it in favour of propaganda and references to the 'Marxian racket spreading dissension and treason'. Now it could be argued that robbing ex-soldiers was a perfect case of being 'un-American'. The film's representation of Marxism makes no reference to capital and labour, except to inform us that Marx wrote *The Capital* [*sic*]. In this and other movies, racial tensions and class hatred are created by Communists, although the intensity of the hatred spectators are encouraged to feel for trade unionists highlights the true political purpose behind these works of propaganda.

Now the films were forced to refer to *real* current social problems in order to displace the centre of gravity and indict Reds. In *The Red Menace* it is housing and race, whereas the Depression, with its poverty and unemployment, provides the starting-point of the action in *Woman on Pier 13* and *Walk East on Beacon* (1952). Unemployment may well be exploited by Reds in the former, but there is no discussion of what it means to be unemployed. However, the hero is an ex-Communist and clearly still very liberal, so the true significance of raising the question is exposed: it was fine to be radical – even Red! – in the 1930s but irrelevant at best after the war. The film thus sounds a warning to liberals with a nostalgia for the past: no compromise with the comrades can be tolerated. In *Walk East on Beacon* it is a taxi-driver, symbol of the proletariat, who joined the Party during the Depression. When he tries to leave, he is murdered. As the old anti-Communist cliché had it: 'nobody leaves the Party', which here is taken literally.

On occasion, however, there surfaces something more revelatory than admitting to flaws in America's past, which itself suggests that they no longer existed by the 1950s. Certain films highlight their own contradictions. I shall give briefly four different examples of this. In *Walk East on Beacon* a character is forced to deal with Communists but also collaborates with the FBI.[17] At one point he receives orders to meet a CP member in the middle of the night. When he is walking along the deserted streets, we see a man watching him, then another. Are they his CP contacts or FBI agents there to protect him? This suggests we cannot distinguish between CP thugs and FBI agents, a surely unintended ambiguity.[18] In *The Iron Curtain* access to the cipher room at the Soviet Embassy is via a steel door behind a velvet curtain. This is one way of representing devious Soviet tactics but can also be taken to refer, presumably unconsciously, to President Theodore Roosevelt's remark: 'walk softly but carry a big stick'. In *Invasion USA*, faced with the need for tanks, a government representative threatens the owner of a factory specialising in tractors that the State will take over his business if necessary. Thus an anti-Communist film justifies the control of the means of production by the State. As this is a fundamental notion of communism, the film is once again equating fascism and Communism and simultaneously encouraging a Fascist solution, inasmuch as fascist regimes too controlled the means of production for 'patriotic' purposes.

In *Walk a Crooked Mile* the question of loyalty is raised: all the men guarding a top-secret nuclear research centre are ex-soldiers or Marines 'who had proved their loyalty in battle'. As the film dates from 1948, this refers to World War II, not to Korea. Blacklisted writer Michael Wilson denounced attempts to question the loyalty to the US of CP members. He was contacted on 21 July 1951 by the Marine Corps concerning an inquiry into his background and CP activities (as a former Marine, Wilson was still bound by his oath of allegiance). He produced a letter from his Commandant, dated 12 March 1946, which stated: 'Your patriotism and your fine devotion to duty have been an inspiration to the officers and men who shared the responsibilities for final and complete victory.'[19] By 1951 war duty no longer counted for HUAC, so the film reveals unwittingly that patriotism had become a case of politics.

Two films demand a more detailed analysis, as they not only contain ambiguities and contradictions which can find no resolution, but in their attempts to do so create new sources of confusion: *My Son John* (1952) and *The Whip Hand* (1951).

Writing on the former, one critic has pointed out that director Leo McCarey remained true to certain aspects of the comedies that had made him famous in the 1930s, despite the film being 'desperately solemn' (Sayre 1982: 98).[20] More intriguing is the presumably unconscious satirical dimension of the film. John's father is a member of the American Legion and McCarey turns him into a figure of fun in the way he puts on his Legion cap whenever he waxes patriotic. The scene where he breaks into song – 'If you don't like your Uncle Sammy, go back over the sea' – is a moment where patriotic solemnity and comedy clash ludicrously. It is difficult to take the film seriously, yet in its clichés it betrays a particularly nasty and reactionary philistinism. John is an intellectual, whereas his parents read only the Bible and a cookbook. More sinister is the representation of John as a homosexual 'in a period when sexual or political "deviation" were considered equally disgusting' (Sayre 1982: 96). This is a revealing aspect of the film, as Robert Walker (John) had just played Bruno in Hitchcock's *Strangers on a Train*. In this most complex film, a man comes to fear the police because he is suspected of a murder he did not commit. Thus furtive assignations between two men at night take on the appearance of homosexuality, with the film's homosexual (Walker) being represented as a threat to the nation's security.[21] Significantly, John's two brothers are virile football players (a tribute to John Wayne?) and when the film opens are on their way to fight in Korea.

However, it is the character of the mother that highlights the film's contradictions. Clearly the central figure for McCarey, she goes along with John when he says he loves 'the downtrodden, the minorities', since this is Christian. At the same time she drools over him, telling him how she used to bounce him on her knee and starts gurgling as if he were a newborn baby or she a cretin. It is John the Communist who breaks up the home, but what a home! Is the film suggesting that a mother's influence is negative and that the father must be counted on to make sure sons are strapping, anti-Communist patriots? How does this square with McCarey's obvious affection for the mother and the portrayal of the father? If she hands John over to the FBI, this only highlights the film's contradictions, impossible to solve in a context where subtlety of characterisation must be sacrificed to the new Hollywood doxa, not to mention McCarey's own ideological contradictions. These in turn are part of the contradiction inherent in the ideology of the anti-Red cycle:

> . . . although America is glorified as the land of freedom where everyone can speak and think for himself, the threat of communism is simultaneously located in that very exercise of free thought . . . In short, to preserve our freedom we must relinquish it. Loyalty to motherhood and HUAC must be as absolute as loyalty to the Party. (Roffman and Purdy, 1981: 292–3)

The Whip Hand started out as an anti-Nazi film, but rabid Red-baiter Howard Hughes (who also produced *Woman on Pier 13*) turned it into an anti-Communist one. For Hollywood at this period, Nazis and Communists were identical: one of the characters is a Nazi working for Moscow. Similarly, in *Red Planet Mars* (1952) the Soviets capture a Nazi scientist and get him to work for them. Reality, however, gets in the way here: the US placed Nazis in high places in Germany after the war to help in the crusade against Communism.[22] This helps explain the fascinating ambiguity of *The Whip Hand*. After an accident, a fisherman tries to get help in a nearby town where everyone is unfriendly or frightened or both. And they have every right to be: characters are forever spying on everyone to make sure they say or do nothing out of place. However, it is one thing to inform the film's audience of what is happening by talk of 'dropping an Iron Curtain' around the town; it is quite another to convince the audience that this is what has happened. Something totally different is taking place.

The town used to be prosperous, then a virus killed the trout and its booming industry. This was followed by people moving in and buying everything cheap, with the result that people no longer feel at home. The film is successful in creating a climate of fear and paranoia and I would argue that its sub-text is spying by the FBI on supposedly free American citizens. *Walk East on Beacon*, a paean of praise to Hoover, openly encouraged citizens to spy on their neighbours and write to the FBI.[23] *The Whip Hand* simply shows the result in fictional terms. America in the early 1950s resembled in reality what the film's manifest content claims the Soviets have done to a tiny backwater via wire-tapping, surveillance and other favourite FBI tactics. However, the recourse to the notion of a town being cut off because everyone is in cahoots with the alien forces that have taken it over – the film represents alienation in a disturbing fashion to the point where characters resemble zombies – looks ahead to a film of a very different nature: *Invasion of the Body Snatchers* (1955), where aliens take over people's bodies in the Californian town of Santa Mira when they go to sleep. *The Whip Hand* is really part of the horror/science-fiction corpus of the decade: anti-Communist at one level and a representation of the anxiety brought on by social and psychological alienation on another, more profound and meaningful level. The fact that in *The Whip Hand* the town loses its only industry is surely a reference to fears for jobs in real-life America, whereas people moving in to make a profit from this is a perfect manifestation of the faceless corporate society. The word 'takeover' refers both to aliens and a capitalist ploy to increase profits by laying off 'surplus' workers. In both cases, the worker's body is no longer his own (Humphries 2002a: 62). Similarly, as one critic has astutely written of *Body Snatchers*,

> since America did not, after all, know Communism, but anticommunism and its abyss of universal suspicion, we had just as well consider the ruling ideology rather than its object as emblematic of the disaster that befell Santa Mira. (Kovel 1997: 186)

This sums up perfectly *The Whip Hand* too and highlights the contradictions inherent in the horror/science-fiction cycle of the decade.

The Whip Hand also looks ahead to director William Cameron Menzies' next film, *Invaders from Mars* (1953) which is even more unnerving in its representation of the breakdown of the family unit under pressure – an indication that the discourse devoted to placing the home and success on a pedestal was failing to produce the consensus hoped for – than as a warning about invaders from Moscow.[24] If *The Thing from Another World* (1951) and *Them!* (1954) can easily be interpreted along anti-Communist lines, the tendency to put all films of the period in the same basket is misguided to say the least.[25] The mere evocation of the atom bomb has been sufficient for even so lucid a critic as the late Michael Rogin to interpret *Kiss Me Deadly* (Robert Aldrich, 1955) as an anti-Communist film, although not a shred of evidence is produced (Rogin 1987: 269). It is as if to evoke the Bomb in 1955 is tantamount to adopting the cold-war mentality of the period. Rogin writes that at the end of this apocalyptic movie only private eye Mike Hammer escapes (Rogin 1987: 249). Had he seen the film?[26] In one version of the film – the only version that Aldrich himself recognised – we see Hammer on the beach with his secretary as the bomb explodes; in an alternative version they disappear from sight while still in the house never to reappear and we can only assume they perish. I suspect Rogin's interpretation stems from the fact that the film is based on the novel by Mickey Spillane, an openly Fascist writer.[27] Only by assuming that Spillane's McCarthyism was shared by Aldrich can one consider the film's villain a Red. The comments on *Invasion of the Body Snatchers* that I quote in note 24 can be applied to *Kiss Me Deadly*: the film is not about the bomb but *alienation* and the complete breakdown of values in a society devoted to money and power. The bomb is thus the signifier of America's own self-destructive drives. The pursuit of 'the Great Whatzit' is a manifestation of 'pure' Americanism: unbridled individualism, success at any price, and to hell with society. The film looks ahead to the current suicidal scramble for profits. It would be more productive to see this profoundly disturbing and *radical* film in the context of other Aldrich productions of the period, such as *The Big Knife* (1955) which hints at blacklisting: the actor hero is chided by his agent for writing out a cheque for $200 for an actor friend. The script implies that he is unemployed after being named.[28] The gesture by the hero is seen as misplaced and potentially dangerous for his career.[29]

The kinds of misinterpretations of which *Kiss Me Deadly* was a victim and the reductive readings of key works like *Invasion of the Body Snatchers* stemmed from three regrettable tendencies of the time that have unfortunately continued to plague film studies and histories of the period. Firstly, to see the situation in a 'cause/effect' perspective where the Cold War produced anti-Communist movies in the same way it produced anti-Communism. Secondly, an understandable but misguided desire on the Left generally to give pride of place to films which they can classify as works of 'social comment'. Thirdly, a systematic downgrading of the films of the 1950s, because so much talent had been chased from the studios. All three are intimately interdependent and a proper study is beyond the scope of this book. However, the question is too closely related to our concerns here not to call for some comment. What follows is therefore not an attempt to respond to the above remarks one by one but to offer the beginnings of a synthesis of what was at stake and the negative effects produced.

It is ironic that one director constantly quoted in progressive and radical circles as an example of quality film-making is none other than Kazan. Leaving aside the genuine qualities of certain of his films (including *On the Waterfront*), this admiration is far too often due to the dimension of 'social comment'. Thus *Gentleman's Agreement* (1947) and *A Face in the Crowd* (1957) are praised to the skies. Why? Because the former is anti-anti-Semitic, the latter an attack on a popular demagogue and his sinister influence on those who listen to his ravings. I find both films contrived to the point of becoming ludicrous; what little artistry they have lies in putting over a simplistic message that reduces them to the level of tracts.[30] They are light years removed from the artistic and intellectual subtlety, not to mention the deep and insistent social commitment, that

distinguishes the work of the writers and directors soon to find themselves
without work. This would seem to bring grist to the mill of those who deplore
an absence of serious movies after 1952, but this attitude betrays a regrettable
over-simplification of the situation. 'Social comment' takes many forms, the
most important being that 'commitment' referred to above which cannot be
reduced to some facile message but which must inform the film at all levels.

Now it is surely stating the obvious to point out that the exodus of much
talent from Hollywood in the years following the Hearings of 1947 could only
have negative fallout on the quality of films. I prefer to state the matter positively: if HUAC had never existed, Hollywood in the 1950s would have been
even greater than it was. With the exception of the 1940s, this was the greatest
decade in the industry's history. It was Hitchcock's greatest decade, Lang made
films even more critical than those of the 1940s (but artistically more varied in
overall quality), Ford starting to produce his darkest, most critical and out-
standing work, from *The Searchers* (1956) to *Seven Women* (1965). The work of
Robert Aldrich from 1954 to 1959 was as radical, critical and artistically successful as one could hope for.[31] Nicholas Ray came into his own in the period
1952 to 1958 and the contribution to the cinema of the 1950s of Samuel
Fuller, Anthony Mann, Otto Preminger, Nicholas Ray and Douglas Sirk – to
name the most obvious – cannot be over-stated.[32] I have already drawn attention to the horror and science-fiction movies, so shall state the matter bluntly
and provocatively: there is more artistry, intelligence and – yes! – social
comment in *I Was a Teenage Werewolf* (1957) than in many a supposed 'master-
piece', such as the two films by Kazan referred to earlier.

The matter has been put in a nutshell by one theorist: 'Fifties horror films
display an awareness of the monsters that haunted cold war society, but also an
awareness that many of these monsters were ones that members of that society
had created themselves' (Hendershot 2001: 2). The most important 'monster' was
that social and psychological alienation of which *Body Snatchers* is the supreme
representation. It was the perfect filmic manifestation of that 'eerie conformity'
(Hendershot 2001: 80) that had taken a stranglehold of much of Hollywood and
of a complacent society where the return of the repressed (the trademark of
horror movies) was a constant reality, 'America's desire to set in contrast the corporate world and freedom' (Hendershot 2001: 16). This trenchant remark perfectly encapsulates the refusal to give in to the superficially bland but ferociously
repressive ideology of Eric Johnston, a refusal that saw the light of day in multi-
farious ways in film genres – such as horror and science-fiction and melodrama
(Ray and Sirk) – that transcend completely the depressing tenets of 'realism'
as understood both by Hollywood and, alas, certain left-wing commentators.[33]
Invasion of the Body Snatchers is exceptional because it succeeded in representing
and analysing two mutually exclusive sets of values imposed on Americans

throughout the 1950s. These can be summed up as follows: conform or be considered a subversive; Communists demand conformity. Little wonder that paranoia and schizophrenia were rife, both in films and in reality!

I shall conclude with two more examples: *It Came from Outer Space* (1953) and *I Married a Monster from Outer Space* (1958). The very titles seem an affront to the intelligence and that 'good taste' dear to liberals. The former is a welcome antidote to hysteria: the hero is anxious to contact and protect the alien ship that has landed but is helpless, given the ostracism of which he is a victim on the part of the community which sees him as an outsider and an intellectual. Since the aliens are well-meaning victims of American incomprehension, the film is not a 'Reds from outer space' saga but a rather a call for cooperation between the US and the Soviet Union. The title of the second film is a condensation of *I Married a Communist* (the original title of *The Woman on Pier 13*) and *I Was a Communist for the FBI*. The climate of the time and the ambiguities of many supposed liberals on questions of freedom certainly allow for an anti-Communist reading. In reality the monster's behaviour towards the wife (the alien has 'taken over' the body of the husband) is but an extreme example of the misogyny of human males in the film which thus becomes an implicit attack on sexual complacency and the ideology of 'the woman's place is in the home' redolent of the decade.

NOTES

1. Bernard Gordon, Abraham Polonsky and actor John Randolph led the protests.
2. Members of the Communist group in the SDG, along with Berry, Biberman, Dassin and Tuttle.
3. Gordon, OH, p. 322, UCLA. Interview conducted by Gerard Dessere. Vorhaus, McGilligan and Buhle 1997: 678. Gordon was active in the CP in New York between 1943 and 1946, directing plays not films (OH, p. 328).
4. This was the publishing house of Carey McWilliams.
5. Hedda Hopper Papers, file 583, MHL.
6. Like Buchman, Lees, Rinaldo, Levitt and Huebsch were all writers.
7. Kazan had originally appeared in January 1952 to talk of himself but had refused to name names. He changed his mind in April (Navasky 1980: 199–222).
8. In 1949 he had played a similar role in Dassin's *Thieves' Highway*.
9. The former film was originally entitled *I Married a Communist*, but this was considered insufficiently commercial (the anti-Nazi film *The Man I Married* was originally entitled *I Married a Nazi*). The fact that there is no Pier 13 is less important than the role of the waterfront. For more detailed information on these and other films of the cycle, see Doherty 1998, Humphries 2006 and Sayre 1980.
10. The killer in the pay of the CP in *The Woman on Pier 13* is played by William Talman. The character is a cold, calculating woman chaser. In 1950 Talman played

an identical character in *Armored Car Robbery*, a classic gangster movie with no anti-Communist implications. We can see at work here the codes of representation and narration within the gangster film and *film noir* shifting effortlessly from mainstream productions to the special sub-genre called 'the anti-Red cycle'.

11. The Reds in Hawaii disrupt shipping and communications, which presents them as extensions of Bridges and also assimilates them to the former Japanese enemy: Pearl Harbor is on Hawaii. No phoney parallel between the current US enemy and past enemies is neglected.

12. This was Hollywood's way of turning things upside down: during the 1930 it was the CP who was most active in the fight against poverty and for civil rights.

13. After relegating blacks to menial tasks in the films where they were allowed to be represented, Hollywood had suddenly discovered they could be useful in other ways.

14. That the film, fiction in the strongest sense, was nominated for an Oscar as the best *documentary* of 1951 testifies to the complicity of Hollywood at every level with the FBI and HUAC. *I Was a Communist* was based on the real-life FBI undercover agent, Matt Cvetic (see Leab 2000). Warner Brothers produced both *I Was a Communist* and *Big Jim McLain* where Wayne got members of HUAC to play themselves, and thanked the Committee for its work.

15. This aspect of the film suggests that Communists were just out to make money. This presumably explains why Lawson went to prison in the Deep South when campaigning for civil rights (see Chapter 2, note 39).

16. The American Legion is on record as stating that 'American Legion Junior baseball is a medium through which we can combat Communism' (Schrecker 1998: 62).

17. The film was co-produced by the FBI and stars Republican George Murphy, one of Reagan's colleagues on the Board of the SAG at the time when the Guild threw its weight behind HUAC and blacklisting.

18. This is exploited by director Robert Aldrich in *Kiss Me Deadly* which we discuss below.

19. Michael Wilson Papers, Box 45, folder 2.

20. McCarey worked with Laurel and Hardy and the Marx Brothers and directed Hollywood's greatest screwball comedy, *The Awful Truth* (1937).

21. For a remarkable analysis of the links between homosexuality, homophobia, spying and paranoia in the 1950s, both in Hollywood and Washington, see Corber 1993. For a discussion of the systematic persecution of gays and lesbians in Washington, see Johnson 2004.

22. Soderberg's *The Good German* (2006) provides a fine analysis of this.

23. For a detailed analysis of this film as an example of the active collaboration between Hollywood and Hoover, see Shaw 2007: 52–65.

24. Writing on *Body Snatchers*, Joel Kovel has significantly referred to 'the inability of suburban enclaves . . . to protect against the terror of existential disintegration' (Kovel 1997: 184). This formula perfectly encapsulates the dread at the centre of *Body Snatchers* and *The Whip Hand*. The alien 'pods' in *Body Snatchers* have rightly been interpreted as 'the globules of burgeoning suburban conformism that offered quiet complicity with McCarthyism' (Buhle and Wagner 2003a: 73).

25. *Them!* was a Warner Brothers production directed by Gordon Douglas who also made *Walk a Crooked Mile* and *I Was a Communist for the FBI*. Shot in black and white, the film's title is in colour: red, for both the ants and Communists! An FBI agent is crucial to the plot (Humphries 2002a: 58–60).

26. It would be nice if people took the trouble to *look at* movies. Thus one critic states that 'the protagonist viciously kills the Communist spies' (Schwartz 1998: 160), while another refers to Hammer as 'turning anti-communist and routing atomic spies' (Shaw 2007: 50). This places the film in a totally false perspective and distorts its vision.

27. The progressive Aldrich once stated that Spillane was a fascist with no respect for democracy. His novels were key examples of Cold War hysteria.

28. The hero of *The Big Knife* was once a supporter of the New Deal, considered as anachronistic and worthy only of scorn by the film's representative of contemporary conservatism, a vindictive and mean-minded gossip columnist of the Hedda Hopper and Louella Parsons variety. The film was based on a play by friendly witness and former Communist, Clifford Odets.

29. Aldrich worked as Assistant Director for future blacklistees Chaplin, Polonsky and Losey, and gave financial help to blacklisted writer Hugo Butler and his family, exiled in Mexico. See Jean Rouverol (2000: 51). For more details, see Williams 2004a.

30. Lest readers consider this as proof that I am an unreconstructed adversary of the Great Pretender, I shall go on record as stating that Kazan closed the decade with one of its greatest movies, *Wild River* (1960). It has received less attention than *Gentlemen's Agreement* and *A Face in the Crowd*.

31. The hero of *Ten Seconds to Hell* (1959) is a progressive architect, the villain a neo-Fascist who believes in social status, economic success and the survival of the fittest. The latter represents contemporary American values, the former is the sort of person who would have been hounded from his job at the beginning of the decade. In *Attack!* the heroes are working class or Jews (or both, as in Lawson's *Action in the North Atlantic*), the villains middle class.

32. As early as 1954 Ray's Western *Johnny Guitar* brilliantly allegorised witch hunting, the director offering himself the luxury of casting Red-baiter extraordinary Ward Bond in the role of the leader of the hunters.

33. Thus a Marxist such as Sirk could work away quietly in Hollywood, making films that subverted received notions concerning the family, gender relations and class: *There's Always Tomorrow, All that Heaven Allows* and *Written on the Wind* in the period 1955–56. He burrowed away like a mole and undermined the base from within: an excellent example of the 'termite'. That *All that Heaven Allows* should be remade by Rainer Werner Fassbinder (*Fear Eats the Soul*, 1974) and Todd Haynes (*Far from Heaven*, 2002) testifies to Sirk's exceptional importance when it comes to representing the alienation of the 1950s.

7

Life (and Death) on the Blacklist

In December 1950, just weeks before HUAC's return to Hollywood, there opened a film that was one of the Left's most remarkable and prescient criticisms of the way American society was going – and one of the last: *The Sound of Fury*, written by Jo Pagano and directed by Cyril Endfield whose previous film *The Underworld Story* was an extended allegory on witch hunting.[1] The left-wing themes of class, intolerance and the need for a scapegoat central to *The Underworld Story* are taken to their logical conclusion in the later film where two men – arrested for killing the wealthy man they had kidnapped – are dragged from prison by townspeople, tortured and lynched. One critic has written of this despairing and uncompromising film: 'the story as a whole is such a thoroughgoing indictment of capitalism and liberal complacency that it transcends the ameliorative limits of the social-problem picture' (Naremore 1998: 127). The film shows that it is possible for a society to reach such a pitch of hysteria that a person prevented by the 'laws' of economics from gaining a decent living and caring for his family – he is tempted into the kidnapping fiasco by an unscrupulous drone – can also be deprived of life itself by other members of the same community who identify with those behind such economic exploitation. Seen from that standpoint, *The Sound of Fury* becomes a symbol of the various forms of privation visited on those in Hollywood who refused to bow the knee to the values dominant after the Hearings of 1947.

J. Edward Bromberg, Mady Christians, John Garfield, Canada Lee and Philip Loeb did not have the opportunity to live out the blacklist. Bromberg, after a harrowing interrogation by HUAC that prompted one member of the Committee to suggest a recess because of the witness's ill health, went to London to work and died of a heart attack in December 1951, aged 47 (Kanfer

1973: 134). Christians, who played Joan Fontaine's mother in Max Ophüls' *Letter from an Unknown Woman* (1948: written by future blacklistee Howard Koch), found work impossible to get after being smeared for her activities in so-called Communist fronts (such as helping refugees from the Spanish Civil War), and succumbed to a cerebral haemorrhage as a result of hypertension in October 1951, aged 51. Garfield, long hounded because of his progressive sympathies – in his testimony before HUAC he denounced Communism but named no names – had had heart problems going back to November 1949 (Trumbo 1970: 128). His body was found in a flat in New York in May 1952; he was 39. Lee, who was black, found himself unable to obtain work either in Hollywood or on radio and television; he died the same month as Garfield, aged 45. Loeb, banned from television in the early 1950s and depressed by family problems, committed suicide in a hotel room in 1955, aged 63. Another victim also deserves mention here. Writer Leopold Atlas was a friendly witness in March 1953, but HUAC had been after him since 1949 and he had suffered several heart attacks. By the end of 1954 he was dead, aged 47 (Navasky 1980: 362). Atlas, along with Guy Endore and Philip Stevenson, was nominated for an Oscar in 1946 for the script of *The Story of G.I. Joe* (1945), a war film about foot soldiers which had ironically been made because General Eisenhower considered that such a film was necessary. Stevenson, like Endore, was blacklisted.[2]

In February 1949 actor Roman Bohnen died, aged 54. Although he had been in Hollywood for many years, Bohnen is also an interesting figure here because of his role in the Actors' Lab, a major training-ground for actors and home for radical theatre. It was also an educational centre that welcomed returning GIs and offered them, under the GI Bill of Rights, State-funded education. For many Republicans, this was the same thing as calling the Lab a hive of Communist activity and in February 1948 Jack Tenney, Chairman of California's HUAC, subpoenaed Bohnen, along with Bromberg and Rose Hobart. This elicited a letter of support, dated 24 February and signed by fifty-two veterans of World War II: 'This slur is of a particular personal concern to us inasmuch as it places in possible jeopardy the continuation of our education under the G.I Bill of Rights in the school of our choice'.[3] For Tenney, proof of subversion was the staging of plays by Anton Chekhov and Sean O'Casey.[4] Members of the Executive Board of the Lab included future blacklistees: actors Morris Carnovsky, Howland Chamberlin, Larry Parks and Art Smith, writers Abraham Polonsky, Waldo Salt and John Wexley, and director Michael Gordon. It is worthwhile recording that Smith, a familiar face in *films noirs* in the late 1940s, was named by none other than Elia Kazan, once a defender of radical theatre. Ironically, Kazan had spoken at the Memorial Tribute to Bohnen in March 1949, along with Carnovsky and other future blacklistees, actor Jeff

Corey, director Jules Dassin – and Art Smith.[5] Kazan also named Bromberg, presumably because he was safely dead and could no longer be hurt.

Fortunately, the vast majority of HUAC's victims were healthy. All they had to endure was a form of 'living death': their transformation into non-persons. Perhaps the most extreme case is what befell Howard Da Silva after his unfriendly testimony. He had just acted in a Western, *Slaughter Trail* (1951), so the studio dutifully filmed all the scenes where he appeared, with Brian Donlevy replacing him. More complex is the case of Paul Jarrico whose name was removed from the credits of *The Las Vegas Story* by producer Howard Hughes after Jarrico took the Fifth. Jarrico contested his right to do so, pointing out that it was the SWG which decided who got credit, whereas Hughes claimed that 'the entire story was rewritten and no part of the manuscript written by Jarrico was used in the filming of the picture in question'. Supporting Hughes in his anti-Red campaign, journalist Florabel Muir unwittingly raised an important question: 'Why is it so important to Jarrico to have his name on the screen on this picture?'[6] This is like asking why an author should insist on his or her name appearing on the cover of a novel, but in reality the question refers back to the struggles between unions and studios in the 1930s and the rights won by writers to have their work on a script recognised. Jarrico lost because the SWG caved in over this fundamental issue because of anti-Communist hysteria. Bernard Gordon was luckier. By the time a Western he had written, *The Lawless Breed*, appeared in 1953, word was out about his subpoena and *The Hollywood Reporter* review of the film omitted to mention his name. Gordon learned that Borden Chase (a member of the MPA and a Western specialist) had been hired to rewrite enough of the script for the studio to deny Gordon credit but that producer William Alland had jettisoned the rewrite to force the studio to give Gordon sole screenplay credit. Gordon was soon fired on the grounds that his work was 'unsatisfactory' (Gordon 1999: 40, 46). In the cases of Da Silva and Jarrico, it was a case of 'out of sight, out of mind'. After blacklisting the Ten, Hollywood had adopted the tactic of refusing to buy for adaptation any of their work written outside Hollywood (the writers were also novelists and playwrights).

In the documentary *Legacy of the Blacklist* (1987) actresses Evelyn Keyes and Jane Wyatt, both active in the Committee for the First Amendment, talk of the way their careers faltered in the 1950s, Wyatt stating how she was taken off film after film because of pressures exerted within Hollywood and without. The career of Keyes, who had been married to John Huston from 1946 to 1950, simply evaporated. The American Legion had its own strategy for punishing political incorrectness: picketing films featuring actors, writers and directors who had in some way supported the Ten or continued to defend such progressive opinions as the need to find a *modus vivendi* with the Soviet Union.

They would march up and down in front of cinemas showing films featuring the tainted to dissuade potential spectators whom they also encouraged to mount a boycott. The effect this had on box-office takings frightened the studios and led them to think twice before using certain people again. The climate was such by 1950 that it led certain liberals deliberately to curtail their critical tendencies: 'After *The Asphalt Jungle*, John Huston never again made a film that resonated with the leftist satire of his early work' (Naremore 1998: 130). This did not prevent the Legion from boycotting his film *Moulin Rouge* (1952).[7] Huston actually left Hollywood to settle in Ireland but continued to make films regularly. According to one source he had met with the Legion and pledged support for their fight against Communism (Schwartz 1998: 113). Orson Welles, an early target for the FBI because of his anti-Fascism, simply stopped working in Hollywood in 1948 for a decade, making *Othello* (1952) in Morocco and *Confidential Report* (1955) in Europe.[8]

However peripatetic, Huston and Welles could come and go as they chose, which was not the case for other artists. Thus Chaplin's permit to re-enter the US was revoked by the Attorney General (under pressure from Nixon) while he was out of the country (Schwartz 1998: 88). Chaplin was a favourite target of the FBI and the Legion, self-styled guardians of morality. Their combined forces led him to settle in Europe between 1952 and 1972; his films *Monsieur Verdoux* (1947) and *Limelight* (1951) had suffered at the box office thanks to the systematic persecution of which he was a victim.[9] Chaplin had remained a British subject, but American citizens suffered similar harassment in the form of the withdrawal of their passports. Such treatment was meted out to dissidents too: one American judge 'was refused a passport to visit Germany where he had been Chief Justice of the Allied Control Commission courts, but who had subsequently criticized American policy in Germany'. A fellow judge remarked that

> if an American was not allowed to travel because of what he had said in the United States, not only was his freedom of speech curtailed geographically but also his freedom of speech at home was punished and therefore threatened; hence a violation of the First Amendment. (Caute 1978: 248)

In the context of the blacklistees, interesting information is provided by Cyril Endfield concerning Robert Rossen who had been an unfriendly witness and suffered accordingly. Rossen had left the States for Mexico but made the error of returning to the States where his passport was withdrawn.[10] As a result, he could no longer leave the country. Endfield continues:

> I don't know how long it was – maybe a year or two years he lasted out. But he was stranded in the States, couldn't go abroad, which offered him

the chances we had. In the States he had to use his name, and could not get work. He could not stand it. (Neve 2005: 125)

Rossen finally gave in and named names.[11]

What happened to Chaplin amounted to deportation, the fate also of Mexican actress Rosaura Revueltas while working on *Salt of the Earth*. Launched in 1953 and completed and released in 1954, the film was an attempt by blacklistees to produce an independent film and thus became the focal point of a struggle for artistic and political survival against overwhelming odds. It was directed by Herbert Biberman, written by Michael Wilson, produced by Paul Jarrico, featured actor Will Geer, with a score by Sol Kaplan.[12] The film also starred Clinton Jencks, an official for the Communist-controlled International Union of Mine, Mill and Smelter Workers. The story is based on an actual strike which took place in Silver City, New Mexico in 1951 where the wives of striking union members, including Mrs Jencks, were imprisoned with their babies and children for several hours. This strike had lasted seven months: 'The company procured a court order prohibiting blocking of the road and the pickets were arrested. The women then took over.' They had tear gas bombs thrown at them, then were arrested too.[13] The film, which follows the events faithfully and is of major interest not only for its militant unionism but also for the way it highlights the active role of women, became the immediate target of the enemies of the Left. Jarrico has described the conditions:

> There was vigilante action against us: attempts to burn down our sets, gunfire directed against us, shots taken at a union organizer's car in the middle of the night, our crews assaulted on the streets of the town in New Mexico where we were shooting. Laboratories refused to process our film. (McGilligan and Buhle 1997: 342)

Both HUAC and Hollywood (in the shape of Brewer and *The Hollywood Reporter*) attacked the production constantly. As a result

> no distributor, major or minor, would pick up the film. Ben Margolis [the Ten's lawyer] said that in four decades of legal experience he had never seen a more complete boycott or more egregious violation of the anti-trust laws. He termed it 'a complete breakdown of law and order. And the frustration of it was we couldn't hope to win satisfaction in court'. (Ceplair and Englund 1980: 417)

Those involved with the film were not without support:

> In Chicago, where a conspiracy of the projectionists' union [under instructions from Brewer], the Legion and the major motion picture

companies prevented our opening at all, a very heartening protest developed. Community organizations, clergymen and rabbis, the American Civil Liberties Union, the campus newspapers and many professors, minority group organizations, the liberal Republican press – all declared themselves on our side . . . against the censors.[14]

In a review dated 15 March 1954 the *New York Times* film critic, Bosley Crowther – a liberal opponent of blacklisting – praised and defended the film, calling it 'a strong pro-labor film with a particularly sympathetic interest in the Mexican' and 'a calculated social document'.[15] However, the film was also severely criticised on the Left. Documentary film maker Leo Hurwitz, himself a blacklistee – he was invited to be present during the shooting in an advisory capacity – took Jarrico to task for his 'casualness' and excoriated Biberman for the rigidity, lack of feeling and of artistic integrity evident everywhere in his direction.[16] Hurwitz was particularly keen that those determined to suppress the film at all costs should 'be answered with something more than a well-intentioned failure'. He was referring to its artistic and political qualities and it is true that much of the film looks amateurish, but its failure to reach an audience had nothing to do with its makers but was due to the political climate in general and Brewer in particular.

For those who remained located in California, life was even worse, as we saw earlier in the case of Keyes and Wyatt. At least the makers of *Salt of the Earth* were working. The blacklisters had long memories and pardon came only with the humiliation of disavowing one's convictions. Huston may have escaped to Ireland but it did his career no good aesthetically throughout the 1950s. Others had to choose between exile and self-degradation, although never officially blacklisted; like the two actresses, they found themselves on the 'graylist'. Thus for several years in the 1950s Paul Henreid, made famous overnight for his portrayal of the anti-Fascist resistance fighter in *Casablanca* (1942), found work hard to find. Correspondence with his New York lawyer, dated 18 February 1955, mentioned that a deal with Edward Small Productions was off: 'politically' Henreid was 'too risky'. He had to bend over backwards to dissociate himself from his past activities in the Committee for the First Amendment before being able to return to work, directing for TV.[17] Actor Alexander Knox preferred to go to Europe where he worked with Roberto Rossellini and Ingrid Bergman (who had been chased out of Hollywood for adultery with Rossellini) and blacklistee Joseph Losey (*The Sleeping Tiger*, *The Damned*, *Accident*).[18] Knox was luckier than Rossen: he had a Canadian passport. Although anti-Communist, Knox had been a co-founder of the Committee for the First Amendment and had earlier incurred the wrath of Brewer by encouraging actors not to cross the picket lines during the CSU strikes.[19] Not being a Communist, not being subpoenaed and not being black-listed changed little for some. While in England, Knox wrote to Brewer in an attempt to clear himself. His lawyer, Michael Luddy, wrote to Brewer on 11 March 1954, to the effect that Knox's letter was 'a complete and masterful refu-tation of any and all suggestions which have been made to the effect that Mr. Knox has or ever has had any Communist connections or sympathies'.[20] However, Knox also used the letter to denounce HUAC and the negative image it gave of America in European circles. This was not appreciated. Moreover, the committee of individuals representing the unions, the SAG and the producers felt Knox had not stated strongly enough that he had been used 'by the left-front organization'.[21] This was presumably a reference to Knox's links to the supposedly Communist-dominated Progressive Citizens of America. Knox had also endorsed the candidatures of Cole and Lardner for the executive board of the SWG. It was not until Kirk Douglas gave him a part in *The Vikings* (1958) that the blacklist was broken (Slide 1999: 113). We shall return to Douglas presently.

The long arm of HUAC – in this case that of California Chairman Jack Tenney – and the poisonous pen of Hedda Hopper combined to try to com-promise radical actor Albert Dekker, not in Hollywood, but as candidate (with his wife) for the Presidency of the Parent–Teacher Association in Hastings-on-Hudson, in the State of New York. On 18 March 1954 information from the 1948 Tenney Hearings on Communism was communicated to PTA members referring to Dekker as 'pro-Red', identifying him with two supposedly com-munist organisations and stating his wife had chaired the California branch of the Congress of American Women, considered a communist front by the Attorney General.[22] Hedda Hopper discussed this in her New York *Daily News* column, which led a reader calling herself 'a citizen who wants fairness' to ask Hopper if Dekker and his wife were or had been Communists, as the affair was causing a split within the PTA concerning their candidature. Hopper's reply is a revealing piece of carefully worded cant. Dekker had 'played ball' with organ-isations cited as Communist or subversive, but had never appeared before HUAC. Although 'no one can look into a man's mind or heart and evaluate his loyalty', she raised the question of 'the welfare of children'.[23] Dekker was not blacklisted and was about to play the villain in *Kiss Me Deadly*, but his film career marked time for several years in the 1950s.

An instructive case is that of director William Wyler who, despite being one of the most powerful and influential figures in Hollywood, found his past catching up with him. It was a distinguished and distinctly progressive past. Not only had he co-founded the Committee for the First Amendment, he had voted for Henry Wallace, the progressive Democrat who had stood against Truman in 1948.[24] Both liberals and the Right considered Wallace a

Communist stooge. What other 'crimes' could be laid at Wyler's door? On 1 July 1949, the Acting Chairman of the 'Bill of Rights Conference' had sent a letter of invitation to, among others, Philip Dunne, Huston and Wyler, Rossen, Lardner and Carey McWilliams. Lardner was already one of the Ten and Rossen was to become an unfriendly witness. McWilliams had long been *persona non grata*. On 28 November 1950, Wyler wrote to the Board of Parole in favour of Adrian Scott of the Ten, asking he be allowed to resume his film career.[25] By 1953 Wyler was under attack from the Legion and on 15 January his agent Paul Kohner wrote urging him to 'think very hard, and as quickly as possible, of something very constructive and strongly anti-communist in which you can participate or do to justify your anti-communist attitude'. On 8 April 1953, Art Arthur (who was an ally of Brewer and Reagan) sent Wyler material stating that he had employed blacklisted writers Michael Wilson, Howard Koch and Guy Endore and that he was 'considered to be friendly with' Rossen, Maltz and others. 'Guilt by association' again. On 24 February 1954 Wyler capitulated. He sent a sixteen-page letter to Frank Freeman of Paramount, stating he was 'sincerely anxious to correct any wrong impression of my political convictions' and that he 'would be most grateful to you, or anyone else, if you would take steps to help correct this impression'. Wyler went on to state that 'a clearer course of action and better judgment' had been needed in the past and would be forthcoming in the future. This amounted to an abandonment of the principles he had defended since 1947.[26]

Meanwhile, the exodus of talent was long over; many blacklistees had become exiles.[27] If some chose New York, most went abroad to Mexico, France or London. Both Maltz and Trumbo had already settled in Mexico and they were joined by writer Hugo Butler and his family and writers John Bright and Gordon Kahn.[28] Directors John Berry and Jules Dassin settled in France, as did writers Ben Barzman and Michael Wilson and their families. London became the home of directors Cyril Endfield, Joseph Losey and Bernard Vorhaus, and of actor Sam Wanamaker (who was to play a gangster in Losey's *The Criminal* in 1960). If Vorhaus abandoned the cinema (McGilligan and Buhle 1997), both Endfield and Losey were able to work regularly. Polonsky eventually went to New York where he joined forces with blacklisted writers Walter Bernstein and Arnold Manoff under circumstances to which I shall return presently. A special case was that of actress Betsy Blair who managed to hang on in Hollywood for a number of years. Blair was married to Gene Kelly, who steadfastly refused to become a turncoat, but she was under pressure to conform and to write letters renouncing her past activities because she was to appear in the film *Marty* (1955). She had the support of producer Dore Schary who called the American Legion and vouched for her: 'And so I was in *Marty*' (Blair 2003: 218). Yet two years passed before her next, and last, Hollywood film *The Halliday Brand* (1957) and she knew why: 'the publicly unacknowl-edged blacklist'. She had steadfastly refused to 'write the cringing, betraying letter' that would get her off the hook, as it had Wyler and others (Blair 2003: 313–16). She made films in France and Italy, including Antonioni's *Il Grido* (1957), then married director Karel Reisz and settled in London.

The collaboration between Bernstein, Manoff and Polonsky was crucial for two reasons: working in TV in New York; and the role of fronts. Let us take TV first, although the two are intimately connected. New York was not a party to the blacklist and the stage offered a haven to actors. TV was more compli-cated and for several years after 1951 the pressures brought to bear on spon-sors – TV networks existed thanks to advertising revenue – were sufficient for them to withdraw their advertisements, resulting in the networks refusing to hire those whose earlier support for liberal or anti-Fascist causes now became a burden. Actors cannot use a pseudonym: their face is their trademark. The same can be said of directors: they work openly on the set. Writers, however, were in a different position: they could work at home and, theoretically, never had to appear in public. An example of the reigning confusion and hypocrisy was the situation of Martin Ritt, blacklisted as an actor but able to work as a director in live TV.[29] In his autobiography Bernstein explains what writers had to do to find work. Firstly, they had to convince the TV producer that they were not planning to overthrow the government. Then they had to find either a pseudonym under which to write or else a 'front': a person willing to pass himself off as the author of their prose or another writer known to the network. Each solution brought its own problems. Should the network's rep-resentative wish to meet the blacklisted writer, then the game was up. And sus-picions as to the identity of author X could be raised if the network had doubts because the scripts were suddenly so much better than those to which they were accustomed. The situation was both comical and Kafkaesque and helps explain why so many writers did not succeed in clearing the hurdles.[30]

The first major writer to take advantage of fronts was Dalton Trumbo. He contributed to such essential examples of *film noir* as *Gun Crazy* (1949) and *The Prowler* (1950). His front on the latter was Hugo Butler, himself about to be blacklisted. This situation sums up matters perfectly. Guy Endore fronted for Butler on Garfield's last film, the symbolically titled *He Ran All the Way* (1951), prior to being blacklisted too, along with the director of *He Ran All the Way*, John Berry.[31] Albert Maltz's front on *Broken Arrow* (1950), a major attempt to show the Indian as other than a savage, was Michael Blankfort who became a friendly witness (unlike brother Henry). Of those blacklisted in the second wave of Hearings, the most instructive example is that of Michael Wilson. The winner in 1952 of an Oscar for the Best Script (*A Place in the Sun*, 1951), Wilson had already been blacklisted, although his next script, for *Five Fingers*

(1952), was also nominated. He then joined Jarrico, Gordon and others whose names disappeared from the credits of the films they wrote. Such was the case with Wilson's best-known film, *The Bridge on the River Kwai* (1957), which he co-wrote with Carl Foreman. Although the film's script won an Oscar, it was attributed to Pierre Boulle, author of the original story. As late as 1962, Wilson's name did not figure on the credits of *Lawrence of Arabia*, co-writer Robert Bolt taking sole credit. In 1957 the Academy of Motion Picture Arts and Sciences, fearing that Wilson would be nominated yet again for *Friendly Persuasion* (1956), stipulated that those who had refused to answer HUAC's question about belonging to the CP were ineligible for an Oscar.[32] This decision, supported by the SAG (whose former President, Ronald Reagan, strove to ensure the blacklist worked), was taken to avoid a repetition of the embarrassment the Academy had suffered in 1956 by awarding an Oscar to Robert Rich for the script of *The Brave One*.

For 'Robert Rich' was Dalton Trumbo, one of the numerous pseudonyms the writer used to keep up with demand: he was as sought after and almost as prolific on the blacklist as he had been prior to 1947. The watershed was 1960. In that year Trumbo was given screen credit for *Spartacus*, thanks to actor/producer Kirk Douglas, and director Otto Preminger announced that he had asked Trumbo to write the script of *Exodus*.[33] The outcry amongst blacklisters was predictable but times were changing and Preminger's courageous move paid off. Already in 1958 director/producer Stanley Kramer had made a gesture which, although less spectacular, had been symbolic of a wish to take on the blacklist. The opening shot of his film *The Defiant Ones* is a close-up of two men in the cabin of a lorry, accompanied by the names of the film's two writers. The name 'Nedrick E. Douglas' appears over the face of one of the men, none other than actor Nedrick Young who wrote scripts under this very pseudonym and who had been blacklisted since his clash with Representative Jackson (see Chapter 5).[34] The script won the Oscar in 1958 and when the true identity of Douglas was disclosed this led to the Academy repealing, in January 1959, its earlier decision against honouring blacklistees.[35]

The problems Young encountered with getting credit for the script of *The Train* (1964) are eloquent. A *Hollywood Reporter* article (14 November 1994) discussed the affair and started out by mentioning that the Writers Guild had arbitrated in favour of two screenwriters. The journalist then referred to director John Frankenheimer's comments on the laserdisc of *The Train*. For him the writers were Young and Howard Dimsdale (another blacklistee): Frankenheimer hadn't used a single word of the script by those officially credited. Frankenheimer considered the arbitration a simple mistake and the author of the article cited wrote that blacklisting 'apparently played no part in the credits determination, although no one was sure at the time'. Reference was also made in the article to writer Walter Bernstein who worked on the film for six weeks with director Arthur Penn, who was then sacked by star Burt Lancaster and replaced by Frankenheimer (with whom Lancaster had already worked). Bernstein left with Penn and Young and Dimsdale were brought in. Young was understandably unhappy with the decision of the arbitration.[36]

In 1993, the year before Frankenheimer's comments, Young's widow had written to the Academy as a voting member, Actors' Branch, stating that 'the Academy can help rectify the grave injustice done to him by restoring his name, Nedrick Young, to his 1958 award [for *The Defiant Ones*]'.[37] The fact that everyone knew that Douglas was Young did not therefore automatically lead to his name being restored to the film's credits and to his being given official recognition as writer. The situation was identical for all those who, because of the blacklist, had been forced to use pseudonyms. What was involved was not only a question of authors' legal and moral rights, but also that of possible royalties. This helps explain the attempt by Paul Jarrico to force Howard Hughes to give him screen credit for *The Las Vegas Story* (see Chapter 5). Indeed, Jarrico became the symbol of the struggle to obtain official recognition from the Academy and it was he who, in 1996, contacted Mrs MacRae to inform her that the Writers Guild of America, West (WGA, the current name of the SWG) was in the process of restoring Young's name to his award-winning screenplays, *The Defiant Ones* and *Inherit the Wind* (Stanley Kramer, 1960).[38] Information published that same year showed that Trumbo had been credited for *Gun Crazy*, *The Prowler* and *The Brave One*, Maltz for *Broken Arrow* and *The Robe* (1953), Butler for *Robinson Crusoe*, Polonsky for *Odds against Tomorrow* (1959), Wilson and Foreman for *River Kwai*, Barzman for *El Cid* (1961), Gordon for *The Day of the Triffids* (1963), and so on (Neale and Stanfield 2005: 83). All but Gordon and Polonsky were dead and Jarrico was killed in a car accident in 1997, at the height of his triumph in getting credits where credits are due. For the survivors and the families of the deceased, a battle had been won and the autobiographies of Norma Barzman, Walter Bernstein, Betsy Blair, Bernard Gordon and Jean Rouverol are strikingly sober. Yet Norma Barzman could write: 'Despite Ben's brilliant film career in Europe, he was bitter' (Barzman 2003: 443). And Bernard Gordon, who knew how to be witty, could on occasion show similar bitterness: 'The action by the guild [restoring some of his writing credits] comes about 40 years too late to help my Hollywood career. I sure am angry at the way I was treated by all the major studios. They blacklisted me, and I couldn't get any work in this damn town.'[39]

Perhaps Ben Barzman summed it up best: 'Living through the blacklist was like having gone to war – it was a rich and rewarding experience, but I wouldn't want to go through it again.' Unfortunately, Trumbo's triumph in 1960 did not put an end to the war, as the case of Waldo Salt painfully shows. In

November 1963 he signed in the presence of his lawyer an affidavit where he wrote: 'I am not a Communist in fact or ideological sympathy' and made clear his 'anti-Communist convictions, arrived at after long and painful consideration'.[40] His reasons were Soviet anti-Semitism and aggression, but he made no mention of US aggression against Cuba in 1961. The desire was to placate HUAC: 'I am troubled by the fact that I did not answer the questions [when appearing before the Committee]'. But HUAC was still in the business of the self-degradation of witnesses, as the letter of 17 January 1964 from Edwin E. Willis, Chairman of HUAC, shows:

> In spite of the passage of time much knowledge you possess is still unknown to the Congress or agencies of the Executive Branch of the Government. You, therefore, can still assist in shedding light on many areas of darkness. For the above reasons your affidavit cannot be accepted as a document which clears the record of present and past Communist affiliations. With regrets the document is returned forthwith.[41]

Salt's confession, destined to enable him to obtain a contract with NBC television, was supererogatory: the networks were no longer bothered by the opinion of HUAC. I have not been able to ascertain whether Salt succeeded in placating HUAC, but he was writing for both TV and the cinema by 1964 and for a decade was a leading writer for mainstream Hollywood, earning Oscars for the scripts of *Midnight Cowboy* (1969) and *Coming Home* (1978) and an Oscar nomination for the script of *Serpico* (1973). He died in 1987.

Herbert Biberman returned to Hollywood to write and direct *Slaves* in 1969 but died shortly after. Ring Lardner, Jr was unable to transform the international success of *M.A.S.H.* into a new career. Albert Maltz had a brief career from the late 1960s to the early 1970s but only *Two Mules for Sister Sara* was not written under a pseudonym. Abraham Polonsky returned to Hollywood to write *Madigan* (1968) and write and direct *Tell Them Willie Boy Is Here* (1969), but ill health prevented him from continuing. Trumbo wrote that Maltz, Michael Wilson and himself were better writers after the blacklist than before: 'This is because they deliberately set out to build second careers in the black market' (Trumbo 1970: 483). There is an element of truth in this: much of Trumbo's work after 1947 is more convincing than his work before. And Trumbo was right to insist on the ability to adapt. Yet the situation was more complex. Bernard Gordon exercised the crafts of reader and writer from 1940 and showed a chameleon-like adaptability, but his parallel career was over by 1972. This was hardly due to a lack of talent. Walter Bernstein, on the other hand, managed to work in both film and TV from the early 1960s to the end of the 1990s, sometimes with director Martin Ritt who was lucky: his Hollywood career started up again in 1957 and he worked constantly until his death in 1990. I have already referred to their famous collaboration *The Front*, much of whose success is due to the presence of Woody Allen, but of all the actors who had been blacklisted, only Zero Mostel had succeeded in starting up his career again. Others who succeeded, such as Jeff Corey and Lionel Stander were, alas, also exceptions to the rule.

We shall conclude our investigation with a brief discussion of what the victory of the witch hunters was to mean.

NOTES

1. Written by Henry Blankfort, blacklisted like Endfield. Blankfort was the brother of friendly witness Michael Blankfort.
2. This information is worth recording, since *Mission to Moscow* was singled out by HUAC in 1947 because Roosevelt is supposed to have requested it be made (see Chapter 4). Writing pro-American war films and/or having a distinguished war record cut no ice with HUAC in 1951.
3. Actors' Lab Theater Papers, Box 3, folder 6, UCLA.
4. Statement by Roman Bohnen, Actors' Lab Theater Papers, Box 3, folder 3.
5. Actors' Lab Theater Papers, Box 3, folder 19. Support for the Actors' Lab came from 'Free Theater' spokespersons, including actor John Randolph, a future black-listee who was to participate in the demonstrations against Kazan's special Oscar in 1999.
6. Los Angeles *Mirror*, 19 March 1952. Civil Rights Congress Papers, Box 2, folders 26, 27.
7. Starring José Ferrer. See his testimony, Chapter 5.
8. For the intimate relation between politics and aesthetics in the work of Welles, see Denning 1998: 362–402.
9. The Freedom of Information Act has brought to light how the FBI made people like Chaplin objects of surveillance. Thus a memo dated 11 July 1947 mentions Chaplin, Garfield and Edward G. Robinson in the same sentence as Biberman and Lawson of the Ten as Communists or Communist sympathizers. See http://foia.gov/foiaindex/compic.htm Part 04 contains the information on Chaplin.
10. Passports were refused the blacklistees until a Supreme Court decision of 1958 ruled that this was unconstitutional.
11. Rossen was arguably the finest and most sophisticated writer on the Left. He wrote the feminist and pro-working class *Marked Women* (1937), the anti-Fascist *Sea Wolf* (1941) and the pro-labor and anti-business *The Strange Love of Martha Ivers* (1946). In January 1944 he published an article extolling the anti-Fascist resistance of Spain, France and Russia, argued that the resistance to Nazism had given rise to a new sort of hero and stated that it was necessary to put this hero on the screen (*New Masses* file, SCL). He directed in 1947 Polonsky's script *Body and Soul* (see Chapter 5, note 34).
12. Father of director Jonathan Kaplan.

13. *The New York Times*, 17 June 1951. Michael Wilson Papers, Box 46, folder 3.
14. Letter from Herbert Biberman, Michael Wilson Papers, Box 45, folder 12.
15. Michael Wilson Papers, Box 46, folder 3.
16. In a letter to Jarrico dated 17 May 1953. Michael Wilson Papers, Box 45, folder 12.
17. Paul Henreid Papers, Box 22, MHL.
18. Losey made the first of these films using a pseudonym but was able to use his own name as from 1956.
19. See Chapter 3. Wayne adopted the same attitude towards writer Carl Foreman. Both he and Brewer succeeded.
20. Alexander Knox Papers, Box 2, 'Blacklist' folder, MHL.
21. Letter to Knox, Alexander Knox Papers, Box 2, 'Blacklist' folder.
22. Carey McWilliams Papers, Box 13.
23. Hedda Hopper Papers, folder 538, MHL.
24. As had Chaplin and Edward G. Robinson, Huston and Fritz Lang. Briefly 'graylisted' in 1952, Lang's career did not suffer, despite being Jewish and having been active in Hollywood as an anti-Fascist since arriving in 1936 as a refugee from Nazi Germany. Writer John Wexley was less lucky: never a Communist, he failed to find work in the 1950s because of his collaboration with Scott and Dmytryk (Barzman 2003: 427). He had also worked with Brecht and Lang on *Hangmen Also Die* (1943). That was more than enough.
25. William Wyler Papers, file 694.
26. William Wyler Papers, file 688.
27. One exception was Jeff Corey who set up an actors' school in Hollywood. Among those who attended his classes were future stars James Coburn and Jack Nicholson. Gary Cooper also sat in on some classes, impressed by Corey's work on a film they did together (McGilligan and Buhle 1997: 178–9, 191). Once again, we see the supposedly reactionary Cooper being politically incorrect for the time. The stances taken on certain issues by conservatives such as Cooper and Senator Taft (see Chapter 5) help explain why Abraham Polonsky, discussing Cold War hysteria, witch hunts and blacklisting in all walks of life, could say that 'the worst were the liberals'.
28. Butler worked twice with Luis Bunuel in Mexico: *Robinson Crusoe* (1953) and *The Young One 1960)*. For life in Mexico on the blacklist, see Rouverol 2000 and Anhalt 2001.
29. For full details, see Bernstein 1996, Buhle and Wagner 2003a. Ritt directed Bernstein's script of *The Front*. A number of blacklisted actors appear in the film.
30. A list of who wrote what for TV, along with a bibliography and web sites to consult, is to be found in Neale and Stanfield 2005: 83–103.
31. Joseph H. Lewis, who directed *Gun Crazy*, was a friend of the Left but suffered no harassment. The same remark goes for Edgar G. Ulmer who directed *Ruthless* (1948) from a script by Gordon Kahn, soon to be blacklisted. Alvah Bessie of the Ten contributed anonymously to the script. In 1955 Ulmer directed *The Naked Dawn* from a script by blacklistee Julian Zimet.

32. *Friendly Persuasion* won the Palme d'Or at Cannes in 1957. The French (as Norma Barzman's autobiography makes abundantly clear) were sympathetic to the black-listees and hostile to blacklisting. So it was Wilson, and not Wyler (who refused to support him), whom Cannes was really honouring.
33. The progressive Douglas had already helped Alexander Knox and Preminger had always been opposed to the blacklist. Ingo, his younger brother, was an agent who had helped both Lardner and Trumbo by arranging for them to write using fronts. He also produced *M.A.S.H.*, written by Lardner. He died in 2005, aged 94, and, like his brother, deserves to be remembered.
34. Young played the journalist in *Gun Crazy*.
35. When Young died in 1968, aged 54, *The New York Times* published an obituary outlining his career. My thanks to Elizabeth MacRae, Young's widow, for making certain of his papers available to me.
36. My thanks to Elizabeth MacRae for sending me a copy of *The Hollywood Reporter* cutting.
37. Letter to the President of the Academy, 7 March 1993, Nedrick Young Papers.
38. Letter from Elizabeth MacRae to the Director of the Credits Department, Writers Guild of America West, 2 September 1996.
39. In an interview given to *The New York Times* in 1997 and quoted in the entry on Gordon, www.imdb.com. In private correspondence with me (20 October 2004), he did not mince his words when discussing those who had led the witch hunts in Hollywood, particularly the MPA. Sadly, he died in May 2007.
40. Waldo Salt Papers, Box 77, folder 21, UCLA.
41. Waldo Salt Papers, Box 77, folder 21.

Conclusion

In 1972 there appeared a film which failed lamentably at the box office in the US precisely because it told the truth about the past and the present of that country: Billy Wilder's *Avanti!* I can think of no film that sums up so cogently the climate of the early 1970s and so brilliantly links that climate to the period under discussion in this book. In the film Jack Lemmon rushes to Italy to recover the body of his father, killed in an accident. He discovers that a young woman (Juliet Mills) is also there to recover the body of her dead mother who turns out not only to have died in the same accident but to have had over the years a secret affair with Lemmon Sr. The film's first point of interest lies in the fact that mother and daughter are proletarian, whereas Lemmon comes from a very wealthy family of Republican businessmen. So important is the family that the State Department sends a government representative to help Lemmon expedite matters. One can't trust Europeans.

The State Department official is played by the character actor Edward Andrews who excelled in pompous or unpleasant characters. Here he is both. Frustrated by the fact that everything closes down from midday to the middle of the afternoon (because of the crippling summer heat), he says to his taxi-driver: 'It wasn't like this in the old days.' The man looks at him in awe and reverence and replies: 'You knew Mussolini?' When their paths cross later he gives Andrews the Fascist salute. This, however, is just one interpretation of 'the old days', which we are also entitled to interpret as an example of the nostalgia of big business and the Republican Party for a past where workers had few rights and certainly not the right to have a prolonged lunchtime pause. So the film's insistence on class spreads out to touch on other issues.

Also of the greatest interest is the delightfully neat way in which *Avanti!* suggests that Andrews' opposition to basic democratic principles is not limited to Italy, particularly in the light of an encounter between him and the manager of the hotel where Lemmon and Mills are staying. In an attempt to flatter the official's ego and prevent him from finding out the truth about the clandestine affair, the manager tells him: 'You are the second famous American we have welcomed. Benjamin Franklin stayed here.' Visibly unimpressed, the official replies: 'Benjamin Franklin? Oh yes, no doubt a very good man in his time, but now I doubt he'd get through the security check.' When one remembers that Franklin was one of the founding fathers of America and the Bill of Rights, this remark takes on a somewhat sinister hue. For we are in 1972, Watergate is just round the corner and the President of the United States is the same Richard Nixon whom we have met throughout this book.

Nixon's resignation in 1974 was a suitably ignominious ending to the most disreputable career in post-war American politics, one of Red-baiting, witch hunting, political chicanery and war crimes in Vietnam and Cambodia. He finally fell foul of the public because of a dirty little piece of wire-tapping à la J. Edgar Hoover, brought on by a paranoid belief in conspiracies of which he was meant to be the victim. A fitting ending to a politician who had gained power by claiming to find Red conspiracies everywhere. This is, however, a cautionary tale. Just as we have seen how the anti-Communism of liberals led to the suppression of the very laws concerning freedom of speech and thought they claimed to champion, so the refusal of liberals to oppose witch hunting led straight to the Vietnam war and opened the doors of the White House to Nixon (Hellman 1976: 155).[1] Ultimately, this was due to the attitude of liberals to McCarthy. If he had been a gentleman from the East rather than a yahoo from the mid-West, they would have loved him. Methods, not values, separated them. Nixon was less crude than McCarthy:

> Nixon's subversive activities were not merely the excesses of an out-of-control politician. They had been nurtured in a system that, from the 1940s on, had justified the illegitimate use of state power against the supposed enemies of the state. Nixon simply identified himself with the state and carried on business as usual. Watergate was, thus, the logical result of the tendency to insulate affairs of state from the Constitution. During the McCarthy era, that tendency nullified the First Amendment; during Watergate it overrode much of the rest of the Constitution. (Schrecker 1998: 414)

The perfidy – to put it mildly – of Nixon must not become the tree that hides the forest. For the excesses of McCarthy have become, over the decades since the Senator's death in 1957, a sort of smokescreen that has conveniently hidden from public view the extent of the disaster that hit America after the war. Essential reforms in the fields of housing and, especially, healthcare bit the dust, their advocates tarred with the brush of Communism, 'thus ensuring that the United States would be the only major industrial nation that did not provide medical insurance to all its citizens' (Schrecker 1998: 384). In the documentary on Los Angeles, *Shotgun Freeway: Drives through Lost L.A.* (1995), Frank Wilkinson (in charge of Los Angeles city housing after the war) tells of how he was smeared on television by McCarthy sidekick Gordon Scherer and driven from office. The film includes a brief extract of Scherer's diatribe against Wilkinson; it is not a pretty sight.[2]

Nor is America since 9/11. In 2005 the USA Patriot Act, voted in the wake of the terrorist attacks of September 2001, was renewed; among other powers it upholds the right of the FBI to order both public and private institutions to hand over their records on designated individuals, without the targeted people being informed of this government intrusion into their personal affairs. Receiving the Laurel Award in 1976 from his SWG peers, blacklistee Michael Wilson evoked blacklisting and made the following unsettlingly prophetic remarks:

> unless you remember this dark epoch and understand it, you may be doomed to replay it, not with the same cast of characters, of course, or on the same issues. But I foresee a day coming in your lifetime, if not in mine, when a new crisis of belief will grip this republic; when diversity of opinion will be labeled disloyalty; when chilling decisions affecting our culture will be made in the board rooms of conglomerates and networks; when the powers of the programmers and the censors will be expanded; and when extraordinary pressures will be put on writers in the mass media to conform to administration policy on the key issues of the time, whatever they may be. (McBride 2002: 29)

During the Nixon years (1968–74) labour leaders happily rubbed shoulders with him, hoping that support for the war in Vietnam would lead to wage increases, but decided he was too 'dovish' and rallied round those conservative Democrats who 'stood against defense cuts and the ongoing retreat from Vietnam' (Buhle 1999: 210). Thirty years later Americans who denounce the invasion of Iraq are accused of aiding and supporting Bin Laden. The mass murders committed by Stalin and his henchmen have enabled the current occupant of the White House to drag from mothballs the old equation 'Communism = Nazism' and to herald in new forms of McCarthyism, as one writer foretold several years ago (Anhalt 2001: 2004).[3] In January 2007 the new Chief of New York's Metropolitan Transit Authority was awarded a pay rise of $42,000, equivalent to the annual salary of many of the transit workers. During a strike a year earlier by said transit workers, the press denounced them as 'thugs' and 'rats' – sixty years ago they would have been called 'hoodlums' and 'commie rats' – and the *Daily News* went so far as to call for the union president to be thrown off a train or over the side of Brooklyn Bridge.[4] This hysteria and verbal violence recall certain excesses to which we have referred throughout this book and illustrate that the hatred and prejudice of which so many were victims, in Hollywood and elsewhere, can return at a time of crisis. We live, after all, in an age where the most powerful person in the world can justify torture, after having lied about 'weapons of mass destruction' in order to invade Iraq and thus precipitate a new crisis, all with the blessing of the supposedly liberal press.

In 1979, several years after American troops had ignominiously left Vietnam, attempts were made to make actress Jane Fonda the object of a witch hunt because of her support for the struggle of North Vietnam. To their ever-lasting credit large numbers of Hollywood personalities took out a full-page advertisement in *Variety* to denounce what they rightly saw as the return of McCarthyism. Eighteen months later Ronald Reagan was safely installed in the White House. In 1984 he nominated fellow witch hunter Roy Brewer to the 'Federal Impasses Panel for adjudication of labor disputes with the government' (Wills 2000: 307). The above quote on Nixon applies equally to Reagan and the late Michael Wilson's warning is peculiarly appropriate in the Bush era. I am reminded of a remark that is quoted almost as frequently as that of Ginger Rogers' mother on *Tender Comrade*. Billy Wilder, it is claimed, said of the Ten: 'Only two were talented; the others were just unfriendly.' However, nobody has ever given the source for this remark. When and where did Wilder make it? Was it made after the condemnation of the Ten? After the collapse of the Committee for the First Amendment? In the years following the refusal of Wilder and Huston to support the 'loyalty oath' called for by the SDG? Was Wilder, like Huston, under pressure to conform? In short: who was Wilder's interlocutor and why is there no source for this remark? Knowing his penchant for humour both caustic and in bad taste, the remark, assuming he made it, could be interpreted as an ironic reference to the pernicious climate created by the Waldorf Astoria Statement of November 1947.

Actor Charlton Heston, a noted Reagan supporter, resorted to this quote in order to defend Kazan and his Oscar and denounce the director's detractors. We are surely entitled to be on our guard. In particular, now that so few victims of the blacklists are still alive, we owe it to them and to those who have passed away never to forget the lessons learned.[5]

NOTES

1. Hellman includes in her book a photo taken in 1948 of members of HUAC, including Nixon, Thomas and Stripling. Dressed like businessmen, they bear an

uncanny resemblance to the gangsters and hoodlums to whom they and Hollywood compared Communists. Kanfer also reproduces this photo.

2. Wilkinson had refused to testify before HUAC. On Wilkinson, see Caute 1978. The film also contains interviews with radical historian Mike Davis.

3. I have already drawn attention to the close links between the Republican Party and those who collaborated with Nazism during the war, amply and chillingly documented (Bellant 1991). Post-war politicians in America were also happy to thwart attempts to bring Nazi war criminals to justice: they were too valuable in the great fight against Communism. The most notorious example is Klaus Barbie, Nazi torturer employed by the US to maintain Fascist regimes in Latin America (see the documentary *My Enemy's Enemy*, 2007). We might note that Dr Strangelove, advisor to the American President in Kubrick's film, is a former Nazi.

4. See www.wsws.org for article dated 9 January 2007.

5. Recently that admirable and underrated film *The Majestic* (2001), starring Jim Carrey, attempted to remind audiences of the events of the period and to convey some idea of the attacks on freedom of thought and speech. The film not only includes footage from the Hearings of 1947, notably the appearance of John Howard Lawson, but sets most of the action in a small California town called – Lawson. The fact that the local newspaper is called *The Lawson Beacon* makes it abundantly clear that writer Michael Sloane wished to rehabilitate a man who was 'much maligned' (Norma Barzman in a private conversation with me, August 2002).

Archival Sources

American Film Institute, Los Angeles (AFI)
 Oral Histories (OH): Howard Koch, Abraham Polonsky, Vincent Sherman, Donald
  Ogden Stewart, James G. Stewart
 AFI Seminar: Leonard Spigelgass

**Academy of Motion Picture Arts and Sciences, Margaret Herrick Library,
Beverly Hills (MHL)**
 The Michael Blankfort Papers
 The Howard Estabrook Papers
 The Paul Henreid Papers
 The Hedda Hopper Papers
 The John Huston Papers
 The Alexander Knox Papers
 The Ring Lardner, Jr. Papers
 The Roger MacDonald Papers
 The William Wyler Papers
 The War Films Hearings
 The Motion Picture Industry Council (MPIC) Papers
 The American Legion folder
 Files on: Willie Bioff, Rupert Hughes, James Kevin McGuinness, Ronald Reagan,
  the Motion Picture Alliance for the Preservation of American Ideals (MPA)
 The Production Code Association (PCA) files

Southern California Library for Social Studies and Research, Los Angeles (SCL)
 The Civil Rights Congress Papers
 The Leo Gallagher Papers
 New Masses

University of California at Los Angeles (UCLA)
Special Collections, Young Reading Library:
    The Actors' Lab Papers
    The American Civil Liberties Union (ACLU) Papers
    The Guy Endore Papers
    The Carey McWilliams Papers
    Oral Histories (OH): Edward Biberman, Roy Brewer, John Bright, Jack Dales, Mary Davenport, Edmond DePatie, Father George Dunne, Guy Endore, William Fadiman, Donald Gordon, Michael Gordon, Dorothy Healey, Paul Jarrico, Robert Kenny, Emmet Lavery, Alfred Lewis Levitt, Helen Slote Levitt, Albert Maltz, Ben Margolis, Carey McWilliams, Edmund North, Herb Sorrell, Jack Tenney, Michael Wilson, Zelma Wilson
    Articles by Martin Dies
    Pamphlets on HUAC and 'hate groups'
    Red Channels
Special Collections, Arts Library:
    The Emmet Lavery Papers
    The Waldo Salt Papers
    The Michael Wilson Papers

University of Southern California, Los Angeles (USC)
    The Edward G. Robinson Papers
    The Jack L. Warner Papers

Bibliography

Adler, Les K. (1974), 'The Politics of Culture. Hollywood and the Cold War', in Griffith and Theoharis (eds), *The Specter*, pp. 240–60.

Andersen, Thom and Noël Burch (1994), *Les Communistes de Hollywood. Autre chose que des martyrs*, Paris: Presses de la Sorbonne Nouvelle.

Anhalt, Diana (2001), *A Gathering of Fugitives. American Political Expatriates in Mexico, 1948–1965*, Santa Maria, CA: Archer Books.

Aronson, James (1970), *The Press and the Cold War*, New York: The Bobbs-Merrill Company.

Barson, Michael (1992), *'Better Dead Than Red!' A Nostalgic Look at the Golden Years of Russiaphobia, Red-baiting, and Other Commie Matters*, London: Plexus.

Barzman, Norma (2003), *The Red and the Blacklist. The Intimate Memoir of a Hollywood Expatriate*, New York: Thunder's Mouth Press.

Belfrage, Cedric (1989 [1973]), *The American Inquisition 1945–1960. A Profile on the 'McCarthy Era'*, New York: Thunder's Mouth Press.

Bellant, Russ (1991), *Old Nazis, the New Right, and the Republican Party*, Boston, MA: South End Press.

Bennett, David H. (1995), *The Party of Fear. The American Far Right from Nativism to the Militia Movement*, New York: Vintage Books.

Bentley, Eric (ed.) (2002 [1971]), *Thirty Years of Treason. Excerpts from Hearings before the House Committee on Un-American Activities, 1938–1968*, New York: Thunder's Mouth Press.

Bergman, Andrew (1992 [1971]), *We're in the Money. Depression America and Its Films*, Chicago, IL: Ivan R. Dee.

Bernstein, Barton J. (ed.) (1974), *Politics and Policies in the Truman Administration*, New York: New Viewpoints.

Bernstein, Walter (1996), *Inside Out. A Memoir of the Blacklist*, New York: Alfred A. Knopf.

Bessie, Alvah (1967), *Inquisition in Eden*, Berlin (DDR): Seven Seas Books.

Billingsley, Kenneth Lloyd (1998), *Hollywood Party. How Communism Seduced the Film Community in the 1930s and the 1940s*, Rocklin, CA: Prima Publishing.

Biskind, Peter (1983), *Seeing Is Believing. How Hollywood Taught Us to Stop Worrying and Love the Fifties*, New York: Pantheon Books.

Blair, Betsy (2003), *The Memory of All That. Love and Politics in New York, Hollywood and Paris*, New York: Alfred A. Knopf.

Braden, Ann (1963), *Bulwark of Segregation*, anti-HUAC pamphlet published by the Emergency Civil Liberties Committee.

Bright, John (2002), *Worms in the Winecup. A Memoir*, Lanham, MD: The Scarecrow Press.

Buhle, Paul (1995), 'The Hollywood Left: Aesthetics and Politics', in *New Left Review*, no. 212, July/August, pp. 101–19.

Buhle, Paul (1999), *Taking Care of Business. Samuel Gompers, George Meany, Lane Kirkland and the Tragedy of American Labor*, New York: Monthly Review Press.

Buhle, Paul and Dave Wagner (2001), *A Very Dangerous Citizen. Abraham Lincoln Polonsky and the Hollywood Left*, Berkeley, CA, Los Angeles and London: University of California Press.

Buhle, Paul and Dave Wagner (2002), *Radical Hollywood. The Untold Story behind American's Favorite Movies*, New York: The New Press.

Buhle, Paul and Dave Wagner (2003a), *Hide in Plain Sight. The Hollywood Blacklistees in Film and Television, 1950–2002*, New York: Palgrave Macmillan.

Buhle, Paul and Dave Wagner (2003b), *Blacklisted. The Film Lover's Guide to the Hollywood Blacklist*, New York: Palgrave Macmillan.

Byman, Jeremy (2004), *Showdown at High Noon. Witch-hunts, Critics and the End of the Western*, Lanham, MD: The Scarecrow Press.

Caute, David (1978), *The Great Fear. The Anti-Communist Purge under Truman and Eisenhower*, New York: Simon & Schuster.

Ceplair, Larry (1989), 'A Communist Labor Organizer in Hollywood: Jeff Kibre Challenges the IATSE, 1937–1939', in *The Velvet Light Trap*, no. 23, Spring, pp. 64–74.

Ceplair, Larry (2007), *The Marxist and the Movies. A Biography of Paul Jarrico*, Lexington, KY: University of Kentucky Press.

Ceplair, Larry and Steven Englund (1980), *The Inquisition in Hollywood. Politics in the Film Community, 1930–1960*, Garden City, NY: Anchor Press/Doubleday.

Cogley, John (1956), *Report on Blacklisting I: Movies; II: Radio – Television*, n p: The Fund for the Republic.

Cole, Lester (1981), *Hollywood Red. An Autobiography*, Palo Alto, CA: Ramparts Press.

Communist Infiltration of the Hollywood Motion Picture Industry, United States House of Representatives, Committee on Un-American Activities.

Film Culture (1970), special issue on blacklisting, no. 50–1, Fall and Winter.

Corber, Robert J. (1993), *In the Name of National Security. Hitchcock, Homophobia, and the Political Construction of Gender in Postwar America*, Durham, NC, and London: Duke University Press.

Davis, John (1977), 'Notes on Warner Brothers Foreign Policy, 1918–1948', *The Velvet Light Trap*, no. 17, pp. 19–31.

Davis, Mike (1986), *Prisoners of the American Dream. Politics and Economy in the History of the U.S. Working Class*, London: Verso.

Denning, Michael (1998), *The Cultural Front. The Laboring of American Culture in the Twentieth Century*, London and New York: Verso Books.

Dick, Bernard F. (1982), *Hellman in Hollywood*, London and Toronto: Associated University Presses.

Dick, Bernard F. (1989), *Radical Innocence. A Critical Study of the Hollywood Ten*, Lexington, KY: University of Kentucky Press.

Dixon, Wheeler Winston (2006), *American Cinema of the 1940s. Themes and Variations*, New Brunswick, NJ, and London: Rutgers University Press.

Doherty, Thomas (1988), 'Hollywood Agit-Prop: the Anti-Communist Cycle, 1948–1954', in *Journal of Film and Video*, vol. 40, no. 4, Fall, pp. 15–27.

Donner, Frank (1961), *The Un-Americans*, New York: Ballantine Books.

Dunne, Philip (1992 [1980]), *Take Two. A Life in Movies and Politics*, New York: Limelight Editions.

Engelhardt, Tom (1995), *The End of Victory Culture. Cold War America and the Disillusioning of a Generation*, Amherst, MA: University of Massachusetts Press.

Fariello, Griffin (1995), *Red Scare. Memories of the American Inquisition*, New York: Avon Books.

Fraser, Steve and Gary Gerstle (1989), *The Rise and Fall of the New Deal Order*, Princeton, NJ: Princeton University Press.

Freeland, Richard M. (1970), *The Truman Doctrine and the Origins of McCarthyism. Foreign Policy, Domestic Politics, and Internal Security, 1946–1948*, New York: Schocken Books.

Fried, Richard M. (1990), *Nightmare in Red. The McCarthy Era in Perspective*, New York and Oxford: Oxford University Press.

Friedrich, Otto (1987), *City of Nets. A Portrait of Hollywood in the 1940s*, London: Headline Book Publishing.

Gabler, Neal (1988), *An Empire of Their Own. How the Jews Invented Hollywood*, New York: Crown Publishers.

Goldstein, Robert (1978), *Political Repression in Modern America. 1870 to the Present*, Cambridge and New York: Schenkman Publishing; Two Continents Publishing Group.

Gordon, Bernard (1999), *Hollywood Exile, or How I Learned to Love the Blacklist*, Austin, TX: University of Texas Press.

Gordon, Bernard (2004), *The Gordon File. A Screenwriter Recalls Twenty Years of FBI Surveillance*, Austin, TX: University of Texas Press.

Gottlieb, Robert and Irene Wolt (1977), *Thinking Big. The Story of the 'Los Angeles Times', Its Publishers and Their Influence on Southern California*, New York: G. P. Putnam's Sons.

Griffith, Robert and Athan Theoharis (eds) (1974), *The Specter. Original Essays on the Cold War and the Origins of McCarthyism*, New York: New Viewpoints.

Hanson, Peter (2001), *Dalton Trumbo, Hollywood Rebel. A Critical Survey and Filmography*, Jefferson, NC: McFarland and Company.

Haynes, John E. (1996), *Red Scare or Red Menace? American Communism and Anticommunism in the Cold War Era*, Chicago, IL: Ivan R. Dee.

Hellman, Lillian (1976), *Scoundrel Time*, Boston, MA: Little, Brown and Company.

Hendershot, Cyndy (2001), *I Was a Cold War Monster. Horror Films, Eroticism and the Cold War Imagination*, Bowling Green, OH: Bowling Green State University Popular Press.

Horne, Gerald (2001), *Class Struggles in Hollywood, 1930–1950. Moguls, Mobsters, Stars, Reds, and Trade Unionists*, Austin, TX: University of Texas Press.

Horne, Gerald (2006), *The Final Victim of the Blacklist. John Howard Lawson, Dean of the Hollywood Ten*, Berkeley, CA, and Los Angeles: University of California Press.

Humphries, Reynold (2001a), 'Investigators, Undercover Men and the F.B.I.: From Gangsterism to Communism and Back Again', in Pierre Lagayette and Dominique Sipière (eds), *Le Crime organisé à la ville et à l'écran (Etats-Unis, 1929–1951)*, Paris: Ellipses, pp. 212–24.

Humphries, Reynold (2001b), 'When Crime Does Pay: Abraham Polonsky's *Force of Evil* (1948)', *Q/W/E/R/T/Y*, University of Pau (France), No. 11, October, pp. 205–10.

Humphries, Reynold (2002a), *The American Horror Film. An Introduction*, Edinburgh: Edinburgh University Press.

Humphries, Reynold (2002b), 'Jules Dassin: Crime and the City', in John Dean and Jacques Pothier (eds), *Le Crime organisé de la Prohibition à la Guerre Froide*, Nantes: Editions du Temps, pp. 145–59.

Humphries, Reynold (2003), 'Crime and Punishment USA: Mobsters, Hollywood and the Cold War Imperative', in Françoise Clary and John Dean (eds), *Crime & Hollywood Inc.: Le Crime organisé, à la ville et à l'écran*, Rouen: Presses Universitaires de Rouen, pp. 133–48.

Humphries, Reynold (2004), 'The Politics of Crime and the Crime of Politics: Post-war *Noir*, the Liberal Consensus and the Hollywood Left', in Alain Silver and James Ursini (eds), *Film Noir Reader 4*, Pompton Plains, NJ: Limelight Editions, pp. 227–45.

Humphries, Reynold (2006), ' "Documenting" Communist Subversion: The Case of *I Was a Communist for the F.B.I.* (1951)', in Gary D. Rhodes and John Parris Springer (eds), *Docufictions. Essays on the Intersection of Documentary and Fictional Filmmaking*, Jefferson, NC: McFarland and Company, pp. 102–23.

Humphries, Reynold (2007a), 'A Gangster Unlike the Others: Gordon Wiles' *The Gangster*', in *Gangster Film Reader*, Alain Silver and James Ursini (eds), Pompton Plains, NJ: Limelight Editions, pp. 119–32.

Humphries, Reynold (2007b), '*Spartacus*: The Specter of Politics and the Politics of Spectacle', in Gary D. Rhodes (ed.), *Stanley Kubrick: Essays on His Films and Legacy*, Jefferson, NC: McFarland and Company.

Humphries, Reynold (2008), 'Ethical Commitment and Political Dissidence: Huston, HUAC, Hollywood and *Key Largo*', in Anthony Tracy (ed.), *New Reflections. The Cinema of John Huston*, Jefferson, NC: McFarland and Company.

Jancovich, Mark (1996), *Rational Fears. American Horror in the 1950s*, Manchester and New York: Manchester University Press.

Jerome, Fred (2003), *The Einstein File. J. Edgar Hoover's Secret War against the World's Most Famous Scientist*, New York: St Martin's Press.

Jezer, Marty (1982), *The Dark Ages. Life in the United States 1945–1960*, Boston, MA: South End Press.

Johnson, David K. (2004), *The Lavender Scare. The Cold War Persecution of Gays and Lesbians in the Federal Government*, Chicago, IL, and London: University of Chicago Press.

Jones, Dorothy B. (1956), 'Communism and the Movies: A Study of Film Content', in Cogley, *Report on Blacklisting. I. Movies*, pp. 196–304.

Kaenel, André (1995), *Anti-Communism and McCarthyism in the United States (1945–1954). Essays on the Politics and Culture of the Cold War*, Paris: Editions Messene.

Kahn, Gordon (1948), *Hollywood on Trial. The Story of the Ten Who Were Indicted*, New York: Boni & Gaer.

Kanfer, Stefan (1973), *A Journal of the Plague Years*, New York: Atheneum.

Kaplan, Judy and Lynn Shapiro (eds), *Red Diapers. Growing up in the Communist Left*, Urbana, IL, and Chicago: University of Illinois Press.

Koppes, Clayton R. and Gregory D. Black (1987), *Hollywood Goes to War. How Politics, Profits and Propaganda Shaped World War II Movies*, Berkeley, CA, and Los Angeles: University of California Press.

Kovel, Joel (1997), *Red Hunting in the Promised Land. Anticommunism and the Making of America*, London and Washington, DC: Cassell.

Krutnik, Frank, Steve Neale, Brian Neve and Peter Stanfield (eds) (2008), *'Un-American' Hollywood: Politics and Film in the Blacklist Era*, New Brunswick, NJ: Rutgers University Press.

Lardner, Ring, Jr (2000), *I'd Hate Myself in the Morning. A Memoir*. New York: Thunder's Mouth Press.

Latham, Earl (1966), *The Communist Conspiracy in Washington. From the New Deal to McCarthy*, Cambridge, MA: Harvard University Press.

Leab, Daniel J. (2000), *I Was a Communist for the FBI. The Unhappy Life and Times of Matt Cvetic*, University Park, PA: Pennsylvania State University Press.

Leffler, Melvyn P. (1991), 'American's National Security Policy: A Source of Cold War Tensions', in Paterson and McMahon (eds), *The Origins of the Cold War*, pp. 73–92.

Lipsitz, George (1994), *Rainbow at Midnight. Labor and Culture in the 1940s*, Urbana, IL, and Chicago: University of Illinois Press.

Lora, Ronald (1974), 'A View from the Right. Conservative Intellectuals, the Cold War, and McCarthy', in Griffith and Theoharis (eds), *The Specter*, pp. 40–70.

Lyons, Arthur (2000), *Death on the Cheap. The Lost B Movies of Film Noir*, n.p.: Da Capo Press.

McAuliffe, Mary Sperling (1978), *Crisis on the Left. Cold War Politics and American Liberals, 1947–1954*, Amherst, MA: The University of Massachusetts Press.

McBride, Joseph (2002), 'A Very Good American', in *Written By*, The Magazine of the Writers Guild of America, West, pp. 26–33.

McBride, Joseph (2003), *Searching for John Ford. A Life*, London: Faber & Faber.

McCormick, Thomas J. (1991), 'Economic Crisis and American Militarization, 1949–1950', in Paterson and McMahon (eds), *The Origins of the Cold War*, pp. 240–53.

McGilligan, Pat (ed.) (1986), *Backstory. Interviews with Screenwriters of Hollywood's Golden Age*, Berkeley, CA, Los Angeles, and London: University of California Press.

McGilligan, Patrick and Paul Buhle (1997), *Tender Comrades. A Backstory of the Hollywood Blacklist*, New York: St Martin's Press.

McWilliams, Carey (1946), *Southern California Country. An Island on the Land*, Boston, MA: Little, Brown and Company.

McWilliams, Carey (1948), *A Mask for Privilege: Anti-Semitism in America*, Boston, MA: Little, Brown and Company.

McWilliams, Carey (1950), *Witch Hunt. The Revival of Heresy*, Boston, MA: Little, Brown and Company.

May, Lary (ed.) (1989), *Recasting America. Culture and Politics in the Age of Cold War*, Chicago, IL, and London: The University of Chicago Press.

May, Lary (2000), *The Big Tomorrow. Hollywood and the Politics of the American Way*, Chicago, IL, and London: University of Chicago Press.

Miles, Michael W. (1980), *The Odyssey of the American Right*, New York and Oxford: Oxford University Press.

Miller, Merle (1952), *The Judges and the Judged. The Report on Black-listing in Radio and Television for the American Civil Liberties Union*, Garden City, NY: Country Life Press.

Moldea, Dan (1986), *Dark Victory. Ronald Reagan, MCA, and the Mob*, New York: Viking Penguin.

Munby, Jonathan (1999), *Public Enemies, Public Heroes. Screening the Gangster from 'Little Caesar' to 'Touch of Evil'*, Chicago, IL, and London: The University of Chicago Press.

Naremore, James (1998), *More than Night. Film Noir in its Contexts*, Berkeley, CA, Los Angeles and London: University of California Press.

Navasky, Victor (1980), *Naming Names*, New York and London: Penguin.

Neale, Steve and Peter Stanfield (eds) (2005), 'The Hollywood Left: Film and TV', special issue of *Film Studies*, vol. 7, Winter.

Neve, Brian (1992), *Film and Politics in America. A Social Tradition*, London: Routledge.

Neve, Brian (2005), 'An Interview with Cy Endfield', in Neale and Stanfield (eds), *Film Studies*, pp. 116–27.

Nielsen, Mike and Gene Mailes (1995), *Hollywood's Other Blacklist. Union Struggles in the Studio System*, London: British Film Institute.

O'Reilly, Kenneth (1983), *Hoover and the Un-Americans. The FBI, HUAC, and the Red Menace*, Philadelphia, PA: Temple University Press.

Paterson, Thomas G. (ed.) (1971), *Cold War Critics. Alternatives to American Foreign Policy in the Truman Years*, Chicago, IL: Quadrangle Books.

Paterson, Thomas G. and Robert J. McMahon (eds) (1991), *The Origins of the Cold War*, Lexington, MA, and Toronto: D. C. Heath and Company.

Pells, Richard H. (1985), *The Liberal Mind in a Conservative Age. American Intellectuals in the 1940s and 1950s*, New York: Harper and Row.

Pizzitola, Louis (2002), *Hearst over Hollywood. Power, Passion and Propaganda in the Movies*, New York: Columbia University Press.

Pomerantz, Charlotte (ed.) (1963), *A Quarter-Century of Un-Americana, 1938–1963*, New York: Marzani and Munsell.

Powers, Richard Gid (1987), *Secrecy and Power. The Life of J. Edgar Hoover*, New York and London: The Free Press.

Prindle, David F. (1988), *The Politics of Glamor. Ideology and Democracy in the Screen Actors' Guild*, Madison, WI: University of Wisconsin Press.

Rhodes, Gary D. (2007), *Bela Lugosi. Dreams and Nightmares*, Narberth, PA: Collectables.

Roddick, Nick (1983), *A New Deal in Entertainment. Warner Brothers in the 1930s*, London: British Film Institute.

Roffman, Peter and Jim Purdy (1981), *The Hollywood Social Problem Film. Madness, Despair, and Politics from the Depression to the Fifties*, Bloomington, IN: Indiana University Press.

Rogin, Michael (1987), *Ronald Reagan, the Movie and Other Episodes in Political Demonology*, Berkeley, CA, and Los Angeles: University of California Press.

Rose, Lisle A. (1999), *The Cold War Comes to Main Street. America in 1950*, Lawrence, KS: University Press of Kansas.

Rouverol, Jean (2000), *Refugees from Hollywood. A Journal of the Blacklist Years*, Albuquerque, NM: University of New Mexico Press.

Saunders, Frances Stonor (1999), *Who Paid the Piper? The CIA and the Cultural Cold War*, London: Granta Books.

Savage, William W., Jr (1990), *Commies, Cowboys, and Jungle Queens. Comic Books and America, 1945–1954*, Hanover, NH, and London: Wesleyan University Press.

Sayre, Nora (1980), *Running Time: Films of the Cold War*, New York: The Dial Press.

Schrecker, Ellen (1998), *Many Are the Crimes. McCarthyism in America*, Princeton, NJ: Princeton University Press.

Schupurra, Kurt (1998), *Triumph of the Right. The Rise of the California Conservative Movement, 1945–1966*, New York and London: M. E. Sharpe.

Schwartz, Nancy Lynn (1982, completed by Sheila Schwartz), *The Hollywood Writers' Wars*, New York: Alfred A. Knopf.

Schwartz, Richard Alan (1997), *The Cold War Reference Guide*, Jefferson, NC: McFarland & Company.

Schwartz, Richard A. (1998), *Cold War Culture. Media and the Arts, 1945–1990*, New York: Checkmark Books; Facts on File.

Shaw, Tony (2007), *Hollywood's Cold War*, Edinburgh: Edinburgh University Press.

Sklar, Robert (1992), *City Boys. Cagney, Bogart, Garfield*, Princeton, NJ: Princeton University Press.

Slide, Anthony (1991), 'Hollywood's Fascist Follies', in *Film Comment*, vol. 27, no. 4, July/August, pp. 62–7.

Slide, Anthony (1999), *Actors on Red Alert*, Lanham, MD: The Scarecrow Press.

Slide, Anthony (2007), *Incorrect Entertainment*, Albany, GA: Bear Manor Media.

Starobin, Joseph R. (1972), *American Communism in Crisis, 1943–1957*, Cambridge, MA: Harvard University Press.

Suber, Howard (1966), 'The 1947 Hearings of the House Committee on Un-American Activities into Communism in the Hollywood Motion Picture Industry', unpublished MA thesis, UCLA.

Talbot, David, and Barbara Zheutlin (1978), *Creative Differences. Profiles of Hollywood Dissidents*, Boston, MA: South End Press.

Theoharis, Athan (1971), *Seeds of Repression. Harry S. Truman and the Origins of McCarthyism*, New York: The New York Times Book Co.

Theoharis, Athan (1991), *From the Secret Files of J. Edgar Hoover*, Chicago, IL: Ivan R. Dee.

Theoharis, Athan (2002), *Chasing Spies. How the FBI Failed in Counterintelligence but Promoted the Politics of McCarthy in the Cold War Years*, Chicago, IL: Ivan R. Dee.

Theoharis, Athan G. and John Stuart Cox (1993 [1988]), *The Boss. J. Edgar Hoover and the Great American Inquisition*, London: Virgin.

Trumbo, Dalton (1970), *Additional Dialogue. Letters of Dalton Trumbo, 1942–1962*, ed. Helen Manfull, New York: M. Evans and Company.

Vaughan, Stephen (1994), *Ronald Reagan in Hollywood. Movies and Politics*, Cambridge: Cambridge University Press.

Vaughn, Robert (1996 [1972]), *Only Victims. A Study of Show Business Blacklisting*, New York: Limelight Editions.

Wagman, Robert J. (1991), *The First Amendment Book*, New York: Pharos Books.

Wasserman, Harry (1974), 'Ideological Gunfight at the RKO Corral. Howard Hughes' *I Married a Communist*', in *The Velvet Light Trap*, no. 11, pp. 7–11.

Wesley, David (1961), *Hate Groups and HUAC*, pamphlet published by the Emergency Civil Liberties Committee.

Whitfield, Stephen (1996), *The Culture of the Cold War*, Baltimore, MD, and London: The Johns Hopkins University Press.

Williams, Tony (2004a), *Body and Soul. The Cinematic Vision of Robert Aldrich*, Lanham, MD: The Scarecrow Press.

Williams, Tony (2004b), 'An Interview with Kim Hunter', *Quarterly Review of Film and Video*, vol. 21, no. 2, April–June, pp. 89–94.

Williams, Tony (2005), 'Alexander Knox: The Lost Interview', *Quarterly Review of Film and Video*, vol. 22, no. 1, January–March, pp. 73–81.

Wills, Garry (1976), 'Introduction', in Hellman, *Scoundrel Time*, pp. 3–34.

Wills, Garry (1997), *John Wayne's America. The Politics of Celebrity*, New York: Simon & Schuster.

Wills, Garry (2000 [1988]), *Reagan's America*, London: Penguin.

Written By (2002), the Magazine of the Writers Guild of America, West, special issue on blacklisting, vol. 6, no. 2, February.

Freedom of Information Act, FBI Investigation of Communism in Motion Pictures: www.foia.fbi.gov/foiaindex/compic.htm

Internet Movie Database: www.imdb.com

World Socialist Web Site: www.wsws.org

Index